Corporate Social Responsibility

Published by
ACADEMIC FOUNDATION
in association with

Institute of Public Enterprise

Corporate Social Responsibility

Driving a Sustainable Future

Editors

R.K. Mishra

Shulagna Sarkar

ACADEMIC FOUNDATION

NEW DELHI

www.academicfoundation.org

First published in 2017
by

ACADEMIC FOUNDATION
4772-73 / 23 Bharat Ram Road, (23 Ansari Road),
Darya Ganj, New Delhi - 110 002 (India).
Phones : 23245001 / 02 / 03 / 04.
Fax : +91-11-23245005.
E-mail : booksaf@gmail.com
www.academicfoundation.org

in association with
Institute of Public Enterprise, Hyderabad.

Disclaimer:
The findings/views/opinions expressed in this book are solely those of the authors and do not necessarily reflect the views of the publisher.

Cataloging in Publication Data--DK
Courtesy: D.K. Agencies (P) Ltd. <docinfo@dkagencies.com>

Corporate social responsibility : driving a sustainable future /
editors, R.K. Mishra, Shulagna Sarkar.
pages cm
ISBN 9789332704114

1. Social responsibility of business--India. 2. Social responsibility of business--India--Case studies. 3. Sustainable development--India. I. Mishra, R. K., 1948- editor. II. Sarkar, Shulagna, editor. III. Institute of Public Enterprise (Hyderabad, India), publisher.

HD60.5.I5C67 2017 DDC 658.408 23

Typeset, printed and bound by The Book Mint, New Delhi.
www.thebookmint.in

CONTENTS

Sectoral Perspectives to Corporate Social Responsibility

Corporate Social Responsibility: The Emerging Discussions

Best Practices in Corporate Social Responsibility

LIST OF TABLES AND FIGURES

TABLES

FIGURES

About the Editors/Contributors

Editors:

R.K. Mishra, Senior Professor and Director, Institute of Public Enterprise (IPE), Hyderabad, is a graduate of International Management Programme, SDA Boccioni, Milan, Italy, and has been a fellow of British Council and Commonwealth Secretariat. He is a member of the UN Task Force on International Taskforce on Standards of Excellence in Public Administration and Education and associated with the UNDP project on Macro Economics of Poverty Reduction carried out by RBI Indira Gandhi Institute of Development Banking and Research. He has also been taskforce member for evaluating CSR (corporate social responsibility) initiatives of CPSEs (central public sector enterprises) as a part of MoU (memorandum of understanding). He has handled assignments for the Ministry of Finance, Ministry of Power, Ministry of Heavy Industries, Ministry of Trade and Commerce, Ministry of Heavy Industry and Public Enterprises, and Ministry of Disinvestment. He has supervised several doctoral researches for several universities in Management, Economics, Commerce and Public Administration. His current interests include: economic reforms, privatisation and restructuring, finance, poverty management and good governance.

Shulagna Sarkar, Assistant Professor, Institute of Public Enterprise, has completed her PhD and MBA (HR) from Rashtrasant Tukadaji Maharaj Nagpur University (RTMNU). She is also a law graduate. She is a certified trainer in the area of CSR by Indian Institute of Corporate Affairs (IICA), Ministry of Human Resource Development (MoHRD) as well as Department of Public Enterprises (DPE). She has published books in the area of CSR and Training Needs Assessment. She has worked on impact assessment and baseline studies for corporates. She has presented papers at National and International conferences. She is involved in teaching, research activities, training and consultancy at the institute. Her areas of interest include: competency management, training and development, and CSR.

Contributors:

Samar Verma, Senior Program Specialist, International Development Research Centre (IDRC) of Canada.

Vivek Vaidyanathan, Research Scientist, CSTEP, Bangalore.

Anshu Bharadwaj, Executive Director, Centre for Study of Science, Technology and Policy (CSTEP), Bangalore.

Sameer Pingle is Associate Professor, Institute of Management, Nirma University, Ahmedabad.

CST Anil Kumar is Fellow Member of the Institute of Company Secretaries of India.

Arun K. Rath is Dean and Professor, International Management Institute, New Delhi.

Punam Singh is Assistant Professor, School of Management Studies, University of Hyderabad.

Deepti Chandra is Assistant Professor, IPE, Hyderabad.

A. Sridhar Raj is Assistant Professor, IPE, Hyderabad.

Manosmita Mahapatra is Faculty, Department of Sociology, Ravenshaw University, Cuttack.

Puneeta Goel is Research Scholar, Jagadguru Sri Shivarathreeshwara Academy of Technical Education (JSSATE), Bangalore, and Assistant Professor, Amity College of Commerce and Finance, Amity University, Noida.

R.S. Ramesh is Professor, Department of Management Studies, JSSATE, Bangalore.

Anup Kumar is Assistant Professor, IPE, Hyderabad.

Khandoker Asef Safa Kabir Upal is Lecturer, Department of Management School of Business and Economics, North South University, Bangladesh.

Tulsi Jayakumar is Professor, Economics and Program Head, PGP-Family Managed Business at S.P. Jain Institute of Management & Research, Mumbai.

Jibitesh Rath is GM-HRD, National Mineral Development Corporation (NMDC) Ltd, Hyderabad.

P. Shyam is DGM-CSR, NMDC Ltd, Hyderabad.

Harendra R. Patel is Joint President (HR), Aditya Birla Group.

R.K. MISHRA and SHULAGNA SARKAR

Preface

> To build and sustain brands people love and trust, one must focus—not only on today but also on tomorrow. It's not easy...but balancing the short and long term is key to delivering sustainable, profitable growth—growth that is good for our shareholders but also good for our consumers, our employees, our business partners, the communities where we live and work, and the planet we inhabit
>
> —Irene B. Rosenfeld, CEO Kraft

Issues relating to CSR (corporate social responsibility) have taken a centre stage in modern societies as organisations worldwide have realised the importance of CSR as a strategic tool for a sustainable business. CSR is an organisation's obligation to consider the interests of their customers, employees, shareholders, communities, and the ecology considering the social and environmental consequences of their business activities. By integrating CSR into core business processes and stakeholder management, organisations can achieve the ultimate goal of creating both social value and corporate value.

India's business sector has generated wealth for shareholders for decades. Yet, the country continues to grapple with problems of poverty, unemployment, illiteracy and malnutrition etc. Salman Khursid has explained that corporate growth is sometimes seen as widening the gap between India and rural India through its income-skewing capability. This gap needs to be bridged. While the government has undertaken extensive developmental initiatives through a series of sectoral programmes, the business sector also needs to take the responsibility of exhibiting socially responsible business practices that ensure the distribution of wealth and the well-being of the communities in which the business operates.

In the 21st century marketplace, businesses are increasingly showing signs of becoming conscious of ethics and human rights as well as being economically, environmentally and socially active and responsible. Social responsibility has become one of the most talked areas in today's world.

1

R.K. MISHRA and SHULAGNA SARKAR

Corporate Social Responsibility in India

Introduction

CSR (corporate social responsibility) is the way companies manage their businesses to produce an overall positive impact on society through economic, environmental and social actions. The totality of CSR can be best understood by three words, 'corporate,' 'social,' and 'responsibility.' In broad terms, CSR relates to responsibilities corporations have towards society within which they are based and operate, not denying the fact that the purview of CSR goes much beyond this. CSR is comprehended differently by different people.

CSR has been explained by numerous researchers and practitioners in their own way and convenience. Yet, the fulcrum of the practice of CSR in organisations extends corporate obligations to include multiple stakeholders such as stockholders, workers, the community, and the natural environment and the outcomes of policies and programmes directed toward those relationships (Clarkson 1995, Donaldson and Preston 1995). Hopkins (1998) has expressed CSR concept being concerned with treating the stakeholders of the firm ethically or in a socially responsible manner.

The corporate world is facing the notion of CSR wherever it turns these days. CSR has been defined much more in terms of a philanthropic or charitable model. Companies make profits, unhindered except by fulfilling their duty to pay taxes. Then they donate a certain share of the profits to charitable causes. It is seen as tainting the act for the company to receive any benefit from the giving. CSR is also known by a number of other names. These include corporate responsibility, corporate accountability, corporate ethics, corporate citizenship or stewardship, responsible entrepreneurship, and 'triple bottom line', to name just a few. As CSR issues become increasingly integrated into modern business practices, there is a trend towards referring to it as 'responsible competitiveness' or 'corporate sustainability.'

India has witnessed a number of phases in the initiation and implementation of CSR. The paper aims to discuss CSR across ages in India along with its future in India.

Table 1.1

Past, Present and Future of CSR in India

	Past	*Present*	*Future*
Approach	Philanthropic	Strategic	Transformative
Organisations undertaking CSR	Any organisation on its own willingness	For public and private who qualify as per Companies Act, 2013	Organisations beyond mandate
Initiation of CSR projects	Based on intentions of organisation	Law based as two per cent of the three-year average annual net profit of the organisation	Need based spent
Implementation of projects	Generalised	Specialised	Integrated

Source: Compiled by the authors.

CSR in India: The Past

CSR is not a new phenomenon to Indian business rather it had always been part of its tradition. Religion, philosophy and history have an influence over how CSR gets articulated within a cultural context and how its definition, understanding and practice evolve over a period of time.

The *Bhagavad Gita* lays utmost emphasis on '*loksamagrah*' which means keeping human beings or the world together, regulating them such that they acquire strength from mutual cooperation. The ancient sculptures like *Vedas*, *Upanishads* preach the virtues of sacrifice and co-existence. In Vedic mythology, business has been seen as legitimate, integral part of society that emphasises work for an economic structure based on contention of *sarva loka hitam* which means 'well-being of all stakeholders'. The references are also available from *Arthashastra* saying, '*praja sukhe sukham*' the concept of '*shreshthadharma*' which means, 'the better off one is in society, the higher should be one's sense of responsibility', e.g., in earlier times wealthy merchants shared a part of their wealth with the wider society by way of setting temples for a religious cause or helping in phases of famine and epidemics and thus securing an integral position in the society. During the independence movement, Mahatma Gandhi advocated the system of trusteeship, which required that in the case of property under the control of a private person, the person must regard himself as its protector not its master, this is derived from the ideal of non-possession influenced by Gandhi and as a result, most businessmen in India saw their business empires as a 'trust' held in the interest of community at large. Businesses made significant contributions to support schools, colleges and hospitals, and emphasis later shifted to supporting technical training, public health and rural development. The operations of the trusts were largely in line with Gandhi's reforms which sought to abolish untouchability, encourage empowerment of women and rural development.

Figure 1.1

CSR across Ages

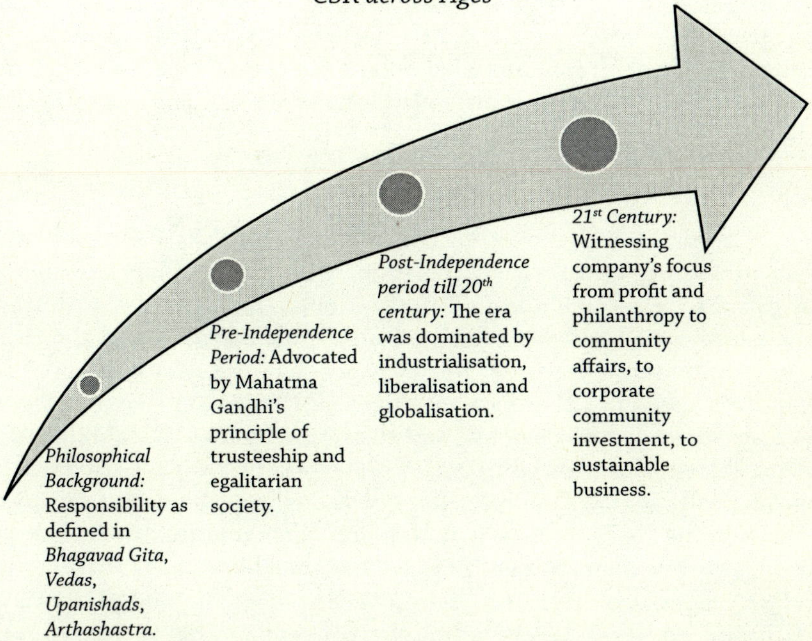

Source: Compiled by the authors.

The post-independence era, the democratic set up and the rights enshrined in the Indian Constitution shaped out a new socio-political order in which development of society required industrialisation. This further led to emergence of PSUs (public sector undertakings), laws relating to labour and environmental standards. The PSUs were conceptualised as the main drivers of community development. However, the public sector was effective only to a certain extent. This led to shift of expectation from public to the private sector and their active involvement in socio-economic development of the country became absolute necessity. Liberalisation of the economy in 1991 saw the private sector become an entity in itself. Increased growth momentum of the economy helped Indian companies grow rapidly and this made them more willing and able to contribute towards social cause. Globalisation transformed India and this led a focus towards labour laws; environment standards in developing countries gave birth to a more structured form of social responsibility whereby organisations took responsibility for the impact of their activities on customer, employees, shareholders, communities and the environment in all aspects of operations. Social responsibility is the responsibility of an organisation for the impact of its decisions and activities on society and the environment through transparent and ethical behaviour that is consistent with sustainable development and the welfare of society. It also takes into account the expectations of stakeholders, its compliance with applicable law, consistency with international norms of behaviour and integration throughout the organisation.

Theoretical Justification to CSR

CSR began with the focus on the role of business leaders, particularly on how they managed their organisations with a view to society and how they gave back local communities. In the 1950s, the focus of CSR shifted to academic debate about what organisations should do to support the society rather than that of individuals. The CSR agenda of organisations have profit orientation as one of the main objective yet, there are two perspectives which are mainly socio-economic and classical school of thoughts. Classical view or shareholder approach holds the view that CSR is for maximisation of profit while socio-economic school of thought believes that businesses owe something to the society that supports them and that the debt to the society is greater than any debt to individual member of the society.

CSR has evolved from the mere concept of giving and philanthropy (Bruch and Walter 2005) to a holistic concept of shared value (Porter and Kramer 2011). Organisations view CSR in different forms like volunteering work, corporations and the community interaction, social and environmental management, cause-related marketing perspective, stakeholder concept and linking CSR policies to business strategy. Yet, these organisations refer CSR activities in various other forms which are as given in Table 1.2.

What is required is a holistic view which ensures giving back to the society to the extent damage or harm is caused. Businesses exist not only for individual/owners growth but there are numerous benefits to the society at large.

Table 1.2

Changing Philosophy of CSR: Philanthropy to Strategic

Philosophy	*Major Researches*	*Other Forms of CSR*
Giving and philanthropy	Bruch and Walter 2005 Sasse and Trahan 2007	Charity
Volunteer work	Freitas and Ventura 2004 Almeida et al. 2005	Individual helping behaviour
Corporations and community interaction	Fonseca, Moori and Alves 2005	Community development
Social and environmental management	Abreu 2001 Pasa 2004	Green wash
Cause related marketing perspective	Sargeant and Woodliffe 2007 Kotler and Lee 2011	Corporate branding
Stakeholder concept	Freeman 1984	Inclusiveness
Linking CSR policies to business strategy	Mcwilliams et al. 2006	Shared value

Source: Compiled by the authors.

CSR in India: The Present Scenario

The Companies Act, 2013: The CSR provisions of the Companies Act, 2013 seek to create an enabling environment by promoting and facilitating far better connect between businesses and communities. It aims at facilitating deeper thought and longer term strategies for addressing some of our most persistent social, economic and environmental problems; they will assist in synergising partnerships between corporates, governments, CSOs (civil society organisations), academic institutions and social entrepreneurs. Business resources can be channelled into a diverse array of programmes to address social, economic and environmental problems, and to bring about a sustainable future for all.

The latest Companies Act, 2013 reflects on the importance of CSR as part of a firms' business strategy. Section 135 contains 5 sub-section on CSR. Schedule VII of the Companies Bill lists out the CSR activities. Section 135(5)—CSR expenditure states that the Board of every company referred to in sub-section (1) shall ensure that the company spends, in every financial year, at least two per cent of the average net profits of the company made during the three immediately preceding financial years, in pursuance of its CSR policy:

> Provided that the company shall give preference to the local area and areas around it where it operates, for spending the amount earmarked for CSR activities.

Provided further that if the company fails to spend such amount, the Board shall, in its report made under clause(o) of sub-section(3) of section 134, specify the reasons for not spending the amount.

Table 1.3

Interpreting Section 135 of the Companies Act, 2013

Challenges: Interpretation and Implementation of the Section 135 of the Act	*Opportunities: The Way Ahead*
Framing of a CSR policy	A reference document to guide structured CSR implementation in organisation, linking CSR with business strategy.
Board level CSR committee	Strategic focus to CSR by incorporating CSR as a part of the structure.
Defining the responsibility of the board	Top management accountability for CSR implementation
Schedule VII	Activities in line with societal and environmental needs.
Mandatory reporting	Informing the stakeholders the reasons for not spending CSR amount. A way to ensure responsible and continuous CSR spending.
Sustainability reporting	A way to showcase responsible business practices to stakeholders, transparency in spending, knowing the impact of company's activities.
Implementing partners	Need for capacity building initiatives at all levels: corporate, NGOs, government and academic institutions.

Source: Compiled by the authors.

CSR implementation post Companies Act 2013: An estimated 14,358 companies fall into this 'mandatory' CSR-reporting category. CSR activities in the first year would be between ₹20,000 crore plus spent in social welfare. Corporates are now required to adopt the 'project mode' to execute their CSR programmes.

Data Analysis

Methodology: Data was collected from top 10 public sectors companies of India. Information on CSR spending, project implementing partners, CSR policy and reporting was collected.

Analysis of CSR Spending

As the Companies Act, 2013 has mandated the spent on CSR in India, an attempt has been made to understand the trend in CSR spent as indicated in Figure 1.2.

The data analysis of the CSR spending of both the public and private sector companies reveals that majorly all companies have an increased CSR spending over the years. There has been a steep rise of CSR spending in Oil and Gas sector companies compared to the rest. Analyses of CSR reports have revealed that most private sector organisations have not reported their unspent CSR budget for the FY 2011-2014. Whereas in the case of public sector organisations, companies have reported their unspent amount due to the existence of Department of Public Enterprises (DPE) CSR Guidelines 2010. The huge CSR fund requires a structured approach to CSR so that CSR funds can be appropriately utilised. Hence, there is a greater emphasis of 'project mode' to CSR programmes for utilisation of CSR funds.

Box 1.1

Schedule VII

1. Eradicating hunger, poverty and malnutrition, promoting preventive healthcare and sanitation and making available safe drinking water.
2. Promoting education, including special education and employment enhancing vocational skills especially among children, women, elderly, and the differently able and livelihood enhancement projects.
3. Promoting gender equality, empowering women, setting up homes and hostels for women and orphans; setting up old age homes, day care centres and such other facilities for senior citizens and measures for reducing inequalities faced by socially and economically backward groups.
4. Ensuring environmental sustainability, ecological balance, protection of flora and fauna, animal welfare, agro-forestry, conservation of natural resources and maintaining quality of soil, air and water.
5. Protection of national heritage, art and culture including restoration of buildings and sites of historical importance and works of art; setting up public libraries; promotion and development of traditional arts and handicrafts.
6. Measures for the benefit of armed forces veterans, war widows and their dependents.
7. Training to promote rural sports, nationally recognised sports, Paralympics sports and Olympic sports.
8. Contribution to the Prime Minister's National Relief Fund or any other fund set up by the Central Government for socio-economic development and relief and welfare of the SC (scheduled caste) and the STs (scheduled tribes), OBCs (other backward classes), minorities and women.
9. Contributions or funds provided to technology incubators located within academic institutions which are approved by the Central Government.
10. Rural development projects.
11. Slum Development.

Figure 1.2

CSR Spending of Public Sector Organisations

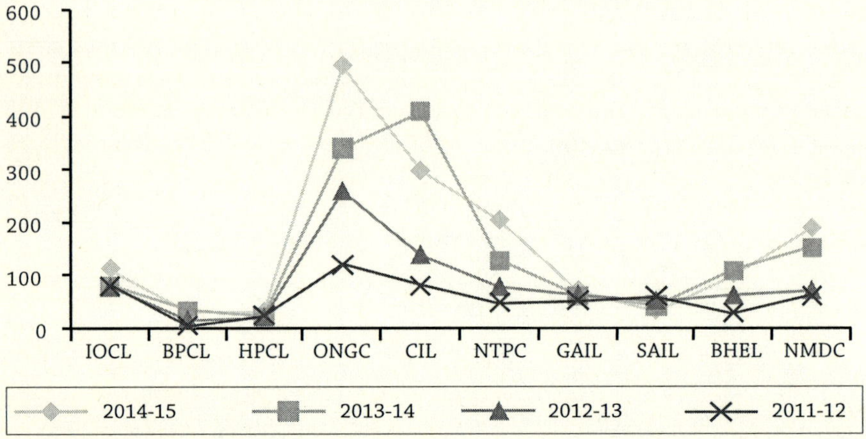

Source: Compiled by the authors.

Analysis of CSR Implementing Partners

Implementing partners play a major role in the successful implementation of CSR initiatives. The detailed analysis in Table 1.4 reflects various preferences of implementing partners.

Table 1.4

Implementing Partners

Company Name Public	*Own Foundation*	*Specialised NGO*	*Local Govt. Agencies*
NTPC	☑	☑	☑
BPCL		☑	☑
IOCL	☑	☑	☑
GAIL	☑	☑	☑
SAIL		☑	☑
BHEL	☑	☑	☑
ONGC		☑	☑
CIL		☑	☑
HPCL		☑	☑
NMDC Ltd.		☑	☑

Source: Compiled by the authors.

Analysis of CSR Policy Document and Reporting

A conscientious corporate for initiating need based CSR assesses the needs of the community and the environment through a consultative mode, formulate a CSR policy as a response to the need and initiate CSR activities through measurable budgets and time lines leading to an impactful society. The CSR, policy documents and CSR and sustainability reports of organisations studied have been referred to make a comparison with regards to enabling CSR with formulation of CSR policy and reporting of CSR initiatives separately as well as a part of sustainability reporting (Table 1.5).

CSR Areas

The CPSEs (central public sector enterprises) are undertaking CSR in all dimensions of education, health, livelihood, rural development as well as environment. The private sector organisations are not undertaking CSR on dimensions like livelihood and environment as rigorous as CPSEs. The study reveals that around 100 per cent of private sector companies studied are implementing CSR initiatives in the area of education, 95 per cent in the area of health, 90 per cent in the area of livelihood, 95 per cent in rural development and 85 per cent in the area of environment.

The various initiatives studied in each of the thrust areas of CSR are:

- *Initiatives under education*: running own school, infrastructure support, quality of education, scholarship, adult education, girl child education.
- *Initiatives under health*: infrastructure and equipment support, water and sanitation, geriatric care, maternal and child health and health camps.
- *Initiatives under livelihood*: skill development and income generation.
- *Initiatives under environment*: green initiatives, water management , water conservation.
- *Initiatives under rural development*: support for differently able, awareness generation, rehabilitation initiatives, infrastructure, youth clubs.

CSR in India: The Future

India both leads the world in some areas of CSR and trails a long way behind in others. In India, CSR has to shift from the extraordinary, to the exceptional, to the expected. It is expected to evolve from a position of vulnerability and 'bolt-on' practice within companies to a position of integration into company strategy, policies, and practices.

Table 1.5

CSR Policy and Reporting

S. No	Company Name	CSR Policy			CSR Board Level Committee			Sustainability Reports			CSR Reporting		
		2014-15	2013-14	2012-13	2014-15	2013-14	2012-13	2014-15	2013-14	2012-13	2014-15	2013-14	2012-13
1	IOCL	☑	☑	☑	☑	☑	☑	☑	☑	☑	☑	☑	☑
2	BPCL	☑	☑	☑	☑	☑	☑	☑	☑	☑	☑	☑	☑
3	HPCL	☑	☑	☑	☑	☑	☑	☑	☑	☑	☑	☑	☑
4	ONGC	☑	☑	☑	☑	☑	☑	☑	☑	☑	☑	☑	☑
5	Coal India Limited	☑	☑	☑	☑	☑	☑	☑	☑	☑	☑	☑	☑
6	GAIL India Limited	☑	☑	☑	☑	☑	☑	☑	☑	☑	☑	☑	☑
7	NTPC	☑	☑	☑	☑	☑	☑	☑	☑	☑	☑	☑	☑
8	BHEL	☑	☑	☑	☑	☑	☑	☑	☑	☑	☑	☑	☑
9	SAIL	☑	☑	☑	☑	☑	☑	☑	☑	☑	☑	☑	☑
10	NMDC	☑	☑	☑	☑	☑	☑				☑	☑	☑

Source: Compiled by the authors.

Its success is attributable to a realisation that CSR is inseparable from reputation, trust, and brand enhancement and risk management, as well as to the organisation's capacity to anticipate and act upon new business opportunities amidst shifting consumer and regulatory environments. Signs of the transformed scenario are new ownership and governance structures that will be challenging conventional practices and introducing new definitions of corporate purposes. The future of CSR is about accelerating a new form of business in India—combining strong financial returns with social good by having CSR which is of transformative, collaborative, integrated, diversified, scalable, reward-based, performance-driven and global. In all, a CSR 2.0 as coined by Visser (2015).

Conclusion

CSR in India is not a new concept; companies have been practicing it in a voluntary spirit with a philanthropic approach. Not all companies were practicing it in a structured manner with many practicing it with the objectives of gaining publicity, tax benefits or goodwill generation. CSR in its current form is in its nascent stage and hence, study like this will help organisations to understand and learn from the CSR practices of the leading companies of the country. The province of corporate social responsibility with the effort to bring India's geographically remote and low-income groups into the mainstream of economic life now has the potential to become the most valuable business opportunity of the next decade. The time is just right for companies to pursue aggressively the agenda of inclusive growth. Inclusive growth for India needs to be assessed from every perspective: personal, societal, cultural, and economic. Inclusiveness is benchmarked against achievement of monitorable targets related to: (i) income and poverty, (ii) education, (iii) health, (iv) women and children, (v) infrastructure, and (vi) environment. It is high time that the Indian organisations initiates CSR 2.0 involving transformative, collaborative, integrated, diversified, scalable, reward-based, performance-driven and global initiatives, as it is the future.

References

Abreu, M.C.S. (2001). *Modelo de Avaliação da Estratégia Ambiental: Uma Ferramenta Para Tomada de Decisão*. Doctoral Thesis. Brazil: Federal University of Santa Catarina.

Almeida, S.L., S.A.G. Lins and R.R. Oliveira (2005). *Benefícios do Capital Social: A Experiência da Escola de Voluntários da Celpe*. Brazil: Anais do Encontro Nacional da Associação Nacional de Pós-Graduação e Pesquisa em Administração, Brasília, DF. September.

Barone, M., A. Miyazaki and K. Taylor (2000). "The Influence of Cause-Related Marketing on Consumer Choice: Does One Good Turn Deserve Another?", *Journal of the Academy of Marketing Science* 28: 248-62.

Bruch, H. and F. Walter (2005). "The Keys to Rethinking Corporate Philanthropy", *MIT Sloan Management Review* 47(1): 48-55.

Clarkson, M.B. (1995). "A Stakeholder Framework for Analyzing and Evaluating Corporate Social Responsibility", *Academy of Management Review* 20: 92-117.

Commission of the European Communities. (2001). *Promoting a European Framework for Corporate Social Responsibilities, COM (2001) 366 Final.* Brussels.

Donaldson, T. and L.E. Preston (1995). "The Stakeholder Theory of the Corporation: Concepts, Evidence, and Implications", *Academy of Management Review* 20(1): 65-91.

Fassin, Y. (2008). "SMEs and the Fallacy of Formalising CSR", *Business Ethics: A European Review* 17: 364-78.

Freeman, R.E. (1984). *Strategic Management: A Stakeholder Approach.* Boston: Pitman.

Fonseca, G.M., R.G. Moori and M.A. Alves (2005, September). *Cooperação intersetorial (empresas privadas e Organizações do Terceiro Setor): Uma Visão Baseada em valor. Anais do Encontro Nacional da Associação Nacional de Pós-Graduação e Pesquisa em Administração*, Brasília, DF. Brazil, 29.

Freitas, F.R. and E.C. Ventura. (2004). *Voluntariado Empresarial: Uma Questão de legitimidade.* Anais do Encontro Nacional da Associação Nacional de Pós-Graduação e Pesquisa em Administração, Curitiba, PR, Brazil. 28 September.

Hopkins, M. (1998). *A Planetary Bargain: CSR Comes of Age.* Macmillan. UK Ethical Corporation Survey (2009). Available at: *www.ethicalcorp.com/csr* (Accessed on 23 February 2014).

Kotler, P. and M.P. Lee (2011). *Social Marketing: Influence Behaviours for Good.* Sage.

Kotler, P. and N. Lee (2005). *Corporate Social Responsibility: Doing the Most Good for your Company and Your Cause.* New Jersey: John Wiley and Sons, Inc.

McWilliams, A., D.S. Siegel and P.M. Wright (2006). "Corporate Social Responsibility: Strategic Implications", *Journal of Management Studies* 43(1): 1-18.

Pasa, C.R.R. (2004). *ECP-Social: Um Modelo de Avaliação da Performance Social Empresarial.* Tese de Doutorado, Universidade Federal de Santa Catarina, Florianópolis, SC, Brazil.

Porter, M. and M.R. Kramer (2011). "Creating Shared Value", *Harvard Business Review* 89(1-2): 62-77, January/February.

Sargeant, A. and L. Woodliffe (2007). "Building Donor Loyalty: The Antecedents and Role of Commitment in the Context of Charity Giving", *Journal of Nonprofit and Public Sector Marketing* 18(2): 47-68.

Sasse, C. M. and R.T. Trahan (2007). "Rethinking the New Corporate Philanthropy", *Business Horizons* 50(1): 29-38.

Visser, W. (2015). *Sustainable Frontiers: Unlocking Change through Business, Leadership and Innovation.* Sheffield, UK: Greenleaf Publishing Limited.

Wagner, T., R. Lutz and B. Weitz (2009). "Corporate Hypocrisy: Overcoming the Threat of Inconsistent Corporate Social Responsibility Perceptions", *Journal of Marketing* 73(1): 77–91

World Business Council for Sustainable Development. (2000). *Corporate Social Responsibility: Making Good Business Sense.* Geneva: World Business Council for Sustainable Development.

Others:

Companies Act 2013, Accessed on 23 July 2014.

DPE, *CSR Guidelines.* March 2010.

2

SAMAR VERMA, VIVEK VAIDYANATHAN
and ANSHU BHARADWAJ

Corporate Social Responsibility in India
Case for Supporting Think Tanks

Corporate Social Responsibility Landscape in India

A number of studies have attempted to research the historical aspects of CSR (corporate social responsibility in India. Many of these studies[1] tended to frame CSR in the context of charity and philanthropic initiatives influenced by family values, traditions, culture and religion, as also industrialisation (Jana Foundation n.d., E&Y 2013). A few of them have even gone a step further in categorising CSR development in India into four phases,[2] namely, philanthropy and charity (Phase 1), CSR as social development during the Independence struggle (Phase 2), CSR by Public Sector Undertakings (Phase 3) and CSR in its current form from 1980 (Phase 4) (E&Y 2013).

There are still debates over whether philanthropy is the same as CSR. However, the authors are of the opinion that philanthropy is an act of giving, essentially a charity, mostly driven by an individual as opposed to a firm, and with personal values of giving back to society as a principal driver. In traditional, family-owned firms, this may take the form of corporate giving, and often mistaken to be CSR.

CSR on the other hand is more about how socially responsible are the firms' operations and activities. In the Indian context, CSR is also often thought of as primarily relating to the question of the business model that the firms employ to create what is often loosely referred to as triple bottom-line, or shared value,[3] across a wide variety of stakeholders—consumers,

1. *http://shodhganga.inflibnet.ac.in/bitstream/10603/15950/12/12_chapter%203.pdf.*
2. Ibid.
3. The term 'shared value' is often used to describe CSR in India, though the concept as originally conceived goes beyond CSR. The creator of this term, Porter and Kramer, however, defined this as generating economic value in a way that also produces value for society by addressing its challenges. A shared value approach reconnects company success with social progress (*https://hbr.org/2011/01/the-big-idea-creating-shared-value*).

employees, suppliers, communities affected by their operations, in addition, of course, to the shareholders. However, one could argue that the very fact that a law had to be enacted to make it mandatory for companies to spend on CSR means that they were otherwise not spending on creating shared value, and yet were referring to it as CSR. Little wonder then that the debate on how much of new money will the CSR law generate remains unsettled. Thus, in the Indian context, such categorisations based on practices of and reporting by firms is in no way water-tight and clear. A large set of activities undertaken by businesses—mostly through their foundations these days — are essentially driven by a need to enhance their markets, or improve their supply chain in other words, they are means to improving their operational effectiveness and profitability. However, these foundations also invest heavily in community work such as building schools and health centres, or providing water and sanitation related infrastructure. In such cases, the distinction between philanthropy and CSR is not clear.

There are multiple studies that have attempted to identify the drivers of philanthropy—ethical or Gandhian values of giving back driven by the owner/CEO, family traditions and the need to create/preserve family names as legacy (think of the Tatas, Birlas—Birla temple is a landmark in many cities and towns in India), commitment to a cause or relationships,[4] etc.

In one sense, one could conceptualise CSR as an umbrella term that has its roots in philanthropy, which then evolved into community development and more recently to strategic CSR. But this historical evolution is not similar across firm size, and certainly different in India compared to the developed countries. A recent study found that larger firms have indeed evolved into strategic CSR, but smaller ones are still into the business of community development. Larger firms use strategic CSR as a means of product differentiation, leading to higher payoffs in the long run (Bansal and Rai 2014).

Recent CSR Spends in India

According to the Kotak Top of the Pyramid 2016 report, the richest of the rich—the UHNIs (ultra-high net worth individuals)—possess a substantial share of the wealth in India. The number of UHNI households has more than doubled in the past five years, and so has their income—the combined net worth of UHNIs has been pegged at ₹135 trillion in the aforementioned report (Manku 2016).

4. In 2014, 3.5 million LinkedIn members indicated on their profiles their wish to volunteer for NPOs (non-profit organisations).

Figure 2.1

Investments and Returns of UHNIs

Optimism Uninterrupted

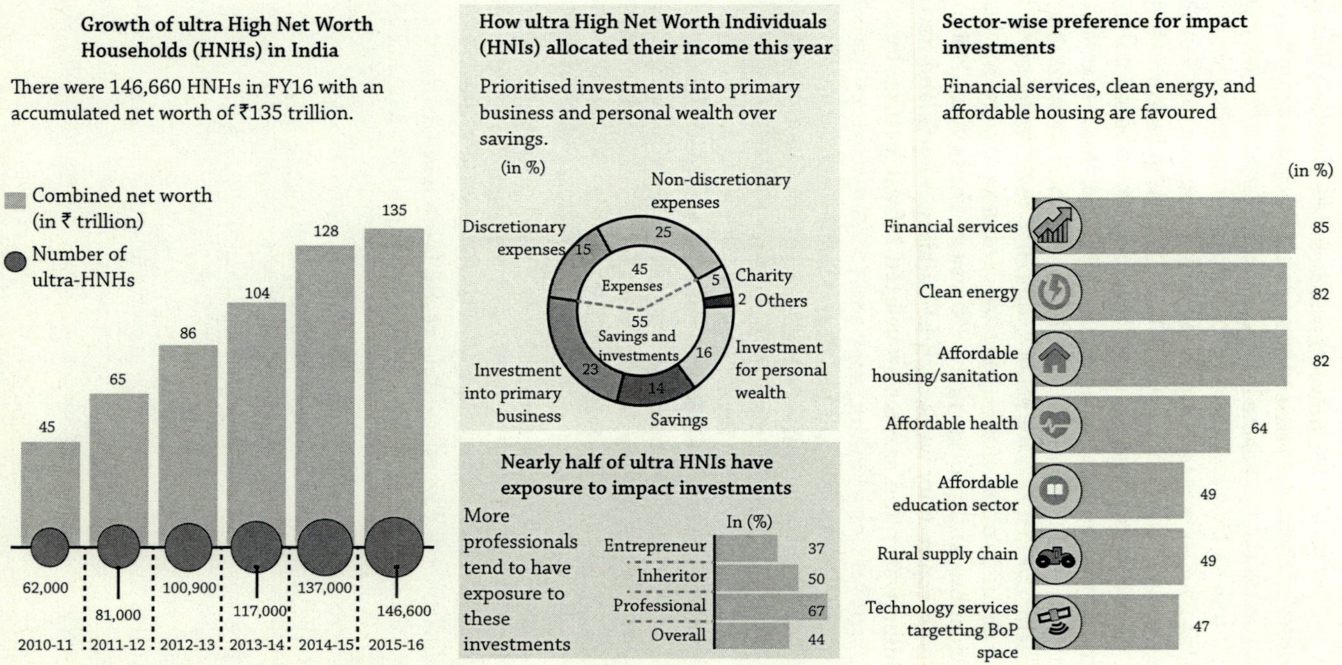

Source: Manku 2016; Kotak Wealth Management, 2016.

According to the FY 2016 report, the number of UHNIs from all three categories—inheritors, entrepreneurs and professionals—is on the rise. While all three categories continue to contribute towards philanthropy, professional UHNIs are investing time and expertise along with money, something the other two find difficult. The report found that UNHIs are increasing investments in the 'impact investing model', where market-based solutions are found for social development issues so that those who invest money get financial returns in addition to making a positive impact on social ills (Figure 2.1). It appears that the UHNIs are giving back more to society than before, but how much?

An analysis of the CSR spending of the top 250 firms for FY 2015-16 revealed that while the prescribed CSR amount to be spent was ₹7,143 crore, the actual spending was ₹6,578 crore, which is an improvement of 13 per cent over the previous fiscal (NGOBOX 2016). The study revealed that corporates prefer to fund themes[5] such as 'education', 'poverty alleviation, healthcare, and water and sanitation', 'rural development' and 'environmental areas' for companies, whereas themes such as 'technology incubation within academic institutions' and 'urban slum development' attracted less enthusiasm from corporates. The study also reveals an interesting paradox—'developed states' like Gujarat, Maharashtra, Andhra Pradesh, Karnataka and Tamil Nadu received more than 35 per cent of CSR funds. A sectoral break-up of the CSR contributions reveals that the Steel sector and the automotive sector contributed 128 per cent and 100 per cent of prescribed funds, respectively, whereas the CSR spending of the pharmaceutical sector with respect to prescribed funds stood at 74 per cent (NGOBOX 2016).

Another study of the CSR spending in FY 2015 of 90 companies revealed that 'health' and 'education' themes are funded to the extent of 45 per cent of the CSR budgets of those companies. A positive sign is that 75 of these companies have also incorporated detailed systems of CSR implementation and monitoring in their policies. These companies carry out their CSR activities through in-house teams, partner NGOs, government agencies or foundations. However, a majority of the companies still seem unsure of CSR spending. Interestingly, of the 90 companies, only 15 spent more than the requisite 2 per cent on CSR activities. Fourteen (14) companies spent exactly 2 per cent and 60 spent less than 2 per cent on CSR (Praxis 2016).

In the first and second years of the enforcement of CSR rules, most companies were focused on compliance rather than the impact of their initiatives. Now, it is mostly about course correction and expansion. Many

5. Themes listed under Section VII of the Companies Act, 2013.

companies are conducting impact assessment studies of their CSR activities to ensure long-lasting impact and optimal use of funds. However, these assessments across firms are largely used for internal purposes and are not in the public domain. One reason for firms to not want such information in the public domain could be their belief that declaring such findings in the public domain could foster a negative perception, especially if the evaluation of a project favours course correction. However, according to Sunil Chavan, Honorary Director at M.L. Dhawle Trust, a philanthropic organisation working on issues of health, livelihood and sustainable agriculture, impact assessment for the sake of conducting one is not the answer. "Many companies do not measure the real impact of their CSR spend. They do it in terms of how many children were given school uniforms or how many mothers were given protein powder, etc. Very few of them have set up mechanisms to measure the real, long-term impact on the community." Sidharth Dutta, Senior Manager, Development Advisory Services at EY India highlighted that current assessments generally focus only on outputs like the number of toilets built. "But to understand the actual impact on the ground, firms need to move from external factors of only counting the number of toilets to analysing qualitative variables in the lives of beneficiaries such as actual usage figures, evaluating status of health indicators along with extent of improvement in sociocultural variables of community life" (Mint 2016a).

However, it is important to put in perspective the euphoria with respect to CSR funding being perceived as a huge opportunity for large amount of funds to flow into the social sector. After the enactment of the new CSR law on 1 April 2014, in the first year of implementation of the Rules[6], it was estimated that close to 16,000 firms qualified to make a contribution of about ₹25,000 crore to the social sector. According to FICCI, even such high estimates only add up to 0.4 per cent of the total social sector spending of the Union government. In March 2016, Corporate Affairs Minister, Arun Jaitley, informed the Rajya Sabha that based on the CSR reports of 460 companies, a total of ₹6,337.36 crore was spent on CSR in 2014-15. This means that just about 3 per cent of the firms expected to spend on CSR had done so, contributing about 25 per cent of the estimated amount. To put this number in perspective, across just 32 social sector schemes, the government spent ₹1.05 trillion in 2014-15 (Manku 2016).

6. The CSR Rules require that firms with a net worth of ₹500 crore or revenue of ₹1,000 crore or net profit of ₹5 crore spend 2 per cent of their average profit in the past three years on social development-related activities listed in Schedule VII of the Rules, Companies Act, 2013.

In this context of CSR funding and focus being predominantly on health and education themes mostly through in-house teams and conventional NGOs, there hasn't been much emphasis on CSR funding for think tanks. Consequently, there isn't much mainstream literature available on CSR spending towards Indian think tanks.[7] The next section analyses think-tank funding in the international scenario.

International Think Tank Funding

In many ways, issues of funding faced by international think tanks mirror those faced by their Indian counterparts. This section details on how think tanks are funded internationally and their experiences in that regard.

Germany has around 135 registered think tanks (half of which are policy research institutes). They receive government funding and provide policy advice to government officials and political parties. These think tanks see themselves as independent from corporate interests, and government funding is regarded as a way to achieve this end. Consequently, many of these think tanks have a narrow focus on government elite. State governments are key financiers of think tanks in Germany, reflecting the country's federal structure. Most German think tanks maintain close ties with universities and avoid being tied to a particular ideology. German think tanks devote significant resources to research and value academic credentials to maintain their funding and reputations. In the recent past, German think tanks were vying for increased cooperation from media houses with a view to influencing decision makers through public opinion (FAS 2008).

A detailed study of think tanks in Canada revealed that funding from non-Canadian money predominantly went to conservative think tanks; however, that represented a small portion of the overall funding. Canadian think tanks usually combine funding efforts from private donations, government, self-generated revenue and investments. The study also showed that the government played a fairly significant role in funding think tanks, and those which obtained 'government grants and contracts' tended to be less political, and contracts reduced the need to bedazzle the funder. One of the findings of the study was that government funding tended to support centrist organisations, whereas private funds went towards conservative think tanks (McLevey 2013).

The case of think tank funding in the developing world is quite different. A study of think tank funding in Latin America reveals that a majority of think tanks have weak finances and are supported by private funding.

7. A few instances of Indian philanthropies spending on Indian think tanks will be expanded upon in a subsequent section.

In addition to private funding, they also receive foreign funding for their projects. Government funding, which is difficult to obtain, is usually in the form of short-term contracts, agreements or, sometimes, bidding for work in government projects. This is generally the case because governments are subject to a yearly budgetary process. Many think tanks in Latin America tend to not avail government funds, citing autonomy and independent agenda as reasons. However, in the recent past, there have been newer forms of public funding including government funding to multilateral agencies, specialised public policy research agencies through which government funds are channelised (Brazil, Costa Rica), and channelling international development funds to think tanks through a bidding process (Bolivia, Colombia) (Lauer 2012).

African think tanks face similar challenges to their Latin American counterparts. The days of 'golden donors' providing multiyear institutional grants are past. Professional philanthropies support short-term, high-impact, project-specific funding (Mungai 2016), whereas governments require 'evidence-based' advice. However, the space for independent voices is shrinking. This seeming contradiction is partly on account of governments wanting to co-opt researchers and experts in their ranks rather than engaging them in public discussions (Mendizabal 2015).

Indian think tanks have traditionally not been very keen in approaching either corporates or government for fund raising. This is on account of multiple factors including the need to maintain research independence, reluctance to deal with a myriad bureaucracy, etc. While the government does have its own think tanks in a few areas such as defence, external affairs and commerce, they tend to approach key non-profit organisations in areas where they do not have sufficient expertise. Corporates, on the other hand, tend to be only interested in funding reputed foreign think tanks. Not surprisingly therefore, Indian think tanks have had to seek support from international donor organisations (Baru 2010). However, the reasons for the corporates reluctance to supporting think tanks seem to run deep. Some of these concerns are discussed later in the paper.

Role of Think Tanks in Policymaking

Little as this might be known among the corporate sector, think tanks play a very critical—and often powerfully influential—role in the public policymaking process. The shape and form, and the pathways of influence, are complex, and think tanks have evolved deftness in handling such processes. A recent comprehensive study (Joe et al. 2017) on the policy impact of social science research in India showed that there is considerable abundance of SSR (social science research) studies and references in various policy documents of the ministries and the five year plans of the Planning Commission in India. For instance, the study found that:

> Out of the total 666 references noted in 200 documents of the Central ministries of human resource development, rural development and women and child development, about 37 per cent are cited for discussing the policy context, whereas about 55 per cent and 43 per cent of the references are used for analysis and inferences respectively. Further, a similar review of 307 references relating to these ministries and observed in the 11th and 12th Plan-related documents shows that about 67 per cent of the total cited references are related to policy design issues, while 38 per cent of the references are cited for their analysis. Also, there is significant involvement of social science researchers as members or chairpersons of important policy forums such as WGs (working groups) and technical committees. Planning Commission was found to be the largest user of SSR: 158 policy documents available on website had 753 SSR references cited in them. Of these, nearly half of the references were made in policy design documents.

This impact is true at level of state policies too. One study (Galab and Reddy 2017) shows that "research by a dedicated and autonomous research institute can play a useful role in giving direction to the policies of the state and help in bringing about changes in the lives of people." The study also highlights "preconditions such as credibility of research and research institute, research design that engages policymakers through the entire research value chain starting from the first stage, robust methodology, innovative research design and advocacy tools, and congenial political climate and policy environment" (Galab and Reddy 2017).

However, think tanks are critical and influential not only in India but in many countries of the world.

Successful International Instances of Think Tank Policy Impact

As illustrative examples, this section highlights only a few of the many stories where the Think Tank Initiative (TTI)[8] could make a difference to think tanks and their effectiveness in their respective contexts. They are all chosen from different countries to illustrate the universality of some core TTI principles that have served all contexts well, while ensuring adequate flexibility at all times to incorporate local contextual realities.

8. *www.thinktankinitiative.org.*

Grupo de Análisis para el Desarrollo (GRADE), Peru: To address the issue of lack of basic infrastructure, the government created the Ministry of Development and Social Inclusion (MIDIS) in 2011. GRADE provided the new ministry with research to support the design of a major new infrastructure investment programme. GRADE demonstrated that making a couple of infrastructure investments in one area leads to a greater total increase in income for beneficiaries than does spreading investments among separate communities. The Ministry used GRADE's findings to design its Infrastructure Combo programme, which is expected to invest US $225 million per year in basic rural infrastructure between 2013 and 2016. Based on GRADE's recommendations, the programme is expected to make simultaneous investments in electricity, clean water, sanitation, telecommunications and roads, and target those who lack at least one of these essential services.[9]

Fundación Salvadoreña para El Desarrollo Económico y Social (FUSADES), El Salvador: In response to a general reduction in El Salvador's economic competitiveness over the past few year (2005 onwards), FUSADES used evidence-based research to establish the competitiveness initiative to bring together a cross-section of social actors concerned with economic competitiveness. As a result of FUSADES's work, the Competitive Initiative network developed an agenda of priority actions for 2012-13 that targets such topics as education, innovation, infrastructure and market access. It was accomplished through collaboration among diverse stakeholders and resulted in several concrete proposals for action.[10]

Centro de Análisis y Difusión de la Economía Paraguaya (CADEP), Paraguay: It launched the Observatory of International Economics, which aims to support the public sector in developing enabling polices and the private sector in making sound business decisions. This initiative is helping to inform debates on how to increase trade and boost economic growth in Paraguay.[11]

Centre for Policy Dialogue (CPD), Bangladesh, and the South Asia Watch on Trade, Economics and Environment (SAWTEE), Nepal: Dedicated evidence-based analysis on issues of interests to the LDCs (least developed countries) in the context of the World Trade Organisation (WTO) negotiations

9. For more information on the project, visit *http://www.thinktankinitiative.org/content/grade-bringing-basic-infrastructure-rural-peru.*

10. For more information on the project, visit *http://www.thinktankinitiative.org/content/fusades-building-networks-strengthen-economic-competitiveness.*

11. For more information on the project, visit *http://www.thinktankinitiative.org/content/cadep-opening-borders-better-data.*

continues to remain under-researched. With a view to remedying this, CPD and SAWTEE are engaged in the process to strengthen the participation of the LDCs in the multilateral trading system of the WTO. This is being done by producing evidence-based policy recommendations in trade-related areas, stimulating knowledge-sharing in trade issues, capacity-building of relevant actors, and effective outreach to promote and secure the trade interests of the LDCs.[12]

Centre for Policy Dialogue (CPD), Bangladesh, and Southern Voice: CPD and Southern Voice have been pursuing research on SSC (South-South Cooperation) and exploring future strategies for the Southern Voice network. The project convened Southern Voice partners to develop a research design including a methodology for implementation of the research and analysis, to identify key themes on which research papers would focus, and to discuss appropriate outreach and engagement activities for sharing research findings and results.[13]

Center for Study of Science, Technology and Policy (CSTEP), India: CSTEP worked with India's Bureau of Energy Efficiency to design the PAT (perform, achieve and trade) mechanism, which promotes energy efficiency among large energy-intensive industries by allowing trade in Energy Saving Certificates. CSTEP worked particularly on developing energy consumption norms for the Indian cement and iron and steel industries. As part of its research, CSTEP also conducted a study to re-assess the potential of wind energy. CSTEP's research enabled the Government of India (GoI) to design and implement PAT, the first market-based mechanism of its kind in India. CSTEP's research in wind energy led to the government's announcement of the National Wind Mission, which is expected to promote wind energy generation.[14]

Although the success stories mentioned above are mostly international and drawn from the countries in which the TTI has been supporting these think tanks in their work, the essence of the argument is that the pathways to influence could work in myriad and often unexpected ways, and the TTI model is now proving to be a useful mechanism to support and strengthen think tanks, research ecosystem and, eventually, the public policymaking

12. For more information on the project, see *http://www.thinktankinitiative.org/sites/default/files/Advancing%20LDCs%20Interests%20in%20the%20WTO%20Strengthening%20Participation%2C%20Securing%20Priorities_CPD_EN_0.pdf.*

13. For more information on the project, see *http://www.thinktankinitiative.org/sites/default/files/Opp_Fund_CPD_April_2015_EN.pdf.*

14. For more information on the project, visit *http://www.thinktankinitiative.org/content/cstep-increasing-energy-efficiency-india.*

in several different contexts and at multiple levels of policy making as the illustrative examples above demonstrate. Indian corporates should be open to the idea of funding such pathways.

Recent Instances of Indian Corporate Support to Think Tanks in India

It would be worthwhile to recall that some of the top Indian institutions were set up through philanthropic support at the time of independence. Institution building was at that time seen as a key ingredient to nation-building, and the generation of Indian philanthropists in 1950s and 1960s played a crucial role in setting up these research institutions which have made India proud and continue to excel in their teaching and research.

One just needs to look at the country's history to see how corporates have shaped some of India's finest institutions—the Tatas funding Tata Institute of Fundamental Research (TIFR), Indian Institute of Science (IISc), Tata Institute of Social Sciences (TISS) and, more recently, the National Institute of Advanced Studies (NIAS); the Lalbhais contribution towards setting up of Indian Space Research Organisation (ISRO), Indian Institute of Management (IIM), Ahmedabad, Centre for Environmental Planning and Technology University (CEPT), Physical Research Laboratories (PRL) in addition to many other philanthropic initiatives. These corporates and the individuals driving them understood the importance of these institutions in the context of nation-building.

However, this tradition of using philanthropic capital for institution building declined and almost disappeared soon after independence, and the role was taken over by a few of the leading international philanthropic foundations, chief among them being the Ford Foundation. It is noteworthy that some of the top think tanks in India were set up through seed money, or similar large-size, long-term, often core grants from the Ford Foundation. However, in the recent past, that declined as well, and at no point did the government step in, to play that role; these institutions were hence left starved of funding and almost completely dependent on project funds, with precious little available for regular operational expenses, let alone institution building. Most think tanks in recent decades therefore became more dependent on project funds, whether from multilateral sources, bilateral agencies or governments. Among the several sources of project funding, it is again noteworthy that external funding played a significant role in supporting Indian think tanks, but largely through project-type research funding, with constraining caps on overheads.

Perhaps that ethos of nation-building needs to be brought back into the CSR narrative. Corporates have to go beyond linking their CSR efforts to their bottom-lines. They have to learn to be on the right side of history, before history bypasses them. We have honourable examples from the Indian context that are already beginning to demonstrate their commitment to this cause. In the recent past, there have been a few instances of corporate philanthropies supporting Indian think tanks. Prominent among these are Nandan Nilekani (Infosys co-founder) and Rohini Nilekani's institutional support to the tune of ₹50 crores each to think tanks such as National Council of Applied Economic Research (NCAER) and the Indian Institute for Human Settlements (IIHS). They have also supported the Takshashila Foundation, a Bengaluru-based think tank. Their philosophy that "it's important to have people of authenticity and integrity speaking up on issues, in a non-polarising way" is what motivates them to fund think tanks which have diverse ideologies. They also see certain issues like urbanisation (crucial to India's economy) requiring core support, which is part of the reason they funded IIHS (Karunakaran 2014).

The funding of think tanks by philanthropists reflects their passion and interest in the concerned areas. Certain industrialists are keen about clean energy and energy efficiency. For instance, Jamshyd Godrej who supported organisations like Shakti Sustainable Energy Foundation (SSEF), the Council on Energy, Environment and Water (CEEW) and the World Resource Institute (WRI) in India. The research and policy work done by these organisations in the energy space directly impacts the government's understanding of these areas, and fed into negotiations and decisions arrived at in the United Nations Climate Change Conference, Paris 2015 (COP 21).

A holistic approach to CSR would necessitate rigorous research into the causes of and solutions for the many economic and social challenges that our country and the world are grappling with. There are limits to insider advocacy as drivers of change. In a dynamic global world that India wants to lead, and belongs to, Indian philanthropists must begin to identify with a larger global public, and begin to think beyond their own generation for a better world that they want to create for their own good. As an important actor in that space of research to policymaking, think tanks have played, and will continue to play, an important and effective role in enabling such solutions through their independent policy research and outreach. They must be supported as institutions that can fiercely protect their independence and increasingly contribute to improved understanding of the world and more evidence-based public policymaking through rigorous research. To even make a difference in the fields of education, corporates need to move from counting the number of school children in uniforms, or change in enrolment and number of teachers, to assessing the real impact on lives and educational outcomes as a result of their intervention. This requires a solid body of rigorous and independent research before designing an intervention and follow-up through meaningful impact assessments. Think tanks are best placed to do that.

The independent policy and research work contributed by Indian think tanks over the years provides evidence-based scientific research which has directly and indirectly contributed to policymaking in multiple dimensions. However, what is probably required is a framework which can articulate this to governments and corporates. The next section provides one such framework and certain success stories in policy application.

The Think Tank Initiative[15] Framework: Making a Case for Corporates (and Government) to Revive their Support to Think Tanks

The TTI is a bold experiment to strengthen think tanks in developing countries, including in South Asia. It's a multi-donor programme dedicated to strengthen the capacity of independent policy research institutions in the developing world. The TTI firmly believes that think tanks or 'policy research institutions' have an important role in strengthening evidence-based decision-making in these countries and hence bear the potential to make sustained improvements in peoples' lives. The governments in these countries face multiple pressing challenges and often lack the capacity for high-quality policy research to take informed decisions. Think tanks can therefore potentially play a crucial role in supporting such informed decisions. However, most think tanks rely on project-based funding, which is often limited and project-specific. Therefore, think tanks are usually restricted to undertaking commissioned research instead of setting an agenda. Further, this prevents them from attracting high-quality talent and developing long-term research capacity, which in turn adversely affects the research quality.

The TTI is on attempt to break this vicious circle: selecting a group of think tanks—over 40 in 20 countries in Latin America, Africa and South Asia, of which 14 in South Asia and 7 think tanks in India—through a rigorous and competitive process of institutional assessment and selection and providing predictable core—unrestricted—support of up to one-third of their annual budget over a period of 10 years since 2009. The objective is to

15. *www.thinktankinitiative.org.*

help them strengthen their research quality and outreach to improve their impact in shaping policy. Therefore, TTI takes a 'leap of faith' on think tanks after selecting them through a long-term and robustly rigorous process. The entire programme is fully owned by the think tanks themselves and they develop their research agenda and programme objectives independently. TTI has developed comprehensive—though light-touch—monitoring and evaluation tools which are used annually. The TTI programme is managed and supported by the International Development Research Centre (IDRC) of Canada and is relevant to note here that TTI itself is a unique example of global public–private partnership between external aid agencies. The UK Department for International Development (DFID), The Norwegian Agency for Development Cooperation (NORAD) and International Development Research Centre (IDRC) and private international foundations like William and Flora Hewlett Foundation and Bill and Melinda Gates Foundation (BMGF) are five institutions that have committed about US $200 million to the programme over 10 years ending in 2019.

The TTI has been a successful programme as it has generated much programme-level and institutional-level learnings around core support, its effectiveness, mechanisms of delivery and assessment of impact on public policy and discourse. The institutions have used the core grant in innovative ways to strengthen research quality, improve organisational performance and improve communications and outreach. The core grant has led to significant improvements in the performance of many of the supported institutions. They have utilised the core grant to incubate innovative research ideas, attract and retain talented researchers, and make important contributions to the national and international policy agenda. The grant has also impacted the institutions and the ecosystem of think tanks beneficially in many different unexpected and indirect ways, as reported by the think tanks themselves. However, discussing programme successes and its impact is beyond the scope of this paper.[16]

The relevant question for the purpose of this paper is the following: Given the success of the global TTI model, can a similar model of providing predictable, core financial support to Indian think tanks be conceived specifically for the Indian context, with domestic philanthropists—either singly or as a consortium of foundations—committing to provide similar support, in congruence with their foundations' thematic priorities? In other words, if leading international donors could take a leap of faith on think tanks in developing countries, can domestic philanthropy not rise to the

16. For a detailed reference to related documents and external programme evaluation, visit *www.thinktankinitiative.org*.

occasion, modifying the model to suit their priorities and relevant to the Indian context? For the limited purpose of this article, the authors would like to propose the idea of 'TTI for India'—called by whatever name—but retaining the commitment in providing full/partial core support to think tanks as part of their research funding. This could include some amount of government contribution as well. This corpus can be used to support think tanks which are selected by a transparent and rigorous competitive process. A promising start has been made with Nilekani's grant to NCAER and IIHS. That story needs to be shared and widely believed in within the country. To be sure, the authors are not proposing core support to the entire annual budget, as that would likely lead to organisational complacency, but an optimum mix of core and project-based support to enable think tanks to develop an independent research agenda, hire talented researchers, but also remain exposed to market realities and continuously innovate to compete in the think tank space. It is important that the core grant only be a fraction of the institutions' budget so as to prevent them from becoming entirely dependent on the grant. Such a model will go a long way in improving the effectiveness of Indian think tanks and also enable them to fiercely protect their independence.

Meaningful engagement with government and policy impact takes effort and time, and requires perseverance and deep pockets. The TTI approach with an emphasis on multi-donor funding (US $200 million) in the form of institutional grants for over a decade in many ways is a game changer. This is a model which corporates might want to follow with adequate and appropriate modifications to suit their needs, priorities and requirements. Given that the CSR budget of the top 250 companies in India for just one fiscal was over ₹7,000 crore raises immense possibilities. One simple and effective approach could be for like minded corporates (in terms of themes that they would like to fund) to come together and pool their resources to fund think tanks. This funding could be in the form of grants or through a competitive process, albeit at least in part institutional in nature, which would allow think tanks to work on core areas of policymaking and also help them retain independence.

Corporates could even adopt an altered model similar to those in Western Europe which provide funding to research organisations—having components of policymaking, hiring researchers (professors, postdoctoral and doctoral positions) and researching questions key to that corporate/ industry. In that sense, think tanks present a unique opportunity for corporates to benefit directly from evidence-based research, and in the larger context, contribute and shape debates on key national issues.

For their part, think tanks should approach corporates with an agenda that they can identify with. For instance, corporates currently operating in the sanitation space (constructing toilets) could be made aware of concepts such as FSM (faecal sludge management) which should ideally be adopted as part of their sanitation CSR agenda. Think tanks working on FSM could suggest FSM strategies for upcoming CSR sanitation projects, while corporates could support studies which could lead to evidence-based decision-making. In the long-term, these learnings could contribute towards a sustainable sanitation policy which would be a win-win for government, think tanks and corporates.

As Ratan Tata—whose family established some of India's top institutions —said recently,

> The only advice I would give (to Indian philanthropists) is there is a lot of money that is probably less effectively used or employed because someone has not done enough research on what the problems are. But a large amount of philanthropy is in the more traditional forms—maybe to build temples or hospitals, not so concerned about what it actually does, but that edifices are created because that establishes that you did A or B or C. I think India has to move like other countries into a more sophisticated form of philanthropy which makes a difference and is designed to make a difference rather than just creating edifices (Mint 2016b).

CSR and Think Tanks: Issues to Consider

Like all partnerships, it is important to ensure that the relationships are strategic in nature and the boundaries of each partner are learnt and fully appreciated in the interest of a long-term credible relationship. While CSR funds offer promising funding potential for think tanks, there are certain caveats which both think tanks and corporates might want to consider while exploring effective, long-term partnerships.

For Corporates

The new regulations for CSR under the Companies Act, 2013, provide a huge opportunity for corporates to support social causes. Historically, Indian corporates have generously supported social causes, including programmes such as education, nutrition, health, tribal welfare and social welfare. However, corporates have been lukewarm in supporting research in general and think tanks in particular. The authors have discussed this issue with several leading corporates and think tank leaders and tried to understand the reason behind this reluctance to support think tanks. Based on this anecdotal evidence, the following appear as the main concerns of the corporates. However, they also need to better understand each of these.

Direct impact: Corporates are normally interested to support activities that create a 'direct impact'. In other words, they are interested in activities that show tangible output for the money spent. This approach is understandable as there are a large number of social issues where direct impact is beneficial to the stakeholder. Therefore, corporates are unclear on why they should support open-ended activities.

In case of think tanks, however, there usually is no immediate or direct impact. Think tanks will use the funding to undertake research programmes which may or may not have a policy impact in the short term. There is a parallel of this discussion among donor agencies too. Globally, increasing number of donor agencies now demand evidence of direct impact of think tanks' work. However, there is also an increasing global push back to this requirement—especially from those on aid effectiveness forums—that a push for evidence of direct impact is considerably diluting the value of aid. It undermines local ownership, leads to competition for 'marquee' issues such as health and education at the expense of more challenging social and institution building issues, and tends to focus spending on outputs rather than outcomes and impacts. All of these are anathema to the kernel of what aid is expected to deliver, let alone the fact that paradigmatic changes or big ideas that require long-term investments will be sacrificed at the altars of poorly conceived designs that focus on direct, often short-term, impacts. Institutions are not built in a day and require sustained investment to thrive, and some leading domestic philanthropic family know that all too well.

Attribution: Corporates would like the money spent on CSR activities to be directly attributable to the donor. Ideally, it should lead to the CEO or CSO 'inaugurating' an event where the beneficiaries can directly attribute the donation, and/or a good public relations opportunity, often in collaboration with key and high-level public officials.

In case of think tanks, this is typically not the case. Think tanks receive donations and grants from several institutions, often making it difficult to attribute a policy influence to a single donor. And that is key in protecting their independence which is not only in the best interest of the think tank, but also in the best interest of the funding agencies, whether government or corporate. Fungibility of grants is critical to protect the reputation and brand of a corporate funding agency. Brands know all too well how the smallest dent in their reputation could quickly translate into huge revenue loss, over a long time. Core support to institutions therefore is best guarantors of corporate brand reputation and enhancement.

Differentiation of Think Tanks: Think tanks are often loosely clubbed under the category of 'NGOs'. This is because most think tanks are non-profit and also charitable institutions. However, most corporate don't realise that a think tank, or policy research institution, is a different entity from most 'NGOs' as commonly understood and loosely referred to in common parlance. The common perception of a NGO is that of an activist group, which typically conducts anti-government protests, or a community organisation that works directly on the ground with communities on service delivery.

However, a policy research institution occupies a small niche in the entire spectrum of civil society space. They usually undertake evidence-based studies to inform public policy debates, with the hope that such evidence and knowledge will eventually inform public policy processes and outcomes, and also inform public discourse and advance knowledge. As integral members of civil society, they value and strongly protect their independence and free expression, though the expression they often use for advancing their cause is in the form of more and better evidence that is disseminated in public spaces and to public authorities.

Research Quality: Corporates are often not confident of the quality of research being undertaken in think tanks. On the face of it, this may not appear without reason. In the absence of an enabling and supporting ecosystem, most think tanks (with honourable exceptions) find it difficult to attract high-quality researchers. This in turn adversely affects their research quality, creating a chicken and egg situation. Corporates are not confident of their investment leading to high-quality research which impacts policy.

However, if one were to look at research quality as value per unit investment and then compare research from Indian think tanks to those from developed countries such as the US, the argument against research quality of Indian think tanks weakens considerably. Think, for instance, how much more expensive it usually is to fund a Professorial Chair in a US-based think tank as opposed to an Indian think tank, and the value of research as an investment—if that is how CSR managers would like to approach this issue—in Indian institutions will rank considerably higher.

Complexity of policymaking process: The policymaking process is usually complex and involves political decision-making. Historically, policymaking has been restricted to the realms of the bureaucracy. Only recently has the bureaucracy started to involve external expertise. Therefore, it is often not clear whether and to what extent will think tanks have a role in the policy process. This also relates to the issue of research quality and communications and outreach. A study on philanthropies in India revealed that donors expect transparency in the application of funds, demonstrated impact and low overheads as key factors with respect to funding the non-profit sector (think tanks being registered as non-profits) (Bain & Company 2015).

For Think Tanks

A few important issues for think tanks to consider could include, inter alia:

Limiting group exposure: Think tanks should diversify their fund base. They would well be served by setting an upper limit for accepting funds from the corporate sector. Even within that limit, it would be prudent to restrict one's exposure (in terms of funding) to a single corporate group. For their part, corporates will avoid suspicions about trying to buy policy influence by paying for research that speaks only to their interests.

Ethics committee: It is also advisable to have an ethics committee whose job is to scrutinise and advise think tanks on CSR funds, and have these discussions on record. This committee should have independent members (drawn from outside the think tanks) and can serve as an internal watchdog.

Have a firewall between funder and programmes: For core support, corporate donors should not know the project that their funding is being channelled to. Typically, think tanks work in multiple domains and it should be made amply clear that the corporate funding can go to any of the work domains, and not necessarily the ones that a corporate might be interested to fund. The potential downside of this approach, however, is that result-oriented corporate donors are likely to keep away, or perhaps a project-type funding could be negotiated with them. In such cases, the contribution of core support in maintaining independence is critical.

Proactive voluntary disclosure of sources of funding: Think tanks should have a policy of making sources of funding public. This will ensure that both the giver (corporate donor) and the taker (think tanks) are perfectly clear in terms of what they are involved in (information in public domain). Corporates should welcome transparency as it will substantiate their commitment to institution building and the desire to avoid perceptions of back room dealings.

Think tanks to retain copyright and intellectual property of research: It's important for think tanks to retain the copyright and Intellectual Property (IP) of their research and not surrender that to the corporates funding them. It's also important for the think tanks to retain the proprietary rights of the research.

Conclusion

Public institutions are severely threatened in the current tumultuous world, which is becoming wealthier, and grossly more unequal, with only eight individuals reported as possessing as much wealth as the bottom half of the world's population. Significant number of people could not enjoy the benefits of globalisation. However, corporates globally have begun to understand and internalise that world-class factories and hubs cannot be built in a city on fire. Global government's collective and unanimous adoption of the 17 Sustainable Development Goals (SDGs), which were arrived at through the largest consultation in the history of United Nations, and formally included private sector and civil society actors in a significant way for the first time, alongside think tanks, is a clear signal of the intent of the people of the world. 'No one must be left behind' is the motto and vision that we have collectively resolved to achieve by 2030. Global partnership has been incorporated into the SDGs as a means of progressing towards this goal, where private sector, alongside civil society actors including think tanks, are committed to playing larger and significant roles.

In this global context, Indian CSR law provides an opportunity and a trigger to thinking more strategically about the enduring contributions that domestic philanthropists could make to Agenda 2030 of the SDGs and help governments of their countries achieve these targets. Data Revolution is what will be required to begin to understand the scale of the SDGs as well as monitor their progress. Knowledge creation will underpin government's efforts all over the world, and think tanks are already playing a central role in enabling governments to create adequate and appropriate knowledge infrastructure within their countries to live up to their global SDG commitment. Indian corporates must rise to this occasion and by meaningfully supporting think tanks, support their governments to achieve the Agenda 2030. For many corporate families, it is a moment to recall and revive their own family legacy and their contributions to institution building. The success of TTI as a bold and unique model in recent times—itself a product of public-private partnership—provides an opportunity for domestic philanthropy to invoke partnership with governments at national and state levels, and enrich the national- and state-level policy environment and processes of decision-making in the government such that together we build a better future for our children.

References

Bain & Company (2015). *India Philanthropy Report 2015*. Retrieved from *http://www.bain.com/Images/BAIN_REPORT_India_Philanthropy_Report_2015.pdf.*

Bansal, S. and S. Rai (2014). "An Analysis of Corporate Social Responsibility in India", *Economic and Political Weekly* 49(50). Retrieved from *http://www.epw.in/journal/2014/50/web-exclusives/analysis-corporate-social-responsibility-expenditure-india.html.*

Baru, S. (2010). "Indian Minds, Foreign Funds"", *Business Standard,* 9 August. Retrieved from *http://www.business-standard.com/article/opinion/sanjaya-baru-indian-minds-foreign-funds-110080900083_1.html.*

E&Y (2013). "Corporate Social Responsibility in India: Potential to Contribute Towards Inclusive Social Development". Retrieved from *http://www.ey.com/Publication/vwLUAssets/EY-Government-and-Public-Sector-Corporate-Social-Responsibility-in-India/$File/EY-Corporate-Social-Responsibility-in-India.pdf.*

FAS. (2008). "OSC Media Aid: German Think Tank Guide". Retrieved from *https://fas.org/irp/dni/osc/german-think.pdf.*

Galab, S., & Reddy, M.G. (2017). *Policy Impact: Evidence from States*. In S. Thorat & S. Verma (Eds.), Social Science Research in India: Status, Issues and Policies. Oxford University Press.

Jana Foundation. (undated). "Evolution of CSR in India". Retrieved from *http://www.janalakshmi.com/wp-content/uploads/evolution_of_csr_in_india.pdf.*

Joe, W., A. Kalra ans M. Panda (2017). "Policy Impact: Evidence on Central Government Policies", in S. Thorat and S. Verma (eds.), *Social Science Research in India: Status, Issues and Policies*. Oxford University Press.

Karunakaran, N. (2014). "Indian Philanthropic Money into Think-Tanks Silencing Foreign Funding Question", *The Economic Times,* 4 November. Retrieved from *http://articles.economictimes.indiatimes.com/2014-11-04/news/55757735_1_rohini-nilekani-foreign-funding-indian-institute.*

Kotak Wealth Management (2016). *Top of the Pyramid India: Decoding the Ultra HNI*. Retrieved from: *http://wealthmanagement.kotak.com/topindia /pdf/topofthepyramid2016.pdf*

Lauer, A. (2012). "Public Funds for Public Policy Research in Latin America: A Study by Lardone and Roggero". 7 June. Retrieved from *https://onthink tanks.org/articles/public-funds-for-public-policy-research-in-latin-america-a-study-by-lardone-and-roggero/.*

Manku, M. (2016). "Everybody Wants a Slice of the (Tiny) CSR Pie", *Mint,* 1 April.

————.(2016). "Growth of Wealth Gives Way for Growth in Charity", *Mint,* 6 October.

McLevey, J. (2013). *Producing and Promoting Policy Ideas: A Study of Think Tanks in Canada.* Doctoral Dissertation. Ontario: McMaster University. 13 May. Retrieved from *https://macsphere.mcmaster.ca/bitstream/11375/13085/1/fulltext.pdf.*

Mendizabal, E. (2015). "The Future of Think Tanks in Africa: Trends to Look Out For", 20 July. Retrieved from *https://onthink tanks.org/articles/the-future-of-think-tanks-in-africa-trends-to-look-out-for/*

Mint (2016a). "Impact Assessment is the CSR Game-Changer", *Mint,* 12 August. Retrieved from *http://www.livemint.com/Companies/GxHsO3nDwf3ziixuSeE39O/Impact-assessment-is-the-CSR-gamechanger.html*

————. (2016b). "You Really Want to be doing Things that Make a Difference: Ratan Tata", *Mint,* 3 October. Retrieved from *http://www.livemint.com/Companies/eZ5raUtIs7kmScXuchQY9M/You-really-want-to-be-doing-things-that-make-a-difference-R.html*

Mungai, C. (2016). "Which are the Top Think Tanks on the Continent? Plus Insights About the Thinking Business in Africa", *Mail & Guardian Africa*. Africa. 12 February. Retrieved from *http://mgafrica.com/article/2016-02-10-think-tanks-in-africa*

NGOBOX (2016). *India CSR Outlook Report 2016*. Retrieved from *http://ngobox.org/media/India%20CSR%20Outlook%20Report%202016-NGOBOX.pdf*

Praxis (2016). *CSR in India, 2016*.

Thorat S. and S. Verma (eds.) (2017). *Social Science Research in India: Status, Issues and Policies*. New Delhi: Oxford University Press.

3

SHULAGNA SARKAR and SAMEER PINGLE

Corporate Social Responsibility
A Cross Country View

Introduction

Organisations by the nature of its operation have both good and bad effect on the society as well as on environment. These effects influence talent acquisition, employee engagement and morale, land acquisition, certifications, recognitions and market reputation of the company. Organisations have realised that they receive a social sanction from society with an assurance that they, in return, contribute to the growth and development of the society. Long-term business success can only be achieved by organisations that recognise CSR (corporate social responsibility) as part of their core value and makes it as a competitive advantage. Global organisations by the nature and vast expanse are expected to take up CSR activities in its areas of operation irrespective of the boundaries.

Though companies are initiating CSR activities yet, a large number of them are inspired by the benefits received due to the emphasis on CSR by the government. Mandating CSR through legislations has a cascading effect on companies in initiating the CSR drive. In spite of large acceptance and presence of CSR across the world, Levitt (1958) set up a base for the debate about the social responsibility of business and emphasised that 'government's job is not business, and business's job is not government'. Friedman (1970) expressed the same sentiment and added that the mere existence of CSR was a signal of an agency problem within the firm. Countries have debated that whether CSR should be mandated by introducing it as a part of legislation or not. CSR by its definition is interpreted to remain voluntary and market-driven whereas today the essence of CSR is revolutionising from voluntary to more obligatory to companies.

Reich (1998) has explained that government should act as arbiter of business responsibility in society. This view is reinforced by another point of view that sees government as helping business to achieve CSR through regulation, control and enforcement (Broberg 1996). The concern of CSR being mandated may lead some individuals and interest groups being in a favourable position whereas others may not. The idea of legislating on company's CSR activities grabs away the essence of CSR and its successful implementation. There is a less possibility of raising standards through standardisation, as this would remove the competitive incentive driving forward CSR activity and would also place an unmanageable onus on organisations. There is large possibility of CSR processes and practices leading to more corruption in such scenario.

Comparative studies of CSR have not been undertaken much, as compared to other related fields, such as corporate governance or corporate law. Researches in the field of CSR are still in its 'emergent' form (McWilliams et al. 2006). Literature review reveals about the lack of constituent definition of CSR. The lack of consistency of CSR definitions across studies makes it difficult to evaluate and compare the findings from different studies because they usually refer to different dimensions of CSR. On the other hand, several countries have employed legislation, regulation and taxation as tools for the government to promote and protect social objectives (Bichta 2003). Yet, there is a lack of literature which measures the social impact of these tools used by the government. There are hardly any researches which discusses the obligatory approach to CSR and its impact.

In the backdrop of the above concern where there is no uniformity in defining and regulating CSR, an attempt has been made to study CSR in an international perspective and understand the approach to CSR adopted across developing and developed countries. Believing in the voluntary nature of CSR, a large number of countries have made reporting mandatory. The support extended from government or legislations in various countries are distinctly different. The role of government is also very country specific, majorly being an enabling entity to more structured CSR implementation. It has been observed that CSR initiatives in developing countries and LDCs (least developed countries) are addressing more on social issues like poverty reduction, employment generation, education, health and environment. Whereas, the rest of the world considers CSR more as conservation of nature based initiatives. There is a large difference in the type of initiatives considered under CSR in developed, developing countries and LDCs. It is in this context the paper intends to discuss the CSR approaches of developed, developing countries and LDCs with special reference to health and education as CSR area. Literature reveals that there are majorly four approaches to CSR: normative, instrumental, descriptive and strategic. The paper clarifies the approach of corporates in implementing CSR in the studied nations.

Objectives

The objectives of the paper are three folded:

- To elaborate the CSR approach in the developed, developing and LDCs.
- To discuss the government initiatives encouraging corporates' to undertake activities for environment and social development.
- To discuss the CSR initiatives towards health and education in the developed, developing and LDCs.

CSR: The Global Perspective

History reveals the journey of legislations supporting social agendas. According to Dossing (2003), there are three generations of CSR, the first being focused on short-term corporate interests and motives and the second on long-term success strategies. The present third generation is aimed at role of businesses in addressing more imperative issues like poverty, exclusion, and environmental degradation. During the 1970s, most social issues became public policy matters and legislations were passed to address health and safety at work, environmental protection and consumer protection rights. Since the earlier 20th century, European member states had developed legislations to control the relationship between employee and the firm, health and safety at work, issues of environmental interest, discrimination and equal opportunities at workplace (Bichta 2003). In Europe, the state-owned companies were expected to focus on both commercial and social objectives compared to the private sector companies whose prime objective was profit.

In Britain and the United States (US), new laws were introduced along with new agencies like the Department of Environment and Environmental Protection Agency. Corporations responded positively to the new legislation as it was evident that they required experts to formulate environmental policy and that a uniform set of national regulations would provide 'a level playing field' for business (Enloe 1975).

In United Kingdom (UK), the first real law of CSR is based on 'Disclose'. Section 172—Companies Act, 2006, UK emphasises on environment, social and economical focus by redefining the duties of the director. Even though the Act does not make spending or implementing CSR activities mandatory yet, the duties of director to promote the success of the company are based on Triple Bottom Line.

Sweden is viewed as a pioneer in the field of CSR. In Sweden, there is no specific regulation system in place concerning CSR of companies in the country. There are however accounting practices that affect CSR to some extent. Irrespective of no specific regulation concerning CSR in 2013, Sweden topped the RobecoSAM Country Sustainability Ranking. Sweden became the first country to demand sustainability reports from state-owned enterprises. The reports have to comply with guidelines from the GRI (global reporting initiative). About half of all the private companies that report on sustainability, use the GRI as a way of communicating CSR efforts (PWC 2010).

The Johannesburg Stock Exchange was the first emerging market stock exchange to create a SRI (socially responsible investing index) in 2004 (Maguire 2011). Emerging markets such as Brazil, India, China and South Africa have initiated higher involvement in CSR-related activities through CSR reporting to promote the listed companies' credibility, transparency and endurance. Though the government in these countries have a vision for implementation of CSR initiatives yet; research of Petkoski and Twose (2003) reveals that government of developing countries are viewing CSR activities as a means:

- To enhance sustainable development strategies.
- As a component of their national competitiveness strategies to compete for foreign direct investment.
- To position their exports globally and to improve poverty focused delivery of public policy goals.

China's policy vision during mid 2000s was building 'a harmonious society' which was adopted as a policy mandate by the Central Committee of the Communist Party in 2006 (Sharma 2013). This policy focused on harmonious and scientific development and motivated the enactment of new labour and environmental legislation and the incorporation of CSR into the 2006 revision to Chinas' Company Law. Although its meaning is much debated, Article 5 of the Company Law now provides that mainland Chinese companies shall comply with the laws and administrative regulations, social morality and business morality and bear social responsibilities (Gongsifa 2005). China has also encouraged CSR reporting in guidelines released through the Shanghai and Shenzhen Stock Exchange (Maguire 2011). Studies consistently find that reporting rates are highest in Europe, followed by Japan, and with the US showing the lowest rates of reporting among comparable companies (Kolk 2003, KPMG 2005, Welford 2004).

Okoye (2012) advised a contextual approach to identifying CSR objectives and recognises the need for frameworks which law can provide by using the example of Nigeria's attempt to pass a CSR bill mandating contributions towards development. A number of studies have compared the CSR practices and have come up with very significant difference in the approach to CSR across countries. Matten and Moon (2004) have compared

CSR in Europe and US, and have proposed a conceptual framework of 'explicit' versus 'implicit' CSR. Explicit CSR is conceptualised as seen in the United States with less stringent legal requirements, as companies volunteer to address important social and economic issues through their CSR policies. In contrast, Europe and the UK, undertake issues such as healthcare provision, employee's rights and environmental protection as part of a company's legal responsibilities, and thus defined as 'implicit' CSR in the way the company does business.

Maignan and Ralston (2002) also show variance across four industrialised Organisation for Economic Co-operation and Development (OECD) countries in undertaking CSR. The findings revealed that UK firms were more performance driven compared to US based on extension of their core company values. Dutch and French firms displayed combination of performance-driven, values-driven, and stakeholder-driven approach. Stakeholders' pressure on companies to address CSR issues also differ across countries. Maignan (2001) studied the consumer attitudes towards CSR and the demands that consumers are willing to make on firms. Research of Maignan and Ralston (2002) reveal that communities and consumers were the primary stakeholder drivers in the UK while customers and regulators were more salient in France Netherlands.

Benefits of CSR: A Cross-Country View

As several counties initiate in making CSR mandatory, it becomes inevitable for governments to measure the impact of CSR activities. It is essential to frame some metrics and measure the impact of CSR initiatives undertaken. Various researches focused on several aspects of business to measure the effects of CSR activities, these includes financial as well as non-financial measures such as brand image, customer satisfaction, customer loyalty, sales growth, market value, financial performance of the firm, talent attraction and management.

Tang et al. (2012) in their meta analysis from 1995 to 2007 of American enterprises with diversified profile found that there was a positive impact of CSR on financial performance (ROA [return on assets]—and ROE [return on equity]). The research clarified that the impact would only be visible at a longer period of time. While Peloza (2006) found that companies with high CSR reputation have low cost implicit claims, while those with poor social responsibility image will face more expensive explicit claims such as law suits, fines from government, demands of shorter payment period from suppliers and higher costs of obtaining capital owing to increased risk perception by banks and investors.

Study of Aupperle et al. (1985) has reported no significant relationship between strong orientation towards social responsibility or concern for society and financial performance in both short as well as long term return on assets. Katneman et al. (1986) have found causal link between CSR and financial performance. Many researchers have found positive relationship between corporate social performance and corporate financial performance (Graves and Waddock 1994, Russo and Fouts 1997, Hillman and Keim 2001, Lo and Sheu 2007). Financial performance of the companies would be measured differently in different researches studied such as NPV ratio, profit margin, sales growth, share price increases, ROA, ROE, ROI etc. Study of Bhattacharya et al. (2009) found that CSR-stakeholder relationship linkage may precede CSR business performance linkage.

Johnson and Greening (1999) has reported that there was a relationship between firms' ownership structure and CSR in developed countries, while in a Chinese study of Li and Zhang (2010), it was evident that there is difference in behaviour of firms controlled by state and privately owned. This also means that there is a relationship between ownership structure and CSR. During study of Indian banks, Singh and Agarwal (2013) found that CSR orientation of banks differs mainly due to ownership, its number of employees and date of its incorporation (age of bank in market). These variation in banks' CSR orientation is manifested not in all areas of CSR, but namely in the areas of environment and rural development. Salmones et al. (2005) has reported that the development of a favourable brand image and the maintenance of loyal stakeholder is related to the maintenance of a responsible behaviour by respecting environment and communities reducing the consumption of natural resources (Manaktola and Jauhari, 2007), engaging in social causes and providing fair treatment of employees (David et al. 2005).

CSR activities of organisations create a good reputation for business and increase its attractiveness as an employer. CSR increases the perceived trustworthiness of an organisation for a job seeker who is lacking any previous interaction with the organisation (Viswesvaran et al. 1998). Maignan et al. (1999) indicated that market oriented and humanistic cultures lead to proactive corporate citizenship, which in turn is associated with improved levels of employee commitment, customer loyalty and business performance. Study by Peterson (2004) shows a link between employee perception of corporate citizenship and organisational commitment.

CSR orientation positively affects several customer related outcomes (Bhattacharya and Sen 2004). Experimental study (Brown and Dacin 1997, Brown 1998) showed that CSR affects either directly or indirectly, also affects customer-company identification (Sen and Bhattacharya 2001), customer donations to nonprofit organisations (Lichtenstein et al. 2004) and customer product attitude (Berens et al. 2005). Strong research of CSR creates a favourable context that positively boosts consumers' evaluations of attitude toward the firm (Sen and Bhattacharya 2001). Research of Bhattacharya and Sen (2004) on customer-company identification suggest that CSR initiatives constitute a key element of corporate identity that can induce customers to identify that means which develop a sense of connection with the company and customers are more likely to be satisfied with a firm's offerings.

Besides the benefits, the penetration of CSR issues as matters of serious institutional investor concern is less advanced in the US than in the UK (Williams and Conley 2005). Institutional investors believe that social, environmental and governance issues can be financially material, either positively or negatively. CSR profiles can be taken care by such investors as they act as competitive advantage if managed well and also backfire if mismanage (Solomon et al. 2004) institutional investors in the UK would more readily perceive the financial significance of CSR issues than their American counterparts (Aguilera et al. 2006).

Study in China by Gao (2009) found that companies in automobile, iron and steel industries prefer legal and ethical responsibilities such as safety of products or services and energy saving, while companies in home electronics and banking and insurance industries underline philanthropic responsibility such as sponsor civilisation or sports and donation to hope project. Companies in electrical power, oil and chemical industries prefer both ethical and philanthropic responsibility. Companies in transportation, business and trade and other industries have no preference for the issues they address. Mostly all companies found to be similar in addressing stakeholder interest foreign companies also addressed all stakeholders except community (Gao 2009).

In a Romanian study by Baleanu et al (2011) comprising of top 100 companies website content, 49 companies had a dedicated CSR section. The study revealed that Romanian firms lacked appearing of CSR in corporate vision and strategic planning as a part of the structured corporate reporting of CSR. Seventeen (17) out of the 49 companies position CSR in the wider strategic framework of the company i.e., mention of social role of business in mission/vision/values. The study also clarified the ways in which the companies define and prioritise their stakeholders. For around 43 companies, the most important stakeholder is community followed by clients, employers, business partner, shareholders, state institutions, competitors, civil society and other respectively. The CSR activities were in majority initiated in the area of community followed by environment, education, health, sports, culture, employees, organisational activities and others. Nyarko and Grigore (2011) studied around 20 companies from Ghana for CSR orientation and found that out of 20 listed companies, only two reported CSR information on their website, only three had separate heading for CSR in their financial reports, CSR activities were more oriented towards community programme such as education, culture, environment, HIV, Malaria prevention, hospital donations, farming activities, sports etc.

Effect of CSR activities on various aspects of business has been studied by researchers and financial as well as non-financial measures have been reported by them. The studies have also found that the impact of CSR can be seen in the long run. Literature indicates that community is the strongest and most looked into stakeholder by companies for CSR activities followed by clients and others. CSR activities are also associated with brand identity in many researches. In countries where CSR activities are mandatory, the companies are reporting CSR information on their websites. CSR has also been reported to improve employer attractiveness in some studies. Thus, CSR also helps the companies for attracting talented employees. Ownership structure and number of employees also plays significant role in successful implementation of CSR activities. The model of non-shareholder interests' representatives is also extensively used in Scandinavia with particular emphasis on employee representation. This model is also imposed by state regulation and necessitates the representation of employees, the local community, consumers and the environment, in the firm's meetings (Broberg 1996).

Methodology

An attempt has been made to study 11 countries classified as 4 developed and 3 developing and 4 LDCs as per OECD. The various legislations of the select countries have also been studied to make an understanding of the CSR perspective of selected legislations of these countries. It is also attempted to study the Health expenditure, Education expenditure, Population, HDI (human develop index), and GDP (gross domestic product) of these countries. Though there are several issues like environment, gender equality, discrimination, fair wages, health, education, and empowerment yet, two major areas of concern for nation development are 'health' and 'education'. The health and education status and expenditure has been broadly studied for making an understanding of the country status as well government support. Secondary data has been analysed to elaborate the issues of the countries based on the development classification. The CSR intervention in health and education has been discussed to explain how CSR can address social issues of countries.

Limitations and scope of further research: The study comprises only 11 countries. There is a large scope for undertaking research which considers a large sample of countries from each category of developed, developing and least developed countries. Only health and education data has been analysed as a part of the study which again leads to a larger scope for further studies on various other issues pertaining to the development of the country. Issues like women empowerment, gender equality status, environment status could be dealt in depth to understand the scope of CSR activities in these areas.

Country Analysis: Encouraging Social Development

CSR spending reflects socio-economic priorities and institutional gaps in skills or infrastructure especially in developing countries and LDCs. Government in various countries offers tax breaks to multinational companies for social investments in return. Some countries have cultures traditionally based on philanthropy whereas others initiate CSR majorly due to the existence of regulatory or corporate governance laws. Table 3.1 clarifies that most of the developed nations have two concerns to be dealt; being 'environment' and 'fair labour practices'. On the other hand for both developing countries and LDCs, social issues are invariably high. Thus, community development is a major agenda apart from others like health and workplace quality.

Table 3.1 broadly reflects the Legislation/programmes encouraging CSR, thrust areas and CSR approach in 9 countries. As described by Jones et al. (2007), the various approaches to CSR are normative, instrumental, descriptive and strategic. The descriptive approach is about focus on transparent accountability on social, environmental, and financial performance. The strategic approach advocates the sustainability and 'license-to-operate' views and describes the behaviours of companies as they interact with stakeholders (Berman et al. 1999). The instrumental approach to CSR attempts to engage those stakeholder groups that can influence corporate performance, thus creating accountability relationships that help them accomplish mutually important goals, as efficiently as possible (Boesso et al. 2013). It also considers CSR as a strategic tool to promote economic objectives (Garriga and Mele 2004).The normative approach to CSR follows the moral obligation justification and prescribes how stakeholders should be treated based on some underlying moral or philosophical principles (Young and Thyil 2008). In the purview of stakeholder approach to CSR, organisations are expected to manage responsibly an extended web of stakeholder interests across increasing organisations boundaries and also acknowledge a duty of care towards traditional interest groups as well as silent stakeholders—such as local communities and the environment (Simmons 2004).

Table 3.1

Legislations Encouraging CSR Focus across Nations

Name of the Country	*Legislation/ Programmes with Regard to CSR*	*Environment*	*Social Issues*	*Business Practices, Work Condition, Rights, Fair Wages*	*Approach*
Australia	The Australian Securities Exchange, 2014	√	√		Descriptive
	Code of Conduct on environmental risks and controls	√		√	
	Corporate Social Responsibility & Human Rights, 2008			√	
Canada	The Environmental Protection Act, 1999	√	√		Descriptive
	Inclusion of Economic Diplomacy to Bill C-300	√	√	√	
	Corruption of Foreign Public Officials Act, 1999			√	
USA	National Action Plan on responsible business conduct	√	√	√	Descriptive
	Emergency Planning and Community Right-to-Know Act (EPCRA), 1986	√			
	Regional Greenhouse Gas Initiative, 2008	√			
Argentina	CSR Law No. 8.488 *Provincial Law, 2012	√	√	√	Descriptive
	National Labour Law No. 25.877, Regarding Social Balance, 2004			√	

	Glacier Law, 2010	√			
	Environment and Climate Change Law, 2014	√			
India	Companies Act, 2013	√	√		Instrumental
	DPE CSR and Sustainability Guidelines, 2013	√	√		
China	Shenzhen Stock Exchange Social Responsibility Guidelines, 2006	√	√	√	Instrumental
	Shanghai Stock Exchange, 2008	√	√	√	
	The State-owned Assets Supervision and Administration Commission of the State Council (SASAC) Guidelines, 2008	√	√	√	
	Environmental, Social and Governance Reporting Guide, 2012	√	√	√	
Myanmar	The Environmental Conservation Law, 2012	√			Strategic
Maldives	The Nasheed Administration, 2010	√	√	√	Strategic
	The UN Anticorruption Convention, 2005			√	
Bhutan	New industrial emission standards set up by the National Environmental Commission (NEC), 2013	√	√		Strategic

Note: Compiled by the authors.

An attempt has been made to understand the GDP, population and HDI by comparing them. Figure 3.1 reveals that economic prosperity has a trend towards the population rank. Lower the population rank reflects more possibility of high poverty, higher unemployment, economic stagnation and environmental degradation. The HDI measures the average achievements in a country in three basic dimensions of human development: a long and healthy life, access to knowledge and a decent standard of living (HDI 2014). The comparison of the GDP, population and HDI reflects how a country would stand in economy, health and prosperity.

Figure 3.1

Country Profiling

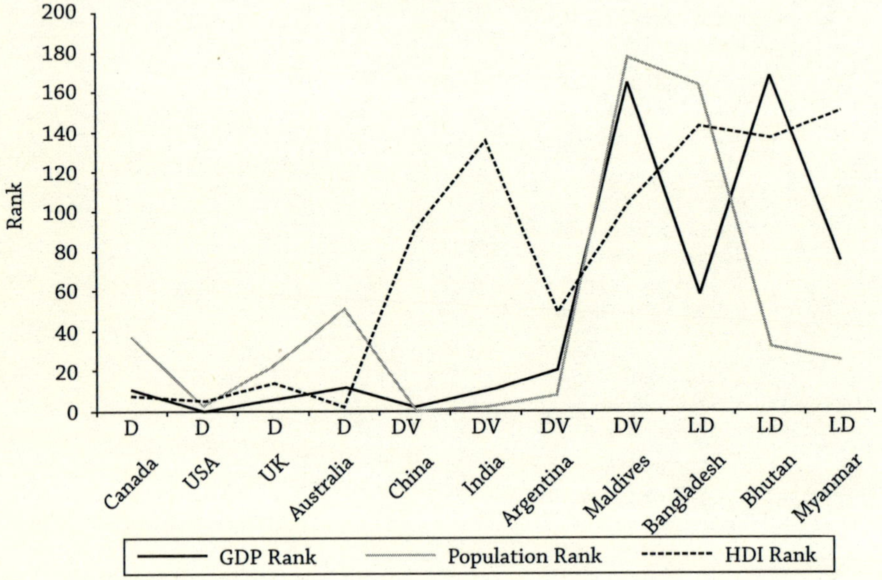

Note: Population rank as on 1 July 2014.

Interpretation: D: Developed, DV: Developing and LD: Least Developed

Source: Compiled by the author based on data from: *www.databank.worldbank.org and www.undp.org*

Health: A Social Issue

The health statuses of men and women, poor and wealthy, or the indigenous and non-indigenous populations reveal the social, economical and cultural status of a country. The living conditions of the country have a significant influence on the chances of its citizens enjoying a long and healthy life. Provisions for health vary across the world. Planning health provision is challenging for countries due to the costs as well as various social, cultural, political and economic conditions.

Table 3.2

Health Profiling of Countries

S. No	*Country*	*Health Index (2013)*	*Infant Mortality Rate (2011) (per 1,000 live births)*	*Maternal Mortality Ratio (2011) (per 1,00,000 live births)*	*Life Expectancy at Birth (2013)*	*Gender Inequality Index Rank (2013)*
1.	Canada	0.946	05	13	81.5	23
2.	United States of America	0.907	06	27	78.9	47
3.	United Kingdom	0.931	04	11	80.5	35
4.	Australia	0.961	04	6	82.5	19
5.	China	0.851	12	36	75.3	37
6.	India	0.714	44	220	66.4	127
7.	Bangladesh	0/779	33	170	70.7	115
8.	Bhutan	0.743	36	120	68.3	102
9.	Argentina	0.866	13	69	76.3	74
10.	Myanmar	0.695	41	220	65.2	83
11.	Maldives	0.891	09	38	77.9	49

Source: Compiled by the authors based on data from: *www.databank.worldbank.org and www.hdr.undp.org*

India, Myanmar, Bangladesh and Bhutan displays a high maternal mortality rate. Infant mortality rate is also high in these countries. Irrespective of the large population of China, the infant mortality rate as well as the maternal mortality ratio is controlled. Australia, Canada and United Kingdom are better than others in health status.

Bangladesh and China show a high growth percentage. Irrespective of India being a developing country, the health expenditure is comparatively low. Canada spends well in health considering its low increase in growth percentage.

CSR Addressing Health Issues

On one hand, countries are heading towards development and advance development while on the other hand, concerns like aging population, decreasing fertility rate, numerous epidemic diseases, rising alcoholism and drugs, deteriorating health conditions of mother and child in several countries are becoming deep concerns which needs close attention. When discussing the CSR issues, 'health based initiatives' clearly stands out as a leader. Countries are spending a considerable part of GDP on improving healthcare quality and accessibility. Corporate spending to global health is 16 times the figure for global education (Brookings 2013). Yet, there is a large gap in the required expenditure on health in both developing countries and LDCs.

Figure 3.2

Health Expenditure

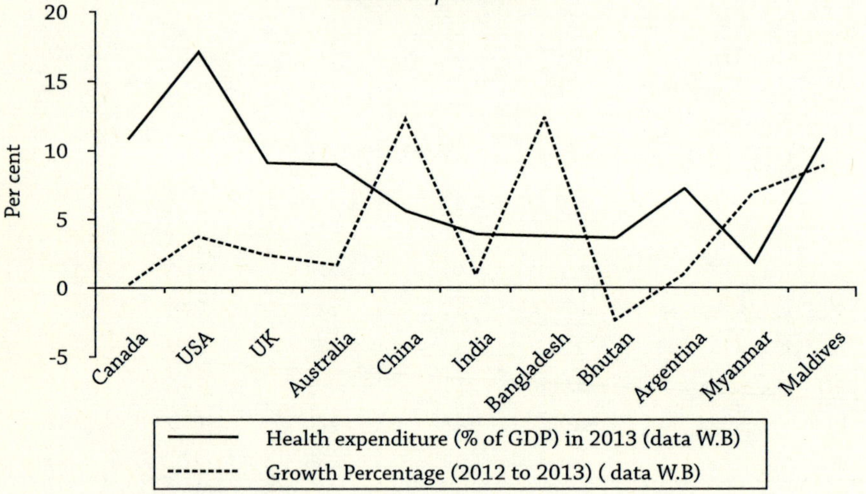

Source: Compiled by the author.

Issues like plague, tuberculosis, malnutrition, infant and child mortality are major issues to least developed nations. Health is not only an issue to developing and least developed nation but also an equal concern to developed countries. Even though countries that have been developed and wealthier over the years are now facing health crisis. However, most of these issues are non-communicable yet; no less deadly on the grand scale. World Health Science (2010) highlights that the western lifestyle is characterised by a high calorie diet, rich in fat and refined sugars and animal proteins. These dietary issues combined with a more sedentary lifestyle, have created an overall energy imbalance leading to cancer, obesity, diabetes, and cardiovascular disease. As the health issues vary from developed, developing countries and least developed nation, the approach to CSR in health also varies in these categorised nations. In majority, the CSR initiatives in least developed and developing countries include: operating mobile medical units in the interiors of the state or country, organising health camps, immunisation drive, providing nutritional supplements to pregnant and lactating mothers including infant and children, creating awareness on health and sanitation and building health infrastructure.

Education: A Social Issue

Education is a dialogue between the past, present and the future, so that the coming generations receive the accumulated lessons of the heritage and carry it forward. Poor education is arguably at the heart of many social problems. Lack of education leads to social issues like crime, unemployment, poverty, sexual attitudes leading to unwanted pregnancies and rising population. Education can bring in a difference to the marriage practices in several counties. Education has the power to abolish early marriages and can make a difference to remove old cultural norms of gender discrimination and empower women. Education has a large impact on the overall life of an individual as it shapes ones attitude.

Figure 3.3

Education Expenditure

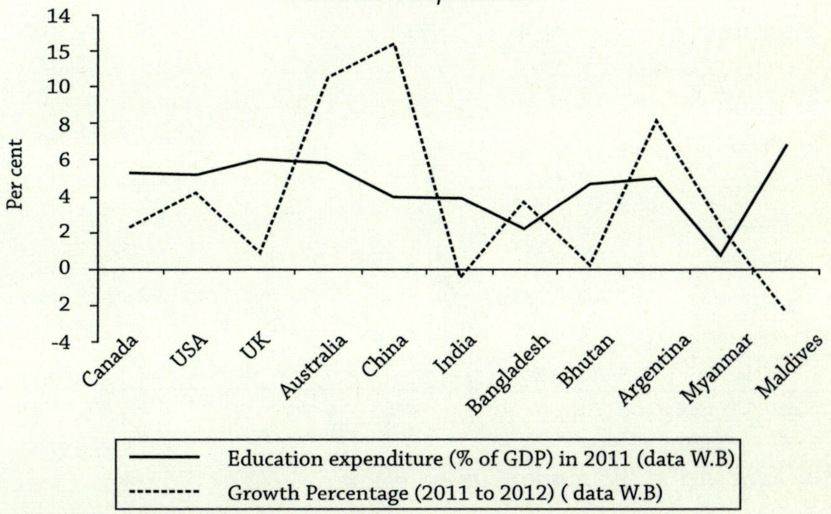

Source: Compiled by the author.

Governments in every country set up the overall framework that shapes their education system and defines its operation. They determine the organisation and structure of the system. Factors like years of compulsory education, students' age for entry in school, grade levels, courses offered, teachers' qualifications, provision of compulsory education (public and/ or private actors), choices of schools available, mechanism of financing education, standards by which education providers are held accountable play a major role in determining the accessibility and quality in accessibility of education of the country. Governments spend on education reveals how valued is education as a factor to the development of the country.

Developed countries spend more on education than developing countries. Countries like Maldives and Argentina are spending high compared to the rest developing countries and LDCs. There are several factors which reflect the education status of the country. Some of the major factors are adult literacy, primary school dropout rate, secondary school dropout rate and Expected years of schooling.

Table 3.3

Education Status

S. No	*Country*	*Education Index*	*Adult Literacy Rate (2013)*	*Gross Secondary Enrolment Rate (2011)*	*Mean Years of Schooling (2013)*	*Expected Years of Schooling (2013)*
1.	Canada	0.850	99	103.40	12.3	15.9
2.	United States	0.890	99	93.55	12.9	16.5
3.	United Kingdom	0.860	99	97.38	12.3	16.2
4.	Australia	0.927	96	133.05	12.8	19.9
5.	China	0.610	95.1	86.61	7.5	12.9
6.	India	0.473	62.8	68.51	4.4	11.7
7.	Bangladesh	0.447	57.7	50.79	5.1	10.0
8.	Bhutan	0.421	52.8	69.69	2.3	12.4
9.	Argentina	0.783	97.9	91.94	9.8	16.4
10.	Myanmar	0.371	92.7	NA	4.0	8.6
11.	Maldives	0.548	98.4	NA	5.8	12.7

Source: Compiled by author based on data from: *http://hdr.undp.org*

CSR Addressing 'Education' as an Issue

Fortune Global 500 are committed to spend at least 20 per cent of their CSR budgets towards education initiatives, total education related CSR spending has risen from US $2.6 bn to US $4 bn. A report of the Business Backs Education (2015) highlights the CSR spend of Fortune 500 companies. The data reveals that a large number of companies are spending a remarkable percentage on education as CSR. Chinese Fortune 500 companies are leading the table in spending 97 per cent of CSR spend on education. Though the average CSR spend of Canada is highest (235.6 million) yet it spends only 31 per cent on education. India is spending 87 per cent of the 81 million on education as per Business Backs Education (2015).

Education is an important issue and Table 3.3 and Figure 3.3 reveals the country status and expenditure on education. The developed countries are far better in the status of education yet; there are a large number of organisations which spends more on education as CSR. Comparatively the least developed nations do not have much corporate to support in undertaking CSR activities as well as the country spend towards CSR is relatively poor which further demeans the status of education in these countries. Access to education, access to quality education, maintaining student teacher ratio, promoting skill based education are some of the areas which corporate focuses as CSR interventions in education.

Conclusion

The concept of CSR is now firmly rooted on the global business agenda. A key challenge facing business in order to move from theory to concrete action is the need for more reliable indicators of progress in the field of CSR, along with the dissemination of CSR strategies. The need for strategising CSR to business growth and opportunity has become inevitable for corporate. Yet, the fact cannot be ignored that CSR is not just about the business recognition and growth but more about the holistic development of society, environment and nation. It is essential that companies understand the essence of true CSR as undertaking initiatives not just to fulfil the legal and ethical requirements. The CSR activities should be undertaken in sync with national issues. This brings in a cohesive effort of government and corporate to deal with the major issues of the country leading to the development of the country as a whole.

The problems of each country differ substantially. The analysis of the status of developed, developing countries and LDCs identifies the issues that can be undertaken as CSR. In developed countries, the focus is majorly on environment and fair labour practices. The developing countries and LDCs majorly focus on community development as an area of concern. Developed countries are found to spend more on education as compared to developing countries. No evident trend was found with regards to health expenditure in developed and developing countries. In some developing countries, the health and education expenditure was found to be considerably low. It is manifested from the data that the issues of developing and developed countries are different and the government expenditure on managing the issues vary from developed, developing and LDCs.

References

Aguilera, R.V., C.A. Williams, J.M. Conley and D.E. Rupp (2006). "Corporate Governance and Social Responsibility: A Comparative Analysis of the UK and the US", *Corporate Governance and Social Responsibility* 14(3): 147-158.

Aupperle, K.E., A.B. Carroll and J.D. Hatfield (1985). "An Empirical Examination of the Relationship between Corporate Social Responsibility and Profitability", *The Academy of Management Journal* 28(2): 446-63.

Baleanu, T. E., L. Chelcea and A. Stancu (2011). "The Social Responsibility of the Top 100 Romanian Companies, An Analysis of Corporate Website", *Corporate Social Responsibility* 13(29): 235-48.

Berens, G., B.M. Cees van Riel and H. Gerrit van B. (2005). "Corporate Associations and Consumer Product Responses: The Moderating Role of Corporate Brand Dominance", *Journal of Marketing* 69(1): 35-18.

Berman, S.L., A.C. Wicks, S. Kotha and T.M. Jones (1999). "Does Stakeholder Orientation Matter? The Relationship Between Stakeholder Management Models and Firm Financial Performance", *The Academy of Management Journal* 42(5): 488-506.

Bhattacharya, C.B. and S. Sen (2004). "Doing Better at Doing Good: When, Why, and How Consumers Respond to Corporate Social Initiatives", *California Management Review* 47(1): 9-24.

Bhattacharya, C.B., D. Korschun and S. Sen (2009). "Strengthening Stakeholder-Company Relationships Through Mutually Beneficial Corporate Social Responsibility Initiatives", *Journal of Business Ethics* 85(2): 257-72.

Bichita, C. (2003). "Corporate Social Responsibility: A Role in Government Policy and Regulation?" *The University of Bath CRI Research Report* No. 16. Bath/UK.

Boesso, G., K. Kumar and G. Michelon (2013). "Descriptive, instrumental and strategic approaches to corporate social responsibility", *Accounting, Auditing & Accountability Journal* 26(3): 399-422.

Broberg, M.P. (1996). "Corporate Social Responsibility in the European Communities: The Scandinavian View", *Journal of Business Ethics* 15 (?): 615-22.

Brookings (2013). *Investment in Global Education: A Strategic Imperative for Business*. R. Winthrop, G. Bulloch, P. Bhatt and A. Wood (eds.). Center for Universal Education, The Brookings Institution. September. p.2

Broberg, M.P. (1996). "Corporate Social Responsibility in the European Communities: The Scandinavian View", *Journal of Business Ethics* 15(1): 615-22.

Brown, T.J. and P.A. Dacin (1997). "The Company and the Product: Corporate Associations and Consumer Product Responses", *Journal of Marketing* 61(1): 68-84.

Brown, T.J. (1998). "Corporate Associations in Marketing: Antecedents and Consequences", *Corporate Reputation Review* 1(3): 215-33.

David, P., S. Kline and Y. Dai (2005). "Corporate Social Responsibility Practices, Corporate Identity and Purchase Intention: A Dual-process Model", *Journal of Public Relations Research* 17(3): 291-313.

Dossing, H. (2003). "The Business Case for CSR", in *International Chamber of Commerce (ICC) UK, Guide to Global Corporate Social Responsibility* 34.

Enloe, C.H. (1975). *The Politics of Pollution in a Comparative Perspective*. London: Longman.

Friedman, M. (1970). "The social responsibility of business is to increase its profits", *New York Times Magazine* 13(32-33): 122-26. September.

Gao, Y. (2009). "Corporate Social Performance in China, Evidence from Large Companies", *Journal of Business Ethics* 59(1): 23-35.

Garriga, E. and D. Mele (2004). "Corporate Social Responsibility Theories: Mapping the Territory", *Journal of Business Ethics* 53(1): 51-71.

Gongsifa (2005). *Company Law* (promulgated by the Standing Comm. Nat'l People's Cong., 27 October 2005, wffective 1 July 1994, amended 1 January 2006). Available at: *http://www.lawinfochina.com* (accessed on 14 April 2016).

Graves, S.B. and S.A. Waddock (1994). "Institutional owners and corporate social performance", *Academy of Management Journal* 37(4): 1034-1046.

Hillman, A.J. and G.D. Keim (2001). "Shareholder Value, Stakeholder Management, and Social Issues: What's the Bottom Line?", *Strategic Management Journal* 22(2): 125-39.

Johnson, R.A. and D.W. Greening (1999). "The Effects of Corporate Governance and Institutional Ownership Types on Corporate Social Performance", *Academy of Management Journal* 42(5): 564-76.

Jones, T.M., W. Felps and G.A. Bigley (2007). "Ethical Theory and Stakeholder-related Decisions: The Role of Stakeholder Culture", *The Academy of Management Review* 32(1): 137-55.

Kahneman, D., J.L. Knetsch and R.H. Thaler (1986). "Fairness and Assumptions of Economies", *Journal of Business* 59(4): 285-300.

Kolk, A. (2003). "Trends in Sustainability Reporting by the Fortune Global 250", *Business Strategy and the Environment* 12 (5): 279-91.

KPMG (2005). *KPMG International Survey of Corporate Responsibility Reporting 2005*. Amsterdam, the Netherlands: KPMG Global Sustainability Services.

Levitt (1958). The Dangers of Social Responsibility. *Harvard Business Review* (Sep/Oct): 41-50.

Li, W. and R. Zhang (2010). "Corporate Social Responsibility, Ownership Structure and Political Interference: Evidence from China", *Journal of Business Ethics* 96(4): 631-45.

Lichtenstein, D.R., E.D. Minette and M.B. Bridgette (2004). "The Effect of Corporate Social Responsibility on Customer Donations to Corporate-Supported Nonprofits", *Journal of Marketing* 68(4): 16-32.

Lo, S. and H. Sheu (2007). "Is Corporate Sustainability a Value-increasing Strategy for Business?", *Corporate Governance-An International Review* 15 (1): 345-58.

Manaktola, K. and V. Jauhari (2007). "Exploring Consumer Attitude and Behaviour Towards Green Practices in the Lodging Industry in India", *International Journal of Contemporary Hospitality Management* 19(5): 364-77.

McWilliams, A., D. Siegel and P. Wright (2006). "Corporate Social Responsibility: Strategic Implications", *Journal of Management Studies* 43(1): 18.

Maignan, I., O.C. Ferrell and G.T. Hult (1999). "Corporate Citizenship: Cultural Antecedents and Business Benefits", *Journal of the Academy of Marketing Science* 27(4): 455-69.

Maignan's (2001). "Consumer Perceptions of Corporate Social Responsibility: A Cross Cultural Comparison", *Journal of Business Ethics* 30(1): 57-73.

Maignan, I. and D. Ralston (2002). "Corporate Social Responsibility in Europe and the U.S.: Insights from Businesses' Self-presentations", *Journal of International Business Studies* 33 (1): 497-514.

Maguire, M. (2011). *The Future of Corporate Social Responsibility Reporting.* The Frederick S. Pardee Center for the Study of the Longer-Range Future. Available at: *http://www.bu.edu/pardee/files/2011/01/PardeeIIB-019-Jan-2011.pdf?PDF=issues-in-brief-no-19* (accessed 27 Jan, 2016).

Matten, D. and J. Moon (2004). "Implicit" and "Explicit" CSR: A Conceptual Framework for Understanding CSR in Europe", in A. Habisch, J. Jonker, M. Wegner and R. Schmidpeter (eds.), *CSR Across Europe*. Berlin, Germany: Springer-Verlag. pp.335-56

Nyarko J. K. and G.F. Grigore (2011). "Corporate Social Responsibility in Developing Countries: The Case of Most Successful Companies in Romania and Ghana". Available at: *http://ssm.com* (accessed 15 DeceOber 2014).

Okoye (2012). "Novel Linkages for Development: Corporate Social Responsibility, Law and Governance: Exploring the Nigerian Petroleum Industry Bill", *Corporate Governance: The International Journal of Business in Society* 12(4): 460-71.

Peloza, J. (2006). Using Corporate Social Responsibility as Insurance for Financial Performance", *California Management Review* 48(1): 52-72.

Peterson, D.K. (2004). "The Relationship Between Perceptions of Corporate Citizenship and Organisational Commitment", *Business & Society* 43(3): 296-319.

Petkoski, D., and N. Twose (eds.) (2003). "Public Policy for Corporate Social Responsibility", *WBI Series on Corporate Responsibility*, 7-25 July. Washington D.C.: World Bank Institute.

PWC (2010). *Hur redovisar svenska bolag hållbarhet 2009?* Available at: *http://www.pwc.com/se/sv/hallbar-utveckling/assets/hur-redovisar-svenska-bolag-hallbarhet-2009.pdf* (accessed on 27th March, 2016)

Reich, R.B. (1998). "The New Meaning of Corporate Social Responsibility", *California Management Review* 40(2): 8-17.

Russo, M. and P. Fouts (1997). "A Resource-based Perspective on Corporate Environmental Performance and Profitability", *Academy of Management Journal* 40(3): 534-59.

Sen, S. and C.B. Bhattacharya (2001). "Does Doing Good Always Lead to Doing Better? Consumer Reactions to Corporate Social Responsibility", *Journal of Marketing Research* 38 (2): 225- 44.

Salmones, G., M.M. Herrero and I. Rodrı´guez Del Bosque (1995). "Influence of Corporate Social Responsibility on Loyalty and Valuation of Services", *Journal of Business Ethics* 61(1): 369-85.

Simmons, J. (2004). "Managing in the Post-Managerialist Era: Towards Socially Responsible Corporate Governance", *Management Decision* 32(3/4): 601-11.

Singh R. and S. Agarwal (2013). "Does CSR Orientation reflect Stakeholders Relationship Marketing Orientation? An Empirical Examination of Indian Banks", *Marketing Intelligence and Planning* 31(4): 405-20.

Sharma, B. (2013). *Contextualising CSR in Asia.* Lien Centre for Social Innovation Social Insight Research Series. Singapore

Solomon, A., J. Solomon and M. Suto (2004). "Can the UK Experience Provide Lessons for the Evolution of SRI in Japan?" *Corporate Governance: An International Review* 12(4): 552-66.

Tang, Z., H. Eirikur, S. Rotenberg (2012). "How Corporate Social Responsibility Engagement Strategy Moderates the CSR—Financial Performance Relationship", *Journal of Management Studies* 49(7): 1274-303.

UNDP (2014) *Human Development Statistical Tables.* Available at: *http://hdr.undp.org/en/data* (accessed on 12 December 2015).

———. (undated). *UNDP Education Index.* Available at: *http://hdr.undp.org/en/content/education-index* (accessed on 12 December 2015).

———. (undated). *UNDP Health Index.* Available at: *http://hdr.undp.org/en/content/health-index* (accessed on 12 December 2015).

UNESCO (2015). *Business Backs Education Report: Creating a Baseline for Corporate CSR Spend on Global Education Initiatives*. January. Available at: *http://www.unesco.org/education/BBE-EPG-Report2015.pdf* (accessed on 12 February, 2016).

Viswesvaran, C., S.P. Deshpande and C. Milman (1998). "The Effect of Corporate Social Responsibility on Employee Counterproductive Behaviour", *Cross Cultural Management* 5 (4): 5-12.

Welford, R. (2004). "Corporate Social Responsibility in Europe, North America and Asia", *Journal of Corporate Citizenship* 17(3): 33-52.

Williams, C. and J. Conley (2005). "An Emerging Third Way? The Erosion of the Anglo-American Shareholder Value Construct", *Cornell International Law Journal* 38(2): 493-551.

World Bank (undated). *World Bank Development Indicators*. Available at: *http://data.worldbank.org* (accessed on 12 December 2015).

World Health Science (2010) "Westernized Societies Have Their Own Health Issues". Available at: *http://www.worldhealthsciences.com/westernized-societies-have-their-own-health-issues.html* (accessed on 12 February 2016)

Young, S. and V. Thyil (2008). "A Holistic Model of Corporate Governance", *Corporate Governance* 8(1): 94-108.

Others:

Companies Act, 2013 (India)—Sec 134, Sec 135.

Companies Act, 2006 (UK)—Sec 172.

4

CST ANIL KUMAR

Corporate Social Responsibility

The Law World Over

Introduction

CSR (corporate social responsibility) world over has taken precedence in the governance of any industry. CSR in simple terms is company's efforts to improve society in some way which could be from donating money to non-profit to implementing environmentally-friendly policies in the workplace. It has become the standard business practice followed by good companies which are into ethical practices. It adds value to the organisation in terms of increased reputation, gives a higher return on the capital employed, high level of employee engagement and an equally satisfied customer base.

It has been debated world over whether CSR falls within the purview of corporates. A few proponents believe that businesses should focus on profits and profits alone and let the government or non-profit organisations deal with social and environmental issues. Milton Friedman and other conservative critics have argued against CSR, saying that the purpose and objective of a corporation is to maximise returns to its shareholders and has no responsibility to serve the society, corporations benefit society best by distributing profits to the owners, who in turn can make charitable donations in diverse areas where they deem fit. The other argument is that the evils in society like pollution, income disparity, to some extent has been contributed by the corporates and they should be held responsible for cleaning up the damage which has been done.

It is the corporates which have the money power to contribute solving the problems of society which the government may be lacking. If corporates become responsible, they can avoid policing by the government by levying fines or crating regulations as in the case of water, air and soil pollution.

It is now fact that lot of corporate have embraced CSR as a part of their agenda. The consensus amongst all the anti-corporate campaigners is that CSR is best if it is left to be done voluntarily. Legislation is to enforce minimum standards and the corporates are free to go beyond what has been legislated and by doing so they can serve best to the society and their company.

India is the only country in the world which has legislated CSR in the Companies Act, 2013. The law mandates that all companies, including foreign firms, with a minimum net worth of ₹500 crore or companies having a turnover of ₹1,000 crore or net profit of at least ₹5 crore, should spend at least 2 per cent of their profit on CSR activity on specified activities but there is a small deviation, and the Act left it to the wisdom of the Board either to spend the money or not to spend it on the CSR activities. There is no penalty for companies for not spending the amounts in spite of the fact that profits are there. Penal provisions are there for not making disclosures in the directors report which is made available to the shareholders and the public. Thus the mandated CSR provisions in the Companies Act, 2013 has been to comply if not explain.

Comparison of the CSR Regulation across the Globe

CSR is not a mandated practice in the United States (US); instead, it is something extra that companies do to improve their local and global communities. The RBC (responsible business conduct) team provides guidance, promotion and support for responsible business practices, engaging the private sector, labour groups, non-governmental organizations, and other governments. The RBC team also manages the Advisory Committee on International Economic Policy (ACIEP) and the Secretary of State's annual Award for Corporate Excellence (ACE) programme, and leads the department's efforts on the National Action Plan on RBC. The team also houses the US National Contact Point, the US government obligation to provide a mechanism for the resolution of disputes arising under the Organization for Economic Cooperation and Development (OECD) guidelines for multinational enterprises.

The Bureau of Economic and Business Affairs (EB) pursues economic diplomacy for America, making the United States of America and its people more prosperous and secure. The CSR team in the EB leads the Department's engagement with US businesses in the promotion of responsible and ethical business practices. It provides guidance and support for US companies to undertake socially responsible corporate activities and ethical business practices that promote sustainable development and engages with business, trade unions, and civil society to adopt and implement exemplary corporate policies. The Department's interaction with the private sector is done under the framework of the OECD guidelines for multinational enterprises and with EB's US National Contact Point for the Guidelines. The state department promotes and recognises exemplary CSR activities of businesses through the annual secretary of State's ACE.

The "process of communicating the social and environmental effects of organisations' economic actions" is done through disclosure. CSR reporting is unregulated in the US. There are different reports such as 'environmental reports', 'social reports', 'climate change reports', 'carbon reports', 'triple bottom line reports' and 'sustainability reports' among others which form part of the CSR report which presents non-financial qualitative and quantitative data.

There are two organisations that have a large influence on CSR reporting, The GRI and Account Ability (AA). The former being more widely used. The GRI frameworks give guidance on what information to include and how to present it in the CSR report.

Several US government agencies, such as the Environmental Protection Agency (EPA), the Securities and Exchange Commission (SEC), and Federal Trade Commission (FTC) are increasing their scope of sustainability disclosure oversight.

In the United Kingdom (UK), CSR is a part of corporate governance. The Companies Act, 2006 requires directors to have regard to community and environmental issues when considering their duty to promote the success of their company and by the disclosures to be included in the business review. CSR is, now, an integral part of good governance, for bigger companies in particular.

The Companies Act, 2006 introduced a mandatory requirement for a business review in the directors' report, which is in line with the provisions of the 2003 European Union (EU) Accounts Modernisation Directive and applies to all companies other than those subject to the small companies' regime. The business review recognises the necessity for companies to provide information for investors and other stakeholders, and a narrative explanation that expands on and complements increasingly complicated financial accounts.

A duty has been cast on the directors to have regard to community and environmental issues when considering their duty to promote the success of their company. The Association of British Insurers, whose members own more than 20 per cent of the companies on the London Stock Exchange, publishes guidance on CSR-related issues for both companies and investors. The 2007 "Socially Responsible Investment Guidelines" requires that the annual report highlights a company's ESG (environmental, social and governance) risks. The remuneration when paid to senior executives, and whether an incentive structure may have an adverse impact on the ESG of the company.

Most companies are keen to talk about social and environmental issues in their annual reports, and many argue that complying with CSR guidelines has become a commercial necessity. At the least, the growing number of 'green' and ethical investment funds needs to find 'green' and ethical businesses to invest in.

The charity business in the community claims a membership of over 850 of the UK's top companies "committed to improving their positive impact on society." It publishes a CRI (corporate responsibility index), which measures the performance of companies in terms of how well they apply CSR values to their business.

The UK Corporate Governance Code is specifically concerned with CSR, as they recognise that a company's duties extend beyond its shareholders: "The board should set the company's values and standards and ensure that its obligations to its shareholders and others are understood and met" (supporting principles, A.1).

The Turnbull Guidance (annexed to the Code) makes clear that risk assessment should cover not only narrow financial risks but also those related to 'health, safety and environmental, reputation, and business probity issues'.

The European Commission promotes CSR in the EU and encourages enterprises to adhere to international guidelines and principles. The EU's policy is built on an agenda for action to support this approach. It includes:

- Enhancing the visibility of CSR and disseminating good practices.
- Improving and tracking levels of trust in business.
- Improving self and co-regulation processes.
- Enhancing market reward for CSR.
- Improving company disclosure of social and environment information.
- Further integrating CSR into education, training and research.
- Emphasising the importance of national and sub-national CSR policies.
- Better aligning European and global approaches to CSR.

The CSR strategy is built upon guidelines and principles laid down by the United Global Compact, United Nations Guiding Principles on Business and Human Rights, ISO 26000 Guidance Standard on Social Responsibility and OECD Guidelines for Multinational Enterprises.

Large public-interest entities (listed companies, banks, insurance undertakings and other companies that are so designated by Member States) with more than 500 employees should disclose in their management report relevant and useful information on their policies, main risks and outcomes relating to at least:

- environmental matters,
- social and employee aspects,
- respect for human rights,
- anticorruption and bribery issues, and
- diversity in their board of directors.

India is the only country which has pioneered the way CSR is carried out by corporate, it persuades the companies to get into the CSR activities but again is voluntary. Laws set minimum standards and leave it to the companies to follow beyond the threshold. There are inherent problems by making it to comply since there is no effective enforcement mechanism for non-compliance, the law is deficient where the 2 per cent allocation if not spent has to be explained to the shareholders in the Directors Report so as to avoid being penalised.

The CSR expenditure of 2 per cent would amount to taxing the company since it is not allowed to claim as an expense. The corporates are already burdened with a high rate of tax 34.61 per cent—already one of the highest, compared to a global average of 24.09 per cent. The increased tax outflow to the corporate will not make India a more 'attractive investment destination'.

Conclusion

In US companies and other developed countries, CSR has not been as heavily regulated as that in India and corporate responsibility is not addressed as a regulatory compliance issue but rather from a social and moral choice perspective. While in India, the regulations make CSR spending a mandate, but by virtue of a rider makes it anfructuous. The defined areas where CSR can be carried is different from other countries which are at will to do differently.

References

Adams, C.A. (2004). "The Ethical, Social and Environmental Reporting: Performance Portrayal Gap", *Accounting, Auditing and Accountability Journal* 17(5): 731-57.

Anne, D. (2009). "Legal Requirements for CSR Reporting in the United Kingdom, Denmark and Australia", *Journal of the Australasian Law Teachers Association:* 11-17.

Ashley, W. (2015). "Corporate Social Responsibility is Now Legal". *https://www.fenwick.com/Publications*. Accessed on 31 December 2016.

Global Reporting Initiative (2002). "Sustainability Reporting Guidelines". URL: *http://www.globareporting.org/guidelines*. Accessed on 12 January 2017.

Lianna, C. (2008). "Corporate Social Responsibility Reporting in the United States", *McNair Scholars Research Journal* 1(1), Article 6.

PWC (2013). "Handbook on Corporate Social Responsibility in India". *https://www.pwc.in/assets/pdfs/publications/2013/handbook-on-corporate-social-*, Accessed on 5 Jan, 2017.

Vives, A. (2008). *Corporate Social Responsibility: The Role of Law and Markets and the Case of Developing Countries.* 83 Chi.-Kent. L. Rev. 199.

Others:

Corporate Social Responsibility: Diplomacy in Action. US Department of State. *http://www.state.gov/e/eb/eppd/csr/* Accessed on 25 December 2016.

OECD Guidelines for Multinational Enterprises, Organisation for Economic Co-operation and Development.

United Nations Guiding Principles on Business and Human Rights, Office of the United Nations High Commissioner for Human Rights.

5

ARUN K. RATH

Analysis of the Ethical Foundation of Corporate Social Responsibility

Introduction

CSR (corporate social responsibility) and business ethics are emerging as major issues of corporate strategy all over the world. A company is formed to carry out business with the objective of earning profit. However, profit is no longer acceptable as the sole purpose of business. The non-profit objectives of ethics, social responsibility and sustainable development have wider implications for society and environment. These factors are increasingly becoming significant for future prospects of business organisations.

There is growing acceptance that, in addition to maximising the wealth of the shareholders, it is imperative for corporations to invest more into human capital, environment and society. Different terminologies are used to describe the emerging non-profit corporate goals. Terms like CSR, corporate citizenship, social issues management, stakeholder management, corporate sustainability, business ethics and sustainable development are used by different countries and companies to cover these objectives. However all these terms have similar philosophical foundations. There is a clear overlap between business ethics, sustainability and social responsibility of business. The concepts concern values, and ethical conduct based on goals other than the mere pursuit of profits. A socially responsible corporation must act ethically and adopt sustainable development as its goal.

Scandals and frauds in high profile corporations have adversely affected the shareholders as well as the other stakeholders. These events have proved beyond doubt that mismanagement and unethical practices in corporations can play havoc with the economic and social order. It has been realised that proper governance of business corporations is as crucial to the world economy as proper governance of countries. There is an increasing demand on the corporations to be fair and ethical and fulfil their responsibility towards society and environment.

Corporate Irresponsible Action: Social Consequences

The modern corporation has emerged as the powerful engine of economic development. The State is gradually withdrawing from industry, business and trade. As a result, the corporations are assuming bigger role in the economy. They have become dominant institution producing goods and services, creating jobs and generating income for the people. However, the track record of corporate responsibility does not give enough confidence. In recent history the Asian financial crisis of 1996-97 and the global financial crisis of 2007-08 have been too costly for the global economy. Further, failures of global corporations like the World.com, Enron, Arthur Andersen, Satyam and Lehman Brothers, to name a few, have shaken the investor confidence.

It is a matter of concern that demolition of the wealth invested in these business enterprises was brought about by the arrogance, personal ambition, unchecked power and above all failure of ethical conduct by the top executives of these companies. Such unfortunate events exposed the deficiencies in the architecture of corporate governance of the failed business enterprises. The questions of responsibility towards society, employees and customers by the top brass of the failed institutions are also being raised.

Cases of fraud and deceit by corporations remind one of the satirist Ambrose Bierce, who described the corporation as "an ingenious device for obtaining individual profit without individual responsibility". In all these cases of corporate fraud, there are not only violations of law, but also breach of trust and failure of ethical conduct by top management.

Very few modern institutions have attracted as much praise and criticism in recent times as the business corporations. On the one hand, the modern corporation has emerged as the powerful engine of economic development. However, the corporations have also been condemned for their pathological obsession for profit (Bakan 2004), low concern for social and environmental interests, damage to nature, reckless exploitation of social capital and labour, violation of laws and unethical conduct. These modern instruments of economic growth have been criticised for being externalising machines, since they use other peoples' money and leave problems for others.

The strongest condemnation of the unethical conduct of the corporations comes in the well researched book, The Corporation (Bakan 2004) in which the business corporation has been labelled as a Frankenstein monster, and a psychopath machine. The separate legal status granted to the corporation as a person through judicial pronouncements is being questioned. The corporation has neither a body nor soul but is pursuing its goals like a killing shark always justifying its actions on the grounds of cost benefit analysis without regard to the social, human and environmental concerns.

Managing 'Other Peoples' Money': The Ethical Issues

Adam Smith (*Wealth of Nations*, 1776) had expressed grave doubts about the future of the corporate form of business. He criticised both the owners, who jointly invested in the companies, and the professional directors, engaged to manage the affairs of the companies on behalf of the owners. He felt that the owners would not pay enough attention to the affairs of the joint business entities so long as they continued to get dividends, and the directors being managers of 'other people's money' would promote their own interests at the cost of the interests of the owners. Smith predicted that such joint stock companies were bound to be mismanaged.

Corporate scandals in modern times due to fraudulent and unethical conduct of directors and managers, constantly remind us of the prophecy of Adam Smith. If unchecked, the errant conduct by corporate executives can cause huge loss to the large number of shareholders and employees.

Emerging Role of Stakeholders

The stakeholder in an organisation is any individual, group or institution who can affect or be affected by the achievement of the organisation's goals (Freeman 1984). Stakeholders are the individuals and groups who are vital for the survival and success of the corporation (Freeman 2004). A stakeholder holds a stake, rather than just a share. This theory raises the fundamental question of purpose of the corporation. The shareholders, employees, customers, creditors, suppliers, community, government, society and environment are stakeholders, since they all contribute to long-term value addition in the company. As such directors and managers should take decisions in the interest of all stakeholders.

Freeman and Evan (1993) suggested two principles to identify stakeholders of a corporation. Principle of corporate rights requires that corporation should not violate rights of others, whereas the principle of corporate effects expects the corporation to be responsible for the consequences of their action on lives of others. Such broad understanding expands the definition of stakeholders into diverse array of individuals, groups and institutions. It is also possible that stakeholders may vary from company to company. Needless to say, the shareholders as the owners of the business enterprise are the dominant stakeholders.

There has been a huge growth in literature on stakeholders theories. According to Donaldson and Preston (1995), all stakeholders theories can be grouped into three categories:

- Normative stakeholder theory provides a rationale as to why corporation should respect interests of stakeholders.
- Descriptive stakeholder theory documents what corporations actually do for the stakeholders.
- Instrumental stakeholder theory examines the benefits accruing to corporations due to their actions in favour of the stakeholders.

The very concept of stakeholders goes beyond profit and financial considerations. It is ultimately an ethical question as to how much of the profits need to be apportioned for the stakeholders.

Ethics in Corporate Governance

Traditionally, providing return on investment to shareholders and investors has been regarded as the objective of corporate governance. Till recent times, business of business was business (Friedman 1970). Doing profitable business was considered to be a social objective by itself. However, there is growing acceptance that it is not enough to just comply with the provisions of law and economics, but to invest more on human capital, environment and society. Business ethics is becoming the cornerstone of corporate conduct. Ethical practices and transparency are expected from business in all dealings and transactions. Ethics permeates different areas of corporate action like production of safe products, healthy marketing practices, non-discriminatory human resource management and reliable financial management. Society expects business corporations to be ethical, sustainable and responsible in harnessing the productive forces of nature, using economic power and deploying human capital for common good of mankind.

Management should take ethics into account in dealing with people. A business is not a machine. It is first and foremost a human construct (Mele 2012). Companies should, therefore, resist seeing people as resources or as simply a means for profit. Making and acting on ethical decisions help to humanise a business, by generating trust, fostering loyalty, encouraging responsibility and helping to develop a strong moral culture.

It is also necessary to be ethical in human resource management. Companies need to avoid discrimination by gender, race, religion and disability even in the absence of a national policy on affirmative action for the private sector. There should be ethical practice in financial management. Companies must avoid creative accounting, misleading financial analysis, insider trading, bribery or kickbacks and accounting scandals as happened in Enron, World.com and Satyam.

The objective of corporate governance has often been debated. Some authors feel that corporate governance should deal with "the ways in which suppliers of finance to corporations assure themselves of getting a return on their investment" (Vishni and Shliefer 1997). Whereas, others strongly believe that corporate governance has several claimants—shareholders and other stakeholders—which include suppliers, customers, creditors, bankers, employees of the company, the government and the society at large. The fundamental objective of corporate governance should be the enhancement of shareholder value, keeping in view the interests of other stakeholders (SEBI, *Birla Committee Report, 1999*). In yet another definition it has been stated that corporate governance is "about promoting corporate fairness, transparency and accountability" (James D. Wolfensohn, the then President World Bank 1998). The ethical dimension of corporate governance is receiving greater acceptability in recent times.

The stakeholder point of view in defining objective of corporate governance is increasingly gaining ground. The stakeholder approach is based upon strong ethical foundation. It lends greater credence to the social relevance of business as against its pure commercial and profit motives.

Corporate Social Responsibility: The Ethical Question

CSR is a multilayered concept having four main aspects namely, (i) economic responsibility required by society (ii) legal responsibilities also required by society (iii) ethical responsibilities as expected by society and (iv) philanthropic responsibilities being desired by society. True CSR requires satisfaction of all four levels consecutively. It leads to definitions of CSR like: "CSR includes the economic, legal, ethical and philanthropic expectations placed on organisations by society at a given point of time".

The other definitions of CSR are:

> A view of the corporation and its role in society that assumes a responsibility among firms to pursue goals in addition to profit maximisation and a responsibility among a firm's stakeholders to hold the firm accountable for its actions.

> A concept whereby companies integrate social and environmental concerns in their business operations and in their interaction with their stakeholders on a voluntary basis.

CSR has remained a voluntary concept all over the world. However, the Indian Companies Act, 2013 has introduced an element of legal compulsion into CSR.

CSR ensures advantages to the company, boosts its brand value, and avoids activists taking on directors in AGM on unethical practices. Employees feel happy to work in an ethical firm. It builds trust among shareholders, employees, customers and society. SRI (socially responsible investment) is now a criteria used by many fund managers for investment decisions. It also helps attract talented people in the company, and retain customers and suppliers. A study by Economist (2000) concluded, "Companies with an eye on their triple bottom line—economic, environmental, and social sustainability—outperform their less fastidious peers on the stock market".

Unethical Business: Adverse Consequences

Unethical business practices may lead to expensive court cases, bad publicity, damage to reputation, loss of brand value, fall in share price. There are examples galore to show that corporate irresponsibility has been costly. Multinational Shell earned bad publicity in 1995 due to: (i) attempted disposal of Brent spar oil rig in North sea and (ii) failure to oppose human rights violations by Nigerian government in spite of Shell's corporate influence. Cases of Nike facing adverse criticism for its supplies using child labour, Dow Chemicals getting involved in 2012 Olympics Sponsorship controversy are few more examples. Monsanto was criticised for aggressively marketing and political lobbying for its GM products. Nestlé's aggressive advertisement and marketing of milk products in developing countries resulted in decrease in breast feeding and use of dirty water in feeding infants. This resulted in boycott of Nestlé's milk products.

Business organisations are increasingly realising the potential risk of their unethical business practices. They are aware that there should be ethics in marketing of dangerous products, transparency about environmental risks, declaration about product ingredients, possible health risks to consumers, honesty in advertising and fairness in pricing.

Corporate Social Responsibility Theories

CSR is an obligation beyond requirement of law and economics. A firm is expected to pursue long term goals that are good for society and environment. It is the continuing commitment by business to behave ethically and contribute to economic development leaving an overall positive impact on society. CSR involves conducting business in an ethical manner and in the interests of the wider community, balancing shareholder interests against the interests of the other stakeholders. It ultimately amounts to being a good citizen in the community. There are a number of drivers of

CSR in the current context. The shrinking role of government, demand for greater corporate disclosures, increased customer interest, growing investor pressure, competitive labour markets and conducive supplier relations force companies to be socially responsible.

There is huge literature on CSR theories. Such theories fall in four groups:

- Instrumental theories, in which the corporation is seen only as an instrument for wealth creation, and its social activities are only a means to achieve economic returns.
- Political theories, which concern with the power of corporations in society and responsible use of this power by the corporation as a political force.
- Integrative theories, in which the corporation is focused on the satisfaction of demands of all stakeholders including society, and
- Ethical theories, based on moral responsibilities of corporation to society as an ethical organisation. These CSR theories present four dimensions related to profits, political performance, social demands and ethical values respectively (Garriga and Mele 2004).

In spite of arguments against deploying shareholders funds on stakeholders, business organisations are decidedly taking a view in favour of CSR. Businesses feel that they do not have an unquestioned right to operate in society. Those managing business realise that they depend on society. Business relies on resources from society and on socially created institutions. There is a social contract between business and society involving mutual obligations. Society and business recognise that they have to depend upon each other. Business can see advantages in adopting a CSR approach in doing business.

Sustainable Development: The Ethical Issues

CSR is also closely linked to the concept of sustainable development. Concept of sustainability is derived from two key sources. First the Brundtland Commission's Report defined it as, 'sustainable development that meets the needs of the present without compromising the ability of future generations to meet their own needs.' Second, Elkington (1999) advised mankind to develop without damaging future generations' prospects. The twin principles of causing least harm and working for long-term while using resources are expected of the corporations engaged in exploitation of natural resources.

Triple Bottom Line

Elkington presented the concept of TBL (triple bottom line) which requires that business goals are inseparable from the interests of societies and environments within which they operate. Corporate strategy must address the concerns for profit, planet and people at the same time. Corporate sustainability must include the three aspects of economic, social and environmental sustainability.

Elkington (1998) was of the opinion that TBL need not be seen only as an accounting exercise. It should measure the commitment of business corporations to promote the cause of society and environment while earning profit out of business. TBL approach is aimed at bringing about a balanced development reconciling the needs of society and nature with the profit motive of the corporations.

Companies should develop and issue EP&L (environment profit and loss) statements which will account for the economic impact of its producer on the ecosystem. Such practices will help stakeholders understand the damage of a product to the environment and also put pressure on companies to internalise costs which have so far been ignored. Higher cost to planet should also translate to higher price to the customer. Simultaneously products that cause the least harm should also have the lowest price.

Corporate sustainability involves adoption of strategy for long term value creation and sustenance of business. Adoption of green strategy, safeguarding social, cultural and environmental interests and pursuing ethical and sustainable values are emerging as the strategy for governing corporate entities.

Millennium Development Goals: The Corporate Agenda

United Nations (UN) (2005) report on *World Social Situation* noted with concern the growing inequality and the widening gap between the rich and the poor across the world. The world body appealed to all to respond to the alarming gap among different groups of people by adopting the eight Millennium Development Goals (MDGs):

- Eradicate extreme poverty and hunger.
- Achieve universal primary education.
- Promote gender equality and empower women.
- Reduce child mortality.
- Improve maternal health.
- Combat HIV/AIDS, malaria and other diseases.
- Ensure environmental sustainability.
- Develop a global partnership for development.

The MDGs were to be achieved by 2015. Since these were not achieved in time, a new set of goals were formulated as a replacement strategy by the UN.

Sustainable Development Goals (SDGs)

The SDGs are a set of 17 global goals with 169 targets between them. These goals are spearheaded by the UN, through a deliberative process involving its 193 member states, and the global civil society. The goals were adopted by the United Nations on 25 September 2015. The SDGs are successor to the MDGs after 2015. The SDGs have become crucial for global society. It is the last chance to save the planet and ensure a just social order. UN Secretary-General Ban Ki-moon aptly stated that "there can be no Plan B, because there is no Planet B".

The SDGs cover the global ideals of: no poverty, zero hunger, good health and well-being, quality education, gender equality, clean water and sanitation, affordable and clean energy, decent work and economic growth, industry, innovation and infrastructure, reduced inequalities, sustainable cities and communities, responsible consumption and production, climate action, protection of life below water and life on land, ensuring peace, justice and strong institutions, as well as partnerships for the goals by strengthening the means of implementation and revitalising the global partnership for sustainable development. These goals are expected to be fulfilled by different governments. However, all of these goals need support of the resources of the business corporations. The profit motives of these business entities are often responsible for the adverse consequences on the socio-economic equilibrium in the world. As such the SDGs cast great responsibility on the business corporations to broaden their scope of social action.

Challenges of Globalisation: Corporate Responsibility

Globalisation has thrown up new challenges before the corporations in respect of their agenda towards society and environment. Every economy in the world has been affected by the forces of globalisation. The poor countries as well as the poorer sections in the rich countries have been hit hardest by the adverse consequences of globalisation. Civil society and opinion makers blame the ruthless economic interests of the multinational companies for the loss of jobs and income among the marginalised sections of the society. The hostile reactions against the global companies have driven the latter to pay more attention to the miseries of the affected groups and alleviate their hardship (Crane and Matten 2010).

Globalisation has brought in new risks and uncertainties for the stakeholders who are not happy with the consequent financial insecurity and instability. The employees are also threatened with job cuts and may have to work with less salaries due to the competitive environment. Consumers are faced with multiple choices of products, but may also face cultural issues due to aggressive marketing and rise in unnecessary consumerism. Small suppliers in developing countries have to face competition from powerful multinational suppliers threatening to cut the income base of the former. Society suffers due to loss of tradition, culture and value systems caused by onslaught of new cultures brought about by foreign business interests.

Issues of sustainable development and business sustainability have grown in prominence in the wake of globalisation. Reckless pursuit of business goals has led to adverse impacts like pollution, climate change, threat to environment and biosphere, waste disposal, threat to traditional culture and values, and fast depletion of earth's resources.

Corporate Citizenship

The power of modern corporation is on the rise. Governments around the world find it difficult to deploy tax payers' funds on economic and industrial activities, which are fraught with risks and uncertainties. The state is gradually withdrawing from production activities. The void is being filled up by enterprising business corporations. Often corporations are taking over functions which were earlier performed by the governments. In the process, people's lives are also being affected by the corporate actions, both in beneficial and adverse manners. While pursuing profits, corporations also come face to face with challenging social and environmental issues.

In this context, the social and political role of corporations are emerging in last two decades, leading to formulation of the concept of CC (corporate citizenship). Although the concept is yet to take a final shape CC is defined (Cranet 2010) as "the corporate function for governing citizenship rights for individuals." CC is arising out of three perspectives (Crane et al. 2008). The limited view of CC is synonymous with corporate philanthropy. The equivalent view of CC is synonymous with CSR, whereas the extended view of CC expects the corporations to play a political role like government in society. CC will be a meaningful and different concept only if the extended view is adopted by corporations to avoid repetition of the two other approaches. In recent times, CC is defined as a set of individual rights (Faulks 2000) comprising of social, civil and political rights of citizens.

Above developments have given a new dimension to the ethical responsibility of corporations towards their stakeholders. Corporation is seen as a political actor in matter of individual rights.

United Nations Global Compact Initiative

The United Nations Global Compact, also known as Compact or UNGC, is a UNs initiative to encourage businesses worldwide to adopt sustainable and socially responsible policies, and to report on their implementation. The Global Compact is a principle-based framework for businesses who are expected to adopt 10 principles to be followed in their corporate activities. These principles concern the areas of human rights, labour, the environment and anti-corruption. A corporation may join the movement by declaring voluntarily to accept these principles of ethical conduct. The Global Compact is the world's largest corporate citizenship initiative.

The Global Compact was first announced by the then UN Secretary-General Kofi Annan in an address to The World Economic Forum on 31 January 1999 and was officially launched at UN headquarters in New York on 26 July 2000. The UNs acknowledged the power and social responsibility of business entities when it was announced, "Let us choose to unite the power of markets with the authority of universal ideals. Let us choose to reconcile the creative forces of private entrepreneurship with the needs of the disadvantaged and the requirements of future generations." The world body promoted the concept of CC among global companies.

Corporate Social Responsibility: Legal or Ethical Responsibility?

India took a bold initiative while amending the company law in 2013. A new provision in the Companies Act was introduced to give a legal status to corporate social action. Directors were also given legal responsibility to ensure implementation of such provisions. Section 135(1) of the Act provides that,

- Board of every company shall make every endeavour to ensure that the company spends, in every financial year, at least two per cent of the average net profits of the company made during the three immediately preceding financial years, in pursuance of its CSR Policy.
- If the company fails to spend such amount, the Board needs to specify the reasons in its report.

Schedule (vii) of the Act lists out the activities to be pursued under CSR. These include education, women and child welfare, social security, health and employment generation. The CSR rules elaborated activities which may be included by companies in their CSR policies:

- eradicating extreme hunger and poverty;
- promotion of education;
- promoting gender equality and empowering women;

- reducing child mortality and improving maternal health;
- combating human immunodeficiency virus, acquired immune deficiency syndrome, malaria and other diseases;
- ensuring environmental sustainability;
- employment enhancing vocational skills;
- social business projects;
- contribution to the Prime Minister's National Relief Fund or any other fund set up by the Central Government or the State governments for socio-economic development and relief and funds for the welfare of the SCs (scheduled castes), the STs (scheduled tribes), other backward classes, minorities and women; and
- such other matters as may be prescribed.

In order to ensure effective and meaningful social action, CSR needs to be integrated with business strategy. CSR initiatives should rise above the limited perspective of resource allocation and expenditure activity. The organisational culture in the corporation should be conducive to acceptance of social responsibility of business. The entire organisation needs to be sensitised. The employees and executives must feel a sense of commitment to society and environment. CSR vision supported by action plan, CSR audit and public reporting would enhance the image and credibility of the company.

Voluntary International Benchmark on Corporate Social Responsibility

International Organization for Standardization, launched (1 November 2010) an International standard providing guidelines for SR (social responsibility) named ISO 26000. Its goal is to contribute to global sustainable development, by encouraging business and other organisations to practice social responsibility to improve their impacts on the workers, natural environment and the communities.

ISO 26000 is a voluntary guidance standard. It does not contain requirements such as those used when a standard is offered for 'certification'. No specific external certification is explicitly tied to ISO 26000. ISO recommends that users say, for example, that they have 'used ISO 26000 as a guide to integrate social responsibility into our values and practices.'

The seven principles of socially responsible behaviour are accountability, transparency, ethical behaviour, respect for stakeholder interests, respect for the rule of law, respect for international norms of behaviour, respect for human rights. Similarly seven core principles prescribed by the ISO 26000 are organisational governance, human rights, labour practices, environment, fair operating practices, consumer issues, community involvement and development. ISO 26000 standards have been kept voluntary to stress on the self regulating principle of good corporate governance. It is expected that, business will adopt these guidelines and enhance their image before the stakeholders.

The OECD Principles of Corporate Governance also lay emphasis on the moral duty of corporations on meaningful stakeholder engagement. The corporate governance framework should recognise the rights of stakeholders established by law or through mutual agreements and encourage active co-operation between corporations and stakeholders in creating wealth, jobs, and the sustainability of financially sound enterprises.

As such, CSR is voluntary all over the world. Companies are under pressure to promote the cause of CSR as part of their strategy to retain their stakeholders in the growth process.

The Ethical Corporation

Traditionally, the objective of corporate governance has been to maximise shareholder value. However, wealth destruction by failure of high profile business corporations has raised many concerns. Primary concern has been the inadequacy of share value maximisation as the primary objective of business strategy. Groups and institutions have emerged, who do not provide capital to the corporations, but contribute to the long term growth of business as stakeholders.

The viability of business itself depends on availability of earth's resources on a sustainable basis. There is need for an ecosystem that continually supply fresh water, clean air, sufficient land and social empowerment. Responsibility towards such factors need to be incorporated into business strategy for corporate growth and sustainability. Business is seen as a social trust aimed at satisfying social expectations. Ethical, well-governed and socially relevant companies are preferred as the investment destinations. Social responsibility of business and ethical conduct are the hallmarks of good corporate governance. In a nutshell, the ethical and socially responsible corporation is emerging as a model for business all over the world.

Business as Social Trust

Profit alone cannot ensure sustainability. Vision, social and ethical values are emerging as crucial factors. Visionary companies with social relevance and contribution to social cause sustain and survive in the long run.

Mahatma Gandhi in his concept of 'Trusteeship of Property' visualised that the rich and wealthy should be trustees of property. They should hold economic power on behalf of society only as custodians. They may enjoy their wealth up to a reasonable limit but major portion of their wealth must be available for benefit of society. *Isopanishad* lays down code of conduct about worldly possessions which inspired Gandhi's theory of trusteeship. The theory is based on detachment or non-possession as in the quote:

Tenā Tyāktenā Bhunjeetah: Ma Gridhā Kasyāswiddhanam?

(Enjoy by renouncing: do not cling to possession; for whose is wealth?)

The concept of trusteeship of property gives a strong philosophical foundation to business ethics and social responsibility.

Profit for Social Good

The objective of business has undergone change in last few decades. In the past, economists led by Nobel laureate Milton Friedman (1970) held the view, "There is one and only one social responsibility of business—to use its resources and engage in activities designed to increase its profits". The ground has now shifted. Issues of business ethics and social responsibility have risen up the corporate governance agenda. It is now accepted that the purpose of business is not just to make profit as an end by itself, but to make profit so that the business can do something more or better: "Profit would be the means to that larger end" (Handy 2002). Peter Drucker (2008) wisely commented, "Profit for a company is like oxygen for a person. If you don't have enough of it, you're out of the game. But if you think your life is about breathing, you're really missing something".

CSR needs to be integrated into the long term corporate plan. The vision should be to earn profit by doing good business ensuring ethical conduct in business activities. Sustainable business strategy must harmonise the twin objectives of profit and social good.

Conclusion

Business corporations are assuming significant role in economic development. They are expected to earn profit and add value to the shareholders' investment. But profit alone is not enough to ensure sustainability of business. In addition to shareholders and investors, there are other stakeholders who contribute to long term value maximisation of the corporation. Society has emerged as a major stakeholder of the corporation. Business is seen as a social trust aimed at satisfying expectations of society. Social good in addition to profit has become the basis for judging the performance of business. The investors, employees, customers, suppliers, community and society expect the corporation to conduct its affairs in an ethical and transparent manner, protecting environment and discharging its social obligations. The ethical corporation as the ultimate goal of business should synergise the twin corporate governance expectations of being both rule-based and principle-based in its growth strategy.

Globalisation is adversely affecting the socio-economic equilibrium of the world. The corporations are largely responsible for the ecological degradation, widening gap between the rich and the poor, and causing social inequalities. In their search for wealth, business entities are causing damages beyond repair. The stakeholders' pressure is increasing on them to be proactive and share their profits with the stakeholders. India has provided legal status to the responsibility of corporations to society. However the provision of two per cent spending on CSR should be regarded as the minimum legal mandate. Corporations need to go beyond this minimum level. They need to address the issues of sustainable development and demonstrate their responsibility as corporate citizens. It is moral duty of the corporations to the people and the planet to adopt sustainable and socially relevant business strategies.

References

Bakan, Joel. (2004). *The Corporation: The Pathological Pursuit of Profit and Power*. New York: Free Press.

Balton, Dianne and Suzanne Benn (2010). *Key Concepts in Corporate Social Responsibility.*

Berle, Adolf A. and Gardiner C. Means (1932, 1967). *Modern Corporation and Private Property.*

Bierce, Ambrose (1906). *Devil's Dictionary.*

Crane, A., D. Matten and J. Moon (2008). *Corporations and Citizenship*. Cambridge: Cambridge University Press.

Crane, Andrew and Dirk Matten (2010). *Business Ethics.* Oxford University Press.

———. (2010). "Carroll's Pyramid of CSR", in *Business Ethics*. Oxford University Press.

Donaldson, L. and James H. Davis (1991). "Stewardship Theory or Agency Theory, *Australian Journal of Management* 16.

Donaldson, T. and L. Preston (1995). "The Stakeholder Theory of the Corporation: Concepts, Evidence, and Implications", *The Academy of Management Review* 20(1): 65-91, January. Published by Academy of Management.

Drucker, Peter (2008). "Peter Senge's Necessary Revolution", *Business Week,* 11 June.

Economist (2000). "Technology Quarterly", *Economist*, 9 December.

Elkington, J. (1999). *The Triple Bottom Line: Reporting from Third Millennium*. CPA Australia. November.

———(1998). "Accounting for the Triple Bottom Line", *Measuring Business Excellence* 2(3): 18-22, doi: 10.1108/eb025539. Published by MCB UP Ltd.

European Commission Green Paper (2001). *Promoting Corporate Social Responsibility.*

Faulks, K. (2000). *Citizenship*. London, Routledge.

Freeman, R.E. (2004). *A Stakeholder Theory of Modern Corporations: Ethical Theory and Business*. 7th edition.

———. (1984). *Strategic Management: A Stakeholder Approach*. Boston: Pitman.

Freeman, R.E. and W.M. Evan (1993). "A Stakeholder Theory of Modern Corporation: Kantian Capitalism", in Tom Beauchamp and Norman E. Bowie (eds.), *Ethical Theory and Business*, Prentice Hall.

Friedman, M. (1970). "The Social Responsibility of Business is to increase its Profits", *New York Time Magazine*: 122-26, 13 September.

Garriga, Elisabet and Domenec Mele (2004). "Corporate Social Responsibility Theories: Mapping the Territory", *Journal of Business Ethics* 53: 51.

Handy, Charles (2002). "What's a Business For?", *Harvard Business Review*: 54, December.

Jensen, Michael C. (2001). *Value Maximisation, Stakeholder Theory and Corporate Objective Function*. Harvard Business School

Jensen, Michael C. and William H. Meckling (1976). *Theory of Firm: Managerial Behaviour, Agency Costs and Ownership Structure*.

Macdonald, Lawrence G. (2012). *A Colossal Failure of Common Sense: The Inside Story of the Collapse of Lehman Brothers*.

Mele, Domenec (2012). *Management Ethics: Placing Ethics at Core of Good Management*. Palgrave-Macmillian.

Monks, Robert A.G. (1998). *The Disconsolate Dawn of the Modern Corporation: The Emperor's Nightingale*.

OECD (1999). *Principles of Corporate Governance*. May.

Ruston, K. (001). *Cracking the Code—IoD Director's Guide: Sustainable Development*. May.

SEBI (1999). *Kumar Mangalam Birla Committee Report*.

Sethi, J.D. (1986).*Trusteeship: The Gandhian Alternative*. Gandhi Peace Foundation.

Smith, Adam (1776). *Wealth of Nations*. Book Five, Chapter 1, Part 3, Article 1.

Solomon, Jill and Aries Solomon (2004). *Corporate Governance and Accountability*. March. pp.23.

Som, Lalita S. (2006). "Corporate Governance Codes in India", *Economic & Political Weekly*, 30 September.

The Economist (ed.) (2010). *Business Ethics*.

Vishny, Robert W. and A. Shleifer (1997). "A Survey of Corporate Governance", *Journal of Finance* 52(2), June.

Werther, William B. Jr. and David Chandler (2010). *Strategic Corporate Social Responsibility*. Sage Publication.

Wolfensohn, James D. (1998). "Battle for Corporate Honesty, World in 1999", *Economist*.

Others:

"CSR the New Mantra", *Harvard Business Review* (August 2009).

Decades of Scam in India, www. fraudtoday. com/decadeofscams.htm.

Sustainable Development: UN Brandtland Commission Report, 1987.

UN Global Compact Website.

6

SHULAGNA SARKAR

Is Corporate Social Responsibility an Approach to Address Social Risks?

Introduction

We live in a world where we are surrounded by issues like climate change, dying species, financial instability, terrorism, unemployment, fatal diseases, water scarcities, malnutrition, and intractable poverty. These issues lie within the society and affect the present and the future generations. Some of these issues are beyond the ability of the nation alone to address it. Social issues tend to develop when negative consequences are neglected over a period. Some of the social issues arise due to the depraved actions of people and organisations and can be avoided or addressed. Thus, there lies an equal responsibility of people and organisations to address these social issues in some form.

Organisations by nature of its operation have both good and bad effect on the society as well as on the environment. These effects influence talent acquisition and engagement, land acquisition, certifications, recognition and market reputation of companies. Organisations have realised that they receive a social sanction from society with an assurance that they, in return, contribute to the growth and development of the society. Long-term business success can only be achieved by organisations that recognise CSR (corporate social responsibility) as part of their core value and create a competitive advantage. Global organisations by nature and vast expanse are expected to take up CSR activities addressing the social issues in its areas of operation irrespective of the boundaries.

Social protection is moving up on the development agenda. The world is increasingly becoming aware that environmental and social issues associated with business activities can create risks to themselves. The environmental and social impacts caused, or perceived to have been caused, by a business can result in consequences such as production delays, negative publicity, threats to operating licenses and unforeseen expenditures.

Social welfare in an economy depends on its ability to satisfy the needs of its members and to manage the risks threatening the well-being of the same people. Outside paradise, the satisfaction of needs require some individual and social actions. But both the ability to act and the possibility to realise positive results are subject to uncertainty and may be threatened by risks. Societies have developed various ways to deal with these basic problems and elsewhere we attempt to analyse and compare the variety in, what we call, the social management of risks.

SRM (social risk management) is a new conceptual framework put forward by the World Bank—that extends the traditional framework of social policies by looking into public actions to improve market-based and non-market based (informal) instruments of social risk management. SRM consists of public interventions to assist individuals, households, and communities to better manage risk, and to provide support to the critically poor (Holzmann and Jorgensen 2000).

The paper outlines the social issues and highlights the development aspects across developed, developing and underdeveloped countries. The paper also presents the SRM concept and explains how CSR programs are a means to provide strategic advantage by managing social risk. The paper also attempts to explain the role of government and corporate in addressing social risks.

The Present Corporate Social Responsibility Statistics

Report on CSR by Times of India (2016) discloses that after the new Companies Act made it mandatory, India's total CSR reporting increased by 27 per cent in 2015, the maximum among 45 countries surveyed by international audit firm KPMG.

Out of the total outlay of ₹6,490 crore towards CSR in India for 2015, companies have spent ₹5,115 crore. The health sector accounts for 20 per cent of the spending followed by education with 19 per cent. Maharashtra has 205 projects under CSR, the maximum among Indian states, followed by Karnataka (152), West Bengal (123) and Tamil Nadu (122). While companies based in India have a target of ₹5,779.68 crore for 2015, they have spent ₹4,708 crore. But out of the target of ₹710.12 crore for foreign-based companies, only ₹406.17 crore has been spent. Among Indian companies, the private sector has performed far better than the public sector. Against the prescribed amount of ₹2,306 crore, PSUs spent ₹1,628 crore (71%). The energy and power sector accounted for the highest expenditure under CSR. Nearly ₹1,994 crore (39%) of total spending is by the power sector followed by banks and IT firms (13% each), mining and metals (11%), and consumer goods (9%).

Figure 6.1

Thematic Priorities in CSR Schedule VII: Theme-wise Number of Companies

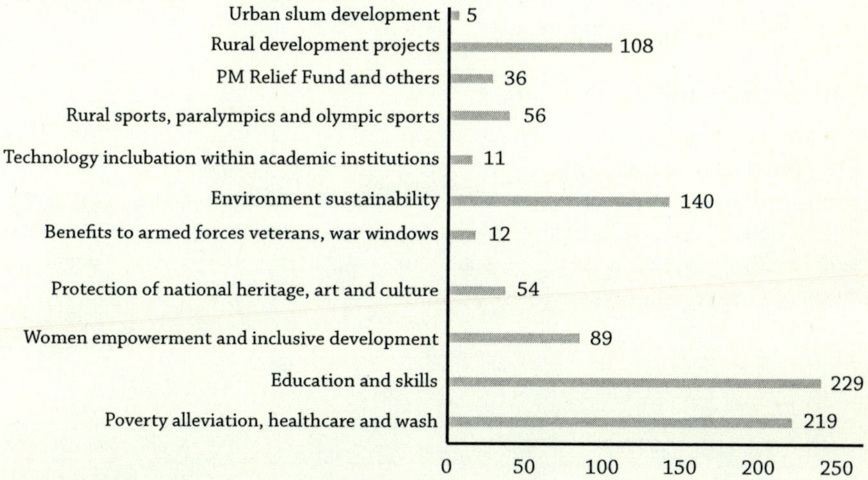

Source: *India CSR Outlook Report, 2016* NGOBOX.

Figure 6.1 reveals that out of the various subjects and activities indicated in Schedule VII of the Companies Act, ₹1,463 crore were spent on activities targeted at promoting education, vocational skills and livelihood enhancement. Eradicating hunger, poverty and healthcare was the next favourite with a spending of ₹1,422 crore. An amount of ₹1,189 crore was spent on environment sustainability activities. Rural development projects saw spending of ₹724 crore. An amount of ₹42.6 crore was contributed to the Swatch Bharat Kosh and ₹15.5 crore to the Clean Ganga Fund. A contribution of ₹125 crore was made to the Prime Minister's National Relief Fund (PMNRF).

The outcomes of the Section 135 of Companies Act, 2013 has surely brought in a change. The *India CSR Outlook Report, 2016* identifies the outcomes as mentioned below.

- The overall quality of reports and availability of data has improved.
- Despite the fact that the Section 135 of the Companies Act mandates companies to prepare CSR report (as part of the annual report) in a particular format, more than 30 companies have not followed the format and went on hiding (moreover ignoring) crucial information like project location, implementing partners, project specific budget and spend etc.
- There is a high discrepancy in the reported data when accounting for actual CSR spend and project-wise CSR spend of companies.

- A few companies spent the unspent amount of last year's CSR budget in this financial year (2015-16) and have calculated it as the actual CSR spend of FY 2015-16, taking their actual CSR spend much higher than the prescribed CSR of this FY.

Risk for Business

The environmental and social are the potential negative consequences to a business that result from its impacts (or perceived impacts) on the natural environment (i.e. air, water, soil) or communities of people (e.g. employees, customers, local residents). Failure to effectively manage environmental and social issues in a business can lead to a range of financial, legal and reputational consequences for the company (Table 6.1).

Table 6.1

Consequences for the Companies Due to its Operations.

	Financial Impact	*Legal impact*	*Reputational impact*
1.	• Costs associated with remedying contaminated land, meet legal requirements or avoid damage to employees' health.	• Fines for non-compliance with environmental, sanitary, health, safety and labour laws.	• Loss of sales due to a poor public perception of the company or its products (e.g. food hygiene scares, labour violations).
2.	• Write-downs of asset value due to irremediable contamination or obsolescence of equipment.	• Legal obligations to restore land used for waste disposal (landfill) or resource extraction at the end of the project's economic life. There may also be unexpected costs associated with such requirements.	• Increased recruitment/ induction costs and lower productivity due to poor reputation or E&S incidents, e.g. chemical spills.
3.	• Low productivity due to lost time caused by a high rate of workplace accidents.	• Damages arising from legal liability for damage to the environment, human health or property (e.g. compensation claims).	
4.	• Unexpected costs associated with meeting regulatory compliance requirements or payment of fines.	• Suspension of operations by regulators or due to an accident or fire.	

Social Issues across Countries

Every society of the world has social issues unique to their society. Some of the countries suffer from extreme poverty where as the others are surrounded by issues of safety and security of women, rising industrial pollution etc. There are many countries which has issues related to water, education, health, waste and food security. On the contrary, there are countries which are affected by the political and economical issues including social exclusions. The United Nations (UN) has set an ending to poverty and hunger as the top two of its 17 Sustainable Development Goals (SDGs) for the year 2030.

Figure 6.2 shares the broad social issues across the world. The social issues that have been considered are based on the work of Ritzer (2003). The social issues considered are then interpreted in relation to the magnitude of the issues to the development status of the countries.

Figure 6.2

Social Issues across the Globe

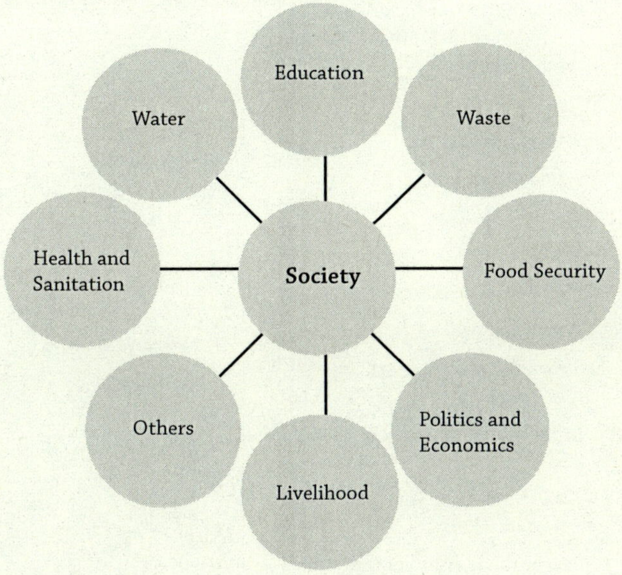

Table 6.2

Social Issues across Countries

	Key Issue in the Area	*Developed*	*Developing*	*Least Developed Countries*
Health and sanitation	Accessibility to health infrastructure			
	Quality of the health facilities			
	Cost of health facilities			
	Malnutrition			
	Infant mortality			
	Existence of communicable diseases			
	Geriatric care			
Water	Water conservation			
	Access to safe drinking water			
Education	Accessibility to education infrastructure including student teacher ratio			
	Quality of the education facilities			
	Cost of education			
	School dropouts			
	Enrolment ratio			
	Literacy rate			
Waste	Waste accumulation			
	Waste disposal			
Food security	Sustainable agriculture and forestry			
Economical and political issues	Economic, financial, and trade issues.			
	Government, politics, and international relations			
	Law and law enforcement issues			
	Rights issues			
	War and military issues			

Livelihood	Skill development			
	Sustainable income generation			
	Entrepreneurship opportunities			
	Technology innovations for development			
	Women empowerment			
Other issues:	Crime and violence			
	Cultural preservation and ethnic heritage			
	Labour and employment issues			
	Science and technology issues.			

Interpretations:

Not an existing issue	Existing issue with low concern	Existing issue with high concern

Source: Compiled by the authors.

The existence of the social issues in the developed, developing and LDCs are as reflected in Table 6.2 are based on the data available on various UN websites. It is interesting to see that not all issues are high concern for the LDCs and there are a relative number of issues which are of high concern even to the developed nations. Identification of social issues provides an understanding of what can be initiated to prioritise and resolve these issues.

Social Risk Management

SRM is a conceptual framework developed by the World Bank under the leadership of Robert Holzmann, about the importance of risk and of risk management instruments for poverty reduction and development. The openness of the SRM approach to empirical validation applies equally to the rights-based approach and the call for minimum provisions. Whether the human rights approach is the best or only feasible approach for guaranteeing basic provisions for the chronic poor and for securing long-term political sustainability of social protection must at the end be left to empirical testing.

The needs that can be considered as mostly prominently to the realm of the social management of risks are:

- access to housing and utilities,
- access to food,
- access to health and healthy sexual reproduction,
- access to security, civil- and human-rights, and
- access to social participation.

The first three are easy to understand ('healthy reproduction' referring to the physical and social circumstances that allows human beings to pro creation). Access to security reflects the need to be protected from criminal activities and the access to human rights; access to social participation refers to the need for individuals to be truly embedded in the social and economic life of the community they live in; when this access is not secured we can speak of 'social exclusion'. Investments in the socio-cultural infrastructure, including 'social capital' (Portes 2000), are appropriate instruments and institutions of an extended social policy. The ESP concepts is also linked to 'capability approach' (Sen 1999) and the 'social rights approach' (Fabre 2000).

Strategising Corporate Social Responsibility by Addressing Social Issues

Every company by the nature of its operation affects the society or nature. This is more obvious in hazardous sector as its operations are more harmful to the environment. Though, a large number of companies work to re-contribute to the environment yet, a considerable number needs to address the society as their operation affects the society too by several means. Companies need to identify the risks arising due to nature of business and address it to the maximum extent possible. We cannot deny the fact the every business in some way affects the society. These effects can be classified in majority as 'incident effects' referring to the effects that are directly related to the event and disappear after a relatively short period of time. Temporary unemployment and short-term illnesses usually have only incident effects. The other major category being 'Lifetime effects' which are related to risks that usually have a long lasting effect on a persons' life. An event can first lead to incident effects, but later lifetime and/or inter-generational effects may result. The challenge lies in identifying the initiatives that can be undertaken to mitigate the hazards caused. The CSR initiatives can be introduced in a manner which either nullifies the negative effects or enhances the reputation of the company and increases its business opportunities.

Role of government in addressing social risks: The role of Government in addressing social issues is very crucial as the government is expected to create an enabling environment for raising awareness and stimulating public debate for the existing social challenges and issues. The government alone cannot make a difference to the society and thus is expected to include more actors in society for defining policies addressing social issues and also encouraging business responsibility in dealing with the social issues. The government is also expected to build capacities of businesses, civil societies and public authorities; fund researches related to social development and engage in PPP (public-private partnerships) for larger social impacts. Social issues can be addressed by initiating structured and sustainable efforts in the form of CSR and the government can act as a facilitator to undertake strategic, structured and impact oriented CSR.

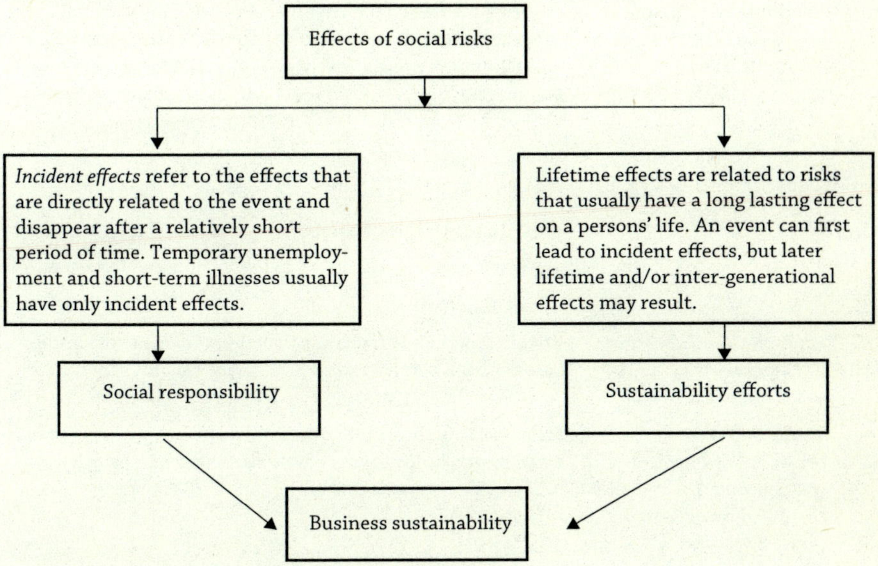

Source: Compiled by the authors.

Role of corporate in addressing social risks: The roles of corporate in addressing social issues primarily lies on first understanding the initiatives undertaken by the government and then design CSR initiatives which are based on real needs in alignment to the government's effort. The corporate effort should not be in conflict with the government. The role of corporate is majorly to dovetail the efforts of the government either by supplementing or complimenting the efforts undertaken by government. Some initiatives that can be undertaken addressing social risks are providing opportunity for skill development, initiating new business chains to create opportunity for employment, creating awareness on various health and hygiene dimensions.

Types of Social Risks

SRM goes beyond public provision of social protection and draws attention to informal and market-based arrangements, and their effectiveness and impact on growth and development. Risk can be defined as the possibility of suffering harm or loss. Managing and controlling risk internally and externally is the key to running a successful organisation.

Table 6.3

Role of Government and Corporate in Addressing Social Risks

Social Risks	*Governmental Initiatives*	*Corporate CSR Initiatives*
	Livelihood Risks	
• Involuntary displacement and resettlement of communities	Creating an enabling environment for raising awareness and stimulating public debate on encouraging new avenues of skill development.	Provide opportunity for skill development essential for industries and also ensuring future employment.
• Lack of skills for employment • Affect on agriculture	Defining policies for addressing livelihood risks.	Initiating new business chains to create opportunity for employment of needy by initiating skill development activities.
	Health Risks	
• Air pollution- Existence of harmful air borne diseases like asthma etc.	Enabling quality infrastructure for health and hygiene.	Supplement and compliment the initiatives of the government.
• Water pollution- Existence of harmful water borne diseases like chronic diarhoea etc.	Stimulating policies for discouraging of products like tobacco, alcohol, drugs etc.	Create awareness against the causes to health related issues.
• Malnutrition, under nutrition	Promoting awareness among all members in the chain for ensuring health system of the country	Creating awareness for acceptance of usage of toilets.
• Tobacco and alcohol related deaths		

Source: Compiled by the authors.

Corporate reputation, governance and ethics are headline issues associated with CSR that have made the news headlines in the last few years. Risks associated with supply chain—country specific such as human rights abuses, or company specific risks such as pollution, operational risks—this covers compliance with regulation, employee satisfaction and dangerous operations, product—this covers use of hazardous raw materials (e.g. nuclear energy) waste during production, health and safety issues and societal expectations—this covers what society demands of a business in the 21st century.

Corporate Case: Addressing Livelihood Risks

Neem project of Gujrat Narmda Valley Fertilisers and Chemical limited (GNFC)

In this project, GNFC Neem Oil is prepared along with neem cakes. The material for the same is collected through local women of SHGs (self-help groups) from around 4,000 villages. Around 2,200 *neem* seed collection centre has been set up in 22 districts of the village. Local women were trained to collect the *neem* seed which is available only during July-August. The project generated 12-15 crore income for 1.25 lakh women as well as created indirect employment for around 50,000 rural people.

Table 6.4

CSR Interventions Addressing Social Risks

	Categorisation of Social Risks	*CSR Interventions*
1	Universal risks are in principle shared by all regardless of their age, gender or position in society. Universal risks can strike theoretically everybody in a society, but that does not imply that everybody is exposed to same degree to the risk.	Road safety, safety and security against terrorism, natural disasters management, environment degradation, water and food security.
2	Life-cycle risks are also in principle shared by all but are specific to a certain age or to specific stages in the course of life for everybody.	Health initiatives for old, children and women. Awareness initiatives towards health and hygiene.
3	Categorical risks (sometimes called class- or group- risks) are risks that are peculiar to certain groups in the society.	Settlement initiatives towards miners, women, underprivileged, children of convicts in jail.

Source: Compiled by the authors.

An impact assessment study by United Nations Development Programme (UNDP) clarifies that the project lead to increased income, reduction in migration, enhanced decision making role of women in their families. The study also reflected that asset creation in form of livestock as well as stoves increased. The women empowerment initiated also addressed the typical issue of domestic violence in villages and reduced it by a considerable percentage.

Corporate Case: Addressing Health Risks

Anti Tobacco Initiative of Bajaj Electricals, Mumbai named "Yes to Life and No to Tobacco"

Tobacco is not just harmful to health but to environment also. It causes soil pollution and fertile lands by clearing tress are used for tobacco cultivation. The anti-tobacco policy of Bajaj Electricals applies the principles of 5As—ask, advice, assess, assist and arrange. The anti-tobacco drive was taken in with project partner Salaam Bombay foundation where the initiatives were taken to increase awareness, empowering school children to refuse tobacco products, building capacity for local stakeholders and engaging policy makers. The mass media outreach initiative included World no tobacco day campaign through Mumbai *dabbawalas*, World no tobacco day campaign with Mumbai BEST transport and World No Tobacco day campaign with Mumbai police personnel. The outcome of the initiative was 250 Mumbai police personnel took a pledge against tobacco and agreed to pass on the message. 1,000 *dabbawalas* workied towards spreading the message to 1 lakh population of Mumbai. Thousands of *zila parishad* schools of rural area of Yavatmal and Wardha were made tobacco free. This is a continuous effort and the impact will be seen over a period of time.

Corporate Case: Strategising Corporate Social Responsibility for Addressing Social Issue

School Hand Wash Programme of Dettol

Health and hygiene is an issue in rural India. Most rural population does not go for hand wash using soap till date. Sadly in India, 1 lakh children die annually from preventable illnesses such as diarrhoea and some of those deaths could have been halted through the very simple act of hand washing with soap. Dettol took an initiative of creating awareness of hand wash using their own products. Dettol is one of the top 10 trusted brands in India which has stood for 'trusted protection' and has completed 75 years in India. In order to spread the good hand washing habits amongst school children, Dettol started 'School Hand wash Programme' with the help of SHARP NGO. The main aim of the programme was to educate students on importance of school hand wash and procedure of 6 steps of proper hand washing. The activity as helped to position Dettol as the best product available for maintaining hygiene. All the students covered under this programme took a pledge to wash their hands properly and to spread the message to their families and community. Posters of 6 steps of hand washing were also displayed near the wash rooms and drinking water sources. The students with 100 per cent attendance were awarded the 'Dettol 100 per cent attendance award'. All the schools were also given a First Kit to the school and Dettol Hand wash Dispensers. The message has been passed to 1.1 million students across 3000 schools.

Conclusion

CSR has emerged as an important tool companies use to fulfil their social responsibilities through their business activities. The emergence of new form of social risks cannot be mitigated through traditional means. The ever changing environment requires innovation by companies in both sensing and understanding these risks. CSR needs to address the real needs of the society. The role of corporate lies in identifying the real needs and design CSR initiatives addressing social issues arising out of their own operations and then cater to other social issues. Molson Coors, a world-wide known beer company initiated a technology oriented initiative working against 'drunken driving'. The company's responsibility lies in identifying social issues and defining the needs of the society. Identification of right partner for implementation, monitoring, evaluation and impact assessment is also integral to the success of the initiatives. The initiative of the government in the form of Companies Act, 2013 has already led the pathway for development but challenge lies in encouraging corporate to follow the true spirit of CSR and initiate needed, sustainable and scalable efforts for future development.

References

Fabre, Cécile (2000). *Social Rights Under the Constitution*. Oxford: Oxford University Press.

Holzmann, Robert and Steen Jørgensen (2000)."Social Risk Management: A New Conceptual Framework for Social Protection and Beyond", *Social Protection Discussion Paper* No. 0006. Washington: World Bank.

IOD CSR Best Practices Report (2017a). *Gujrat Narmda Valley Fertilizers and Chemical Limited (GNFC)*

————. (2017b). *Bajaj Electricals*. Mumbai.

NGOBOX (2016). *India CSR Outlook Report*. Available at: *www.ngobox.org* (accessed on 5 December 2016).

Portes, A. (2000). "Social Capital : Its Origins and Applications in Modern Sociology", in E. Lesser (ed.), *Knowledge and Social Capital*. Boston: Butterworth-Heinemann. pp.43-69

Ritzer, G. (2003). "Rethinking Globalisation: Glocalisation/Grobalisation and Something/Nothing", *Sociological Theory* 21(3): 193-209.

Sen, A. (1999). *Development as Freedom*. New York: Knopf.

Times of India (2016). India Leads in CSR Spending Growth Available at: *http://timesofindia.indiatimes.com/business/India-leads-in-CSR-spending-growth/articleshow/51173712.cms* (accessed on 12 December2016).

Sectoral Perspectives to Corporate Social Responsibility

7

PUNAM SINGH

Addressing Environmental Risk through CSR

Case of Oil and Gas Sector

Introduction

Sectors which have an immense negative impact on environment and society because of the very nature of its operation are referred as 'hazardous sector'. They cause high level of pollution and impose significant costs on society. They cause immense damage to environment and society because of the very nature of operation. These sectors are also among the top contributor to any economy and also the leaders in the area of CSR (corporate social responsibility). One such industrial sector that makes strong claims to business ethics and/or CSR—human rights, employee rights, stakeholder rights, environmental protection, community relations, transparency, corruption, product stewardship, principles and codes of practice—is the oil and gas sector (Frynas 2005).

World Business Council for Sustainable Development (WBCSD) (2002) defined CSR as the commitment of business to contribute to sustainable economic development, working with employees, their families, the local community, and society at large to improve their quality of life, in ways that are good for international development. Business being part of the society has numerous stakeholders. Carroll and Buchholtz (2003) classify some major stakeholder groups into primary and secondary categories. Primary stakeholders include shareholders, employees, customers, business partners, communities, future generations, and the natural environment. The secondary stakeholders include the state, local and federal government, regulatory bodies, civic institutions and groups, special interest groups, trade and industry groups, media, and competitors.

The benefits of adopting CSR can have significant advantages for both shareholders and the environment, particularly when undertaken voluntarily. But another factor in favour of CSR is the oblique pressures brought to bear from a sense of moral obligation, a more ethical approach, sweeping into boardrooms. The mutual relations between CSR and risk management are undisputed. CSR shows how to avoid risk (or minimise it), which is a subject matter of risk management process (Gladys 2008: 2). That is why it needs to be stated that CSR means not only activities connected with reducing likelihood of risk (e.g. reputation loss, sales drop) or its consequences. It is rather more and more frequently observed to be a crucial element of risk management.

To create a model of CSR risk management, we can adopt two approaches: top-down and bottom-up. In top-down approach, international contracts (especially on the area of human rights and natural environment protection), national law and other regulations which organisation must comply with, are factors which decide on paying attention to CSR in risk management. Such an approach is particularly advisable for organisations whose activities are in close relations with these factors. Bottom-up approach is more adequate for organisations, where the main factor is commitment of stakeholders (Gladys 2007: 7).

CSR is a commitment by businesses to consider, not just the shareholders of an enterprise, but the interests of all stakeholders impacted by its activities. These include the employees, the consumers and suppliers of the business, the community in which it operates, and the environment. This paper aims to explore the aspect of CSR as a tool to address environmental risk in hazardous sector with a focus on oil and gas sector in particular. The paper is an exploratory study and is based on secondary data sources. The research question that this paper attempts to explore, Is CSR a tool for addressing environmental risk?

Environmental Risks

The word 'risk' has two distinct meanings. It can mean in one context a hazard or a danger, that is, an exposure to mischance or peril. In the other context, risk is interpreted more narrowly to mean the probability or chance of suffering an adverse consequence, or of encountering some loss. The risks involve a complex series of cause and effect relationships. They are connected from source to impact by pathways involving environmental, technological and social variables which need to be modelled and understood in a specific context.

The risks with which this paper is concerned are all in some way 'environmental'. Environmental risk can be defined as the 'actual or potential threat of adverse effects on living organisms and the environment by effluents, emissions, wastes, resource depletion, etc., arising out of an organisation's activities'.

Environmental risks, as defined here, share a second common feature in addition to being transmitted through environmental media. They cause harm to people who have not voluntarily or specifically chosen to suffer their consequences, and thus they require regulation on the part of some authority above that of an individual citizen—that is, they require managing. These consequences can fall on other groups in the future as well as today, as for example in the mismanagement of natural resources.

The management of risks does require resources—money, skilled manpower, and time—and is itself associated with the risks of cost, delay and inaction. Risk management is not, however, an entirely new or unfamiliar exercise. Social and economic development often leads to the introduction of new processes and products, and to the development of hazard prone areas without any consultation with risk assessors or environmental scientists. The fact that introducing and keeping CSR is 'voluntary' is controversial. It is said that it can be a result of pressure from specific stakeholders, especially local communities (Wisser 2010: 2). This is one of the reasons why in reformed strategy we can find a new definition, according to which CSR is 'companies' responsibility for their influence on society.

The environmental impacts caused by hazardous sector are frequently criticised by environmental groups. These impacts include:

- A huge amount of water is required as it is used in ash disposal to transport pollutants. Mining may also require groundwater levels to be lowered and there is a possibility of leeching, especially from in-situ extraction sites, affecting surrounding forest and arable land.
- Vast areas of land are required for mining, as well as for the disposal of mining waste and spent shale oil. This may cause significant surface disturbance, deforestation, erosion and reduction in traditional land uses.
- An increase in air pollution may also result from the production of particulates during processing. In addition, green house gases are emitted when oil shale is converted into usable oil, as well as from shale oil fired power stations.
- Finite fossils fuel resources, long-term impact from ozone depletion and global warming from greenhouse gas emissions from refining and processing.

- Coastal and marine ecology—impact on corals and marine biodiversity from offshore and coastal operations and tankers (spills).
- Health and safety and environmental risks of major explosions, leaks or spills.
- Destruction or irreversible impacts on critical environmental or social habitats (this could include rainforests, coastal and marine ecology, communities, and any protected areas wetlands, etc).
- Involuntary resettlement/displacement (physical and economic) of peoples as a result of project activities.
- Community health and safety—spread of diseases, prostitution, increase in road accidents, managing HIV/AIDS, etc, and
- Impacts on vulnerable people (the poor, indigenous, women, children—the disadvantaged).

Risk and Corporate Social Responsibility

Recognising the importance of CSR as a strategic tool for sustainable development, the oil and gas sector companies across the globe have initiated focused efforts for championing CSR to gain social sanction and goodwill. Oil companies have successfully implemented various CSR initiatives to mitigate the environmental risks, yet their absolute impact on industry environmental footprint remains questionable. Blowfield and Murray (2008) questioned the importance of 'indirect' impact in determining the role played by the oil companies in sustainable development.

Global companies which include primary operations of extraction and refining of oil and gas resources, mainly British Petroleum, Shell, ExxonMobil, and Total, display similarity which are used to characterise the industry. IEA (2002) has highlighted the importance of the oil and gas industry in managing the global energy consumption. Olje-ogenergidepartementet (2005) has explained that oil and gas cause immense environmental impact, both when produced and used. IPCC (2001) report has raised concern with regards to release of greenhouse gases causing climate change.

Crude oil constitute of substances with high toxicity and eco-toxicity (EPA 2004). Thus, the oil and gas industry is a high risk industry, both in safety and environmental perspective. Tebebba (2003) has talked about the geographical limitations of oil and gas resources and has discussed about the large scale environmental and social challenges related to new extraction fields.

Table 7.1

Understanding Risk and Control in Oil and Gas Sector

Risk (Oil and Gas Sector)	*Controls through CSR Intervention*
Habitat depletion, fragmentation and degradation: • Land clearance/disturbance, loss of vegetation, erosion. • Opening up of previously inaccessible land to agriculture and development—habitat loss. *Natural hazards and risks:* pipeline/pumping station leakage, leading to land/water contamination.	*Habitat and biodiversity management*: biodiversity awareness and conservation. Ecological restoration usually involves the reconstruction of natural and semi-natural ecosystems on degraded lands and ecological rehabilitation involves the repair of ecosystem. *Community/stakeholder relations management:* management of interface between local communities and outsiders/foreign workers through stakeholder identification and consultation(including governmental/national/regional/local stakeholders). *Waste Management*: water disposal and monitoring systems. *Water management*: securing of a sustainable water supply, recycling and reuse wastewater.
Community health and safety: noise, vibration, dust creation, vehicular movement, emissions and air quality. *Strain on infrastructure and public nuisance:* noise, odour, vibration, dust creation, transport movement, and air quality, strain on transport networks and local infrastructure. *Communicable diseases*: spread of diseases to local/foreign populations. *Impacts to existing land use*: eg agriculture, leading to loss of livelihood; changes to access to water resources; impacts to nomadic/grazing routes. Impacts are usually only temporary.	*Health and safety plans:* vaccinations and awareness raising on communicable diseases. *Social /community baseline assessment:* establish community profiles (e.g. livelihoods and employment) in project area, through detailed social baseline assessments to inform mitigation measures and the development of long term agreed community investment/development. *Livelihood generation initiatives*: vocational training/ skill development.

Source: Developed by Author.

Corporate Social Responsibility Drivers in Hazardous Sector

A growing number of companies in a wide range of sectors and geographic regions have discovered concrete value and competitive advantage from taking environmental initiatives, for example, in areas such as pollution prevention, energy efficiency, environmentally oriented design, supply—chain management, waste management, water management, biodiversity management and industrial ecology. In the era of stakeholder activism, a number of factors propel organisations to behave responsibly. In the past, industrial accidents such as Bhopal, Chernobyl and Exxon Valdez, have constituted a great danger for societies and the natural environment, and thus they are used as another reasons to advocate the social responsibilities of business today. Sustainable business, social license to operate, innovation are few reasons for organisations embracing CSR. The prominent CSR drivers in a hazardous sector are discussed in Table 7.2.

Table 7.2

Drivers of CSR

Economic Drivers	*Environmental Drivers*	*Social Drivers*
• Company image	• Legal, Regulatory drivers	• Pressure from NGOs/CSOs
• Risk management	• Pressure from environmentalist	• Social license to operate
• Stakeholder pressure	• Stakeholder activism	• Local community pressure
• Competitive advantage	• License to operate	• Managing social risk
• Business sustainability	• Managing environmental risk	
	• Environmental sustainability	

Source: Developed by Author.

Corporate Social Responsibility: Indian Scenario

The Government of India has passed CSR Act/Guidelines applicable to all companies operating in India which include the social, environmental and economic responsibilities of business, Ministry of Corporate Affairs (MCA), July 2011 and the CSR Mandate as per the latest Companies Act, 2013. The DPE guideline on CSR and Sustainability is applicable to CPSEs (central public sector enterprises) in India w.r.t 1 April 2014. Section 135 of the Companies Act, 2013 deals with CSR provisions and Schedule VII of the Act lists out the CSR activities. Item 4 of the Schedule VII of Section 135 of the Companies Act provides ample scope for companies to work in the thematic area of environmental sustainability. Item 4, of schedule VII of section 135 of the Companies Act states, "Ensuring environmental sustainability, ecological balance, protection of flora and fauna, animal welfare, agro-forestry, conservation of natural resources and maintaining quality of soil, air and water." In the given scenario, it is important to understand the present CSR activities of companies and the thematic areas pursued by them under CSR. It is pertinent to understand the emphasis given by organisation in terms of environmental sustainability and the projects undertaken in the area of the same.

According to the *India CSR Outlook Report* of 2016, which is a survey of 250 companies accounting for one-third of the total CSR spent. The study shows that there is a substantial improvement in the actual CSR spend to prescribed CSR in the FY (financial year) 2015-16. While it was 79 per cent in the FY 2014-15, it has increased to 92 per cent in the last financial year.

Table 7.3

Top 10 Companies in CSR Spending, 2015-16

Company	*Prescribed CSR*	*Actual CSR*	*Actual CSR (%)*
Reliance Industries Ltd.	557.78	651.57	117
NTPC Ltd	349.65	491.80	141
Oil and Natural Gas Corporation Ltd	593.70	421.00	71
Tata Consultancy Services Ltd	360.00	294.00	82
ITC Ltd	246.76	247.50	100
Tata Steel Ltd	150.00	213.24	142
National Mineral Development Corporation	193.28	210.09	109
Infosys Ltd	256.01	202.30	79
Power Finance Corporation Ltd	145.09	196.20	135
ICICI Bank Ltd.	212.00	172.00	81

Source: NGOBOX, *India CSR Outlook Report, 2016.*

The data shows that oil and gas sector which includes both public and private sector are the leaders in CSR spent, followed by services and banking sector in India.

Table 7.4

Thematic Areas of CSR Initiatives of Indian Companies

Thematic Area	*No. of Projects*	*INR Cr.*
Poverty alleviation, healthcare and wash (water, sanitation and hygine)	876	2142
Education and skills	1189	2073
Women empowerment and inclusive development	171	167
Protection of national heritage, art and culture	87	83
Benefits to armed forces veterans, war widows	16	7
Environmental sustainability	345	559
Technology incubators within academic institutions	15	12
Rural sports, paralympics and olympic sports	88	159
Pm relief fund and others	44	162
Rural development projects	206	771
Urban slum development	10	7
Admin expenses	-	437

Source: NGOBOX, *India CSR Outlook Report, 2016.*

Reflection on the Thematic Areas of Corporate Social Responsibility Investment

The data reflects that education (including skilling) and healthcare themes have been the most preferred areas of CSR projects. Environment sustainability stands as the third most preferred area for CSR projects. We can infer from Tables 7.3 and 7.4 that companies in oil and gas sector are the major spender in CSR activities but their initiatives are mostly targeted in the areas of education and healthcare rather as a strategic approach to CSR. Companies in oil and gas need to channelise their CSR initiatives in the area of environmental sustainability.

Environmental Sustainability: CSR Initiatives of Major Oil and Gas Sector Enterprises

Cost benefit language has often been used to excuse the damage caused in one place because it is outweighed by the overall financial benefits (Jenkins 2006). However, in recent years the global mining industry has addressed its social and environmental responsibilities; numerous factors have contributed to this, and the extractive industry is key in debates about social and environmental sustainability (Cowell et al. 1999). The CSR programmes of mining companies tend to focus on community initiatives as their impact in economic, social and environmental terms is felt greatest at the local level. The study conducted by Mishra et al. (2013), reveals that organisations in such sector have undertaken initiatives in terms of reduction of CO_2 and other greenhouse gases. They are members of the United Nations Global Compact, India. All major oil and gas sector companies are certified under the SA 8000 and ISO 14001. The study also reveals that environmental sustainability is one of the major areas of CSR. The paper emphasises the need for better disaster management initiatives. The environmental metric used in the paper includes pollution prevention, environmental safety, biodiversity management, climate change and natural resource management.

Table 7.5 shows that oil and gas sector have initiated activities in the area of environment sustainability. The scope and spent in the area of environment needs to be increased. Integrated projects on rural development with emphasis on addressing environmental and social risk are a good initiative. More such integrated, innovative and sustainable projects need to be designed and implemented. Organisations have to take more projects in the areas of biodiversity management, water management and conservation of natural resource. The projects can also be undertaken in a collaborative approach to increase the scalability of the projects. Companies have to realise the importance of integrating CSR with their business strategy with special emphasis on projects in CSR aimed at addressing environment risks and opportunities.

CSR in Oil and Gas Sector: International Scenario

Environmentally sensitive organisations and leadership companies define corporate environmental responsibility as the duty to cover the environmental implications of the company's operations, products and facilities; eliminate waste and emissions; maximise the efficiency and productivity of its resources; and minimise practices that might adversely affect the enjoyment of the country's resources by future generations.

It is thus, important that organisations have a CSR framework for taking the agenda of CSR ahead which should include as to:

- What has to be done? (e.g.: OECD codes, standards—SA 8000, governance principles—United Nations Global Compact)
- How to be done? (Management—ISO and assurance standards), and
- How to measure progress on a global scale (reporting—GRI)?

The need for holistic framework is required as CSR activities are basically based on a voluntary approach; environmental externalities are observable to stakeholders, but often not verifiable. Generally, the concern about CSR is that, instead of big number of initiatives, there is no comprehensive framework that would cover all at the same time, issues such as: government standards, management systems, codes of conduct, performance standards, performance reporting, and assurance standards. Companies, usually, implement separate components, or join selected initiatives, often forgetting for example about transparent monitoring mechanisms.

In the context of above mentioned CSR framework, Table 7.6 gives an overview of the CSR policies and initiatives of the oil and Gas sector in a global perspective. The table indicates that oil and gas sector have been complying through a number of frameworks and guidelines. Most of the oil and gas companies have a CSR framework in place. The above analysis also reflects of multiple codes and guidelines. Thus, there seems to be a need for a holistic, integrated and comprehensive framework for transparent monitoring, evaluation and reporting.

Table 7.5

CSR Initiatives and Spending of Major Indian Oil and Gas Sector Companies in Environment Sustainability (2015-16)

Corporate	*Name of CSR Activity (15-16)*	*Locations*	*Budget Outlay (Crores)*	*Budget Spent (Crores)*
GAIL	GAIL has approve setting up of two waste plastic to fuel oil plants of 10 TPD capacity each	Haridwar and Ujjain	-	-
	The hugely successful Integrated Watershed Development and Management Programme, Project Jaldhar has resulted in functioning of over 48 SHGs (self help groups) which have in turn facilitated Income generation and promote saving among tribal women of Jhabua, creation of 15 watershed structures and plantation of trees/saplings.	Jhabua, Madhya Pradesh	-	-
RIL	Rural Transformation – Reliance Foundation Bharat India Jodo – Enhancing Rural Livelihoods	Andhra Pradesh, Gujarat, Jharkhand, Karnataka, Madhya Pradesh, Maharashtra, Orissa, Rajasthan, Tamil Nadu	84.35	69.69
	Rural Transformation - Information Services - Enable access to need based locale-specific content in agriculture, marine fisheries, public health, disaster response and other areas by leveraging technology	Andhra Pradesh, Gujarat, Maharashtra and Tamil Nadu	20.12	14.00

ONGC	Harit Moksha: Green Cremation System: To reduce wood consumption during traditional cremations through MGCS (mokshda green cremation systems).	Delhi and Mumbai	20% of the CSR Budget for environmental sustainability projects	-
	Ringal Plantation in Upper Himalayas	Upper Himalayas		
	ONGC-Eastern Swamp Deer Conservation Project in Kaziranga National Park: The project aims at successfully conserving the species of the Eastern swamp deer.	Kaziranga National Park, Assam		
Essar Oil Ltd.	Maximising the impact of interventions on water, recharging aquifer system, enhanced quality of water on a sustainable basis.	Dwaraka and Jamnagar district, Gujarat	.35	.33
IOCL	MoP and NG LPG Schemes for BPL families	Local/Other: All India	21.09	31.62
Oil India Limited	Environment Conservation – Project on Solar Energy & Bio-diversity	OIL operational areas of Tinsukia, Dibrugarh & parts of Sivasagar districts of Assam	0.08	0.08
HPCL	LPG Connections to BPL Families	Pan India	17.87	17.87
BPCL	BOOND - Rain water harvesting project mokhada	Other: DistPalghar, Maharashtra	6.26	1.28
	BOOND - Rain water harvesting project -Kolar Ramanagara	Local: Dist - Kolar &Ramanagara, Karnataka	3.02	.44

Source: Compiled by the author.

Table 7.6

Summary of CSR Policies and Initiatives: Oil and Gas Sector

	CSR Policies			*CSR Multi-Stakeholder Initiatives*			
	Reductions in CO_2 Emissions	*Community Development Projects*	*Government Revenue Transparency*	*United Nations Global Compact*	*Voluntary Principles on Security and Human Rights*	*Extractive Industries Transparency Initiative*	*World Business Council for Sustainable Development*
Shell	Yes	Yes	Yes	Yes	Yes	Yes	Yes
BP	Yes	Yes	Yes	Yes	Yes	Yes	Yes
Exxon	Yes	Yes	Yes	No	Yes	Yes	No
Chevron	Yes	Yes	Yes	No	Yes	Yes	Yes
Petrobras	Yes	Yes	Yes	Yes	No	No	Yes
Indian Oil	No	Yes	No	Yes	No	No	No
PDVSA	No	Yes	No	No	No	No	No
Kuwait Petroleum	No	Yes	No	No	No	No	No

Source: Frynas (2009).

Environmental Sustainability: Case of Shell Oil Company, US

Shell Oil Company, US, is the subsidiary of Royal Dutch Shell. Along with its consolidated companies, it is considered one of America's largest oil and natural gas producers. Taking cognisance of the fact that oil production and distribution involves processes that can lead to environmental hazards and can adversely impact on the ecosystem, Shell is involved in various activities that directly and indirectly lead to environmental protection and sustainability.

Shell and Environment Sustainability

Shell articulated its General Business Principles in the year 1976 and became one of the first multinationals to do so. These principles clearly mention the company's commitment to sustainable development and its resolve to integrate environmental and social considerations in decision-making and policy formulation. To offset the possible impact of their activities on environment, Shell focuses on protecting biodiversity. An impact assessment is done before starting a new project and the results are kept in view throughout the project operation process. In areas which are rich in biodiversity, the company interacts with the community, initiate discussions, and invite their inputs before making their plans. This is done particularly to identify any adverse impact the project can bring about to disturb the ecosystem. The impact assessment also ensures that the operations adhere to the company's laid down biodiversity standards.

Sustainability has always been of particular concern for Shell. One of the most significant steps taken by the company is the establishment of the Shell Centre for Sustainability at Rice University in Houston with an endowment of USD 3.5 million. This was started in the year 2002. Experts work in collaboration with the Centre on societal and environmental issues that arise as a result of economic activities. Other activities and initiatives of Shell towards environment include: Educational funding of America's wetland campaign to save coastal Louisiana; setting up of a Shell Marine Habitat Programme that will support projects to conserve, protect and enhance the Gulf of Mexico ecosystem; and setting up the Cape Floral Kingdom (CFK) in South Africa with the objectives of conserving biodiversity and resources and to provide the people of the community with sustainable livelihood. The company is also continuously engaged in its efforts to reduce oil spills and also reduce greenhouse gas emissions.

Observation: Primarily the analysis of the study of the CSR scenario of Indian companies, global players and also that of Shell shows that the organisations have shown commitment to the protection of the environment. Companies understand the importance of business sustainability and the relevance of environmental sustainability as a tool for the achievement of business sustainability. This is a paradigm shift which is growing in importance and the value of the shift cannot be overstated. Companies also understand the relevance of CSR as a tool to mitigate environmental risk and hence they are spending their CSR budget in activities leading to environmental sustainability. The trend will grow faster than ever in coming future as more and more companies will realise the importance of integrating CSR with business objectives.

Integration of CSR in Business Model

The concept of integrating CSR in business model is about creating a culture of not just about what corporate do with their profits but also about how they make profit. The ultimate goal of integrating CSR in business model is business sustainability. The dimensions of CSR are not limited to what industries do outside their organisation but also about how do they align their production and business process in environmentally sustainable ways.

Figure 7.1

Model Integrating CSR and Business

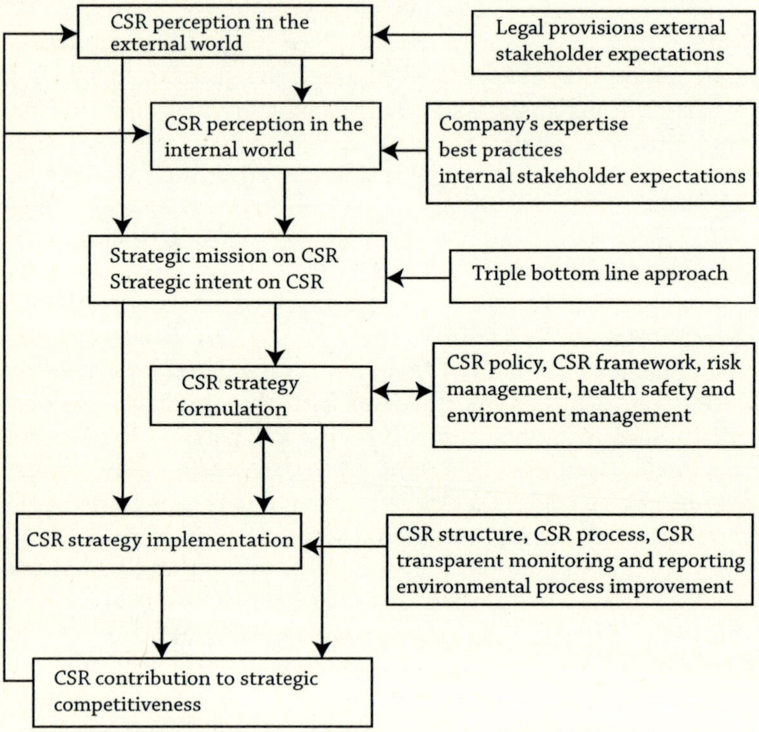

Source: Developed by the Author.

The model in Figure 7.1, proposes CSR as a part of the core business operations of a company, rather than a separate 'add on', distinguishing it from corporate philanthropy, which may be funded out of operations that are damaging to the communities in which business is conducted. The above model of integrating CSR in business model is based on the strategic management process by Hitt et al. (2003).

In the process of integration of CSR in business model, organisations should define very specifically the strategic importance of CSR either by enhancing the intangible assets of their firm (e.g. reputation, social capital, trust) or by minimising production costs (e.g. through better risk management or improved production processes). This is important as it will decide the CSR strategies. Involvement of internal and external stakeholder is important in developing a sound CSR strategy. After the development of a sound CSR strategy, implementation requires a variety of resource commitment, intangible (commitment, communication, and training) as well as tangible such as equipments. Incentives such as financial benefits, audit can also prove beneficial.

Dentchev (2005) reflect on the strategic integration of CSR in business model and states that the concept is still underdeveloped. The process of integration is a challenge for practitioners but it is worth the pain as it has a strategic relevance for firms. In case of oil and gas sector, the model will result in integration of environmental aspect as part of CSR strategy and thus, will address the environmental implications of the company's operations, products and facilities; eliminate waste and emissions; maximise the efficiency and productivity of its resources; and minimise practices that might adversely affect the enjoyment of the country's resources by future generations.

Figure 7.2

Collaborative Approach to CSR

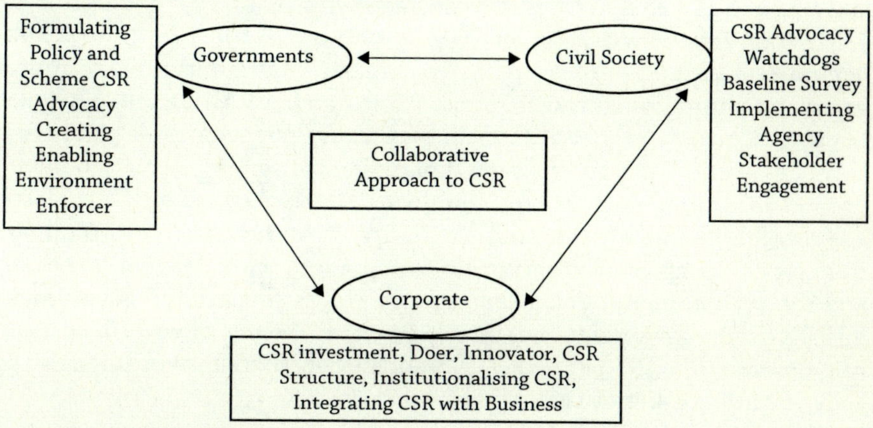

Source: Developed by Author.

Addressing Environmental Risk through CSR-Collaborative Approach

Role of Corporate: The corporates are required to envision CSR as a tool for environmental sustainability and for sustainable tomorrow. This requires them to formulate a CSR policy in line with their organisational strategy. Governance-level discussion needs to take place about how CSR should be integrated into business strategy and to make sure that CSR objectives and the supporting metrics are clear, well understood, and embedded throughout the organisation. Corporates need to design CSR projects by understanding the environmental risks and opportunities and synergise/dovetail the initiatives of the government. They have to partner with the civil society organisations to understand the ground realities and with their help, develop a successful implementation model with the involvement of the local government.

CSR managers: Needs to learn the language of risk management, including categories, tolerances, and outcomes. Quantify activities so they can more easily be used in risk models. Understand how social and environmental trends can become risks and opportunities. Knowledge of the risk climate change poses to their business, their clients, and the communities in which they operate and acceptance of responsibility to mitigate environmental risk and work towards environmental sustainability.

Role of NGOs (non-governmental organisations): NGOs play a variety of role. NGOs play roles from advocates for the poor to implementers of corporate or government programmes. NGOs work as critics to partners and advisors as well as locates and mediates with sponsors of pilot projects. The major role of NGO can be highlighted as: supporting innovation, demonstration and pilot projects, facilitating communication, technical assistance and training, research, monitoring and evaluation and advocacy. CSOs (civil society organisation) can play a very important role right from awareness generation and information dissemination, to capacity building to implementation partners to monitoring and evaluation of the projects. The Swachh Bharat Mission and the Ganga Cleaning Mission in India are two classic examples of government taking a lead with clear set objectives and the corporate and CSOs coming forward to support the government initiatives. The government has also appreciated the role of government and has announced a 100 per cent tax reduction on contribution towards the above mentioned initiatives.

Role of Government: At the macro level discussion, government sector is expected to play the roles as the driver of CSR initiatives by the corporation for the benefit of the society (Moon et al. 2004, Fox et al. 2002). However, at the micro level, the roles are reflected in the implementation strategy which is known among others as public-private partnership CSR strategy. The aims of the partnership are to share resources, knowledge and capability between business corporations and the government agency. The government sectors are expected to provide enabling environment to assist and encourage the business corporation to undertake CSR effort as one of the business strategy in the country. The enabling role played by the government sector would refer to the four key roles that are mandating, facilitating, partnering and endorsing (Fox et al. 2002).

Conclusion

The sustainability performance of a company is generally measured by assessing three aspects of sustainability: economic, social and environmental performance. There are clear rules and broad understanding of measuring the economic pulse of a company at any given point in time.

The assessment of environmental performance is still very limited since it is mainly based on primary environmental impact such as natural resource depletion, land degradation, pollution emissions, energy consumption and waste generation. What really needs to be done and is missing is a long term perspective where-in organisations should study the impact assessment of their business and work upon to mitigate the negative impact of the business caused to the environment.

Oil and gas sector needs to have a more integrated and strategic approach to mitigate environmental risk through CSR. The development of better and more sophisticated CSR programmes, fed and nurtured by a more transparent, receptive approach to stakeholder engagement, represents their response to the changing expectations of governments, NGOs and neighbours over the last several decades. In the past few years, it has been observed that oil and gas sector in India have made great strides towards doing business in a most sustainable and socially and environmentally responsible way. The business of exploring entails environmental cause and social challenges. Therefore, governments, NGO's and community will continue to pressurise hazardous sector to respond to the evolving environmental and social risk and hence, the only way to sustainable business is to make CSR a way of business.

References

Bharat Petroleum Corp. Ltd. (2016). *CSR Report (2015-16)*. Mumbai.

Blowfield, M. and A. Murray (2008). *Corporate Responsibility: A Critical Introduction*. Oxford: Oxford University Press.

Carroll, A.B. and A.K. Buchholtz (2003). *Business and Society: Ethics and Stakeholder Management*. 5th ed. Australia: Thomson South-Western.

Crane, A.W., Abagail, D. Matten, J. Moon and D. Siegel (2009). *The Oxford Handbook of CSR*. Oxford: Oxford University Press.

Cowell, S.J., W. Wehrmeyer, P.W. Argust, J. Graham and S. Robertson (1999). "Sustainability and the Primary Extraction Industries: Theories and Practice", *Resources Policy* 25(4): 277-86.

Dentchev, A. Nikolay (2005). "Integrating CSR in Business Model", *Working Paper*. Hoveniersberg, Belgium: Ghent University. p.28.

EPA (Environmental Protection Agency) (2004). *Environmental Protection Agency Guidelines*. Retrieved from *http://www.epa.gov/oswer/ riskassessment/ragse/index.htm*

Fox, T., H. Ward and B. Howard (2002). *Public Sector Roles in Strengthening Corporate Social Responsibility: A Baseline Study*. Washington, DC: World Bank.

Frynas, J. (2005). "The False Developmental Promise of Corporate Social Responsibility: Evidence from Multinational Oil Companies", *International Affairs* 81(3): 581-598. *http://dx.doi.org/10.1111/j.1468-2346.2005.00470.x*

Frynas, G.J. (2009). *Beyond CSR, Oil Multinationals and Social Challenges*. UK: Cambridge University Press. p.25.

Gladys, J. (2007). "CSR: A Risky Business—Risk Management and CSR", Available at: *http://www.wbs.ac.uk/downloads/news/2007/10/csr-a-risky-business.pdf*

Hindustan Petroleum Corporation Ltd. (2016). *CSR Report (2015-16)*. Mumbai.

Hitt, M. A., R.D. Ireland and R.E. Hoskisson (2003). *Strategic Management: Competitiveness and Globalization*. 5th edition. Mason, Ohio: Thomson South-Western.

IEA (International Energy Agency) (2002). *World Energy Outlook* 2002. Paris: OECD/IEA.

IPCC (Intergovernmental Panel on Climate Change) (2001). *Climate Change (2001) Synthesis Report: Summary for Policymakers*. Retrieved from http://www.ipcc.ch/pub/un/syreng/spm.pdf

Jenkins, Heledd and Natalia Yakovleva (2006). "CSR in the Mining Industry: Exploring Trends in Social and Environmental Disclosure", *Journal of Cleaner Production* 14: 271-84.

Mishra,R.K., P. Singh, Shulagna Sarkar (2013). "CSR: Interventions of Oil and Gas Central Public Sector Enterprises in India", *International Journal of Business Ethics in Developing Economies* 2(2).

Moon, J., A. Crane and D. Matten (2005). "Can Corporations be Citizens? Corporate Citizenship as a Metaphor for Business Participation in Society", *Business Ethics Quarterly* 15(3): 427-51.

Oil and Natural Gas Corporation Ltd. (2016). *CSR Report (2015-16)*. New Delhi.

Oil India Ltd. (2016). *CSR Report (2015-16)*. New Delhi.

Olje-ogenergidepartementet (2005). *Miljø–Xrskpetroleumvirksomhet 2005*. Oslo.

Wisser, W. (2010). "CSR Naświecie—Odrodzenie", *Media Planet: Kompendium CSR—Niezależny Dodatek Tematyczny Dystrybuowany Wraz Z Dziennikiem Gazeta Prawna* 4/Czerwiec.

World Business Council for Sustainable Development (2002). *Business Case for Sustainable Development*. Retrieved from *http://www.wbcsd.ch/DocRoot/rZNj49UF0okxGvdLfDte/ business-case.pdf)*.

Others:

http://www.shell.com/home/content/environment_society/environment/biodiversity

8

DEEPTI CHANDRA

Role of Corporate Social Responsibility and Sustainability in the Small and Medium Enterprises Sector

Introduction: The Indian Story

CSR (corporate social responsibility) in India has conventionally been seen as a philanthropic activity. As a result, there is limited documentation on specific activities related to this concept. As pointed out by some observers, the practice of CSR in India still remains within the philanthropic space, but has moved from institutional building (educational, research and cultural) to community development through various projects. With globalisation and with communities becoming more and more dynamic, it is apparent that while CSR remains largely constrained to community development, it is getting more tactical in nature (that is, getting linked with business) than philanthropic, and a large number of companies are reporting the activities they are undertaking in this space in their official websites, annual reports, sustainability reports and even publishing CSR reports.

India has a very young population of youth with about 65 per cent of the population below the age of 35. With youth come more openings and India need to focus on sustainable opportunities for them and the future generations. CSR is not the social responsibility limited only to corporations. It may have been defined for companies but it needs to be blended with the government or the local government structure as well. India also cannot contradict with the need for configuration of technology with social sector. Social responsibility for the corporation must not start and finish with allocation of percentage of profit and to invest in few projects. It needs to extend into the overall functionality of the organisation.

The Companies Act, 2013

The Companies Act, 2013 has introduced the concept of CSR to the forefront and through its disclose-or-explain mandate, is promoting greater transparency and disclosure. Schedule VII of the Act, which lists out the various CSR activities recommends communities to be at the central point. On the other hand, by discussing a company's relationship to its stakeholders and integrating CSR into its core operations, the draft rules suggest that CSR needs to go beyond communities and beyond the concept of philanthropy. It will be interesting to observe the ways in which this will translate into action at the ground level, and how the understanding of CSR is set to undergo a transformation.

Table 8.1

Evolution of CSR and its Transformation since Independence

Era	*Happenings*
Before 1947	The concept manifested itself through charity carried out by businessmen and philanthropists with a strong spiritual sentiment.
Post 1947	The Gandhian values and beliefs of trusteeship were accepted. It advocated the role of PSUs (public sector units) as important.
Post 1991	The period permitted the entry of global players which enhanced competition in the market. The global standards of CSR provoked the local players to counter to the needs and enhance brand value and meet consumer satisfaction.
Post 2000	The global information sharing allowed the Indian Government to slot in the best practices that made India the first country to authorise CSR. It focused not only on monetary alliance but also on partnership and engagement.

Corporate Social Responsibility and Sustainability

Sustainability or rightly called 'corporate sustainability' is derived from the concept of sustainable development which is defined by the Brundtland Commission as "development that meets the needs of the present without compromising the ability of future generations to meet their own needs".

Corporate sustainability essentially refers to the role that companies can play in meeting the scheme of sustainable development and involves a objective approach to economic progress, social progress and environmental concerns. CSR in India focuses on what is done with profits after they are made. On the other hand, sustainability is about featuring the social and environmental impacts of conducting business, that is, how profits are made. Hence, much of the Indian practice of CSR is a significant constituent of sustainability or responsible business. A fascinating case in point is the NVGs (national voluntary guidelines) for social, environmental and economic responsibilities of business issued by the Ministry of Corporate Affairs in June 2011. The 8 principles relating to inclusive development encompasses the majority of the aspects covered by the CSR clause of the Companies Act, 2013. However, the remaining 8 principles pertain to other aspects of the business. The UN Global Compact, a widely used sustainability framework has 10 principles covering social, environmental, human rights and governance issues, and what is described as CSR is implied rather than cleared in these principles.

What is Corporate Social Responsibility?

The Global Context

Although the core of CSR lie in philanthropic activities, donations, charity, relief work, and the like of corporations, globally, the notion of CSR has evolved and presently includes all interrelated concepts such as triple bottom line, corporate citizenship, philanthropy, strategic philanthropy, shared value, corporate sustainability and business responsibility. This is evident in some of the definitions presented below.

The European Commission (EC) defines CSR as:

> The responsibility of enterprises for their impacts on society. To completely meet their social responsibility, enterprises should have in place a process to integrate social, environmental, ethical human rights and consumer concerns into their business operations and core strategy in close collaboration with their stakeholders.

The World Business Council for Sustainable Development (WBCSD) defines CSR as:

> The continuing commitment by business to contribute to economic development while improving the quality of life of the workforce and their families as well as of the community and society at large.

According to the United Nations Industrial Development Organisation (UNIDO):

> CSR is a management concept whereby companies integrate social and environmental concerns in their business operations and interactions with their stakeholders. CSR is generally understood as being the way through which a company achieves a balance of economic, environmental and social imperatives (Triple-Bottom-Line Approach), while at the same time addressing the expectations of shareholders and stakeholders. In this sense, it is important to draw a distinction between CSR, which can be a strategic business management concept, and charity, sponsorships or philanthropy.

Even in the global context, the notion of CSR and sustainability seems to be converging, as is evident from the various definitions of CSR. The origin of this convergence can be observed from the preamble to the recently released draft rules relating to the CSR clause within the Companies Act 2013 which discusses about the stakeholders and incorporating it with the social, environmental and economic objectives, all of which constitute the idea of a triple bottom line approach.

It is also recognised in the Guidelines on CSR and Sustainability for Central Public Sector Enterprises issued by the DPE in April 2013. The new guidelines, which have replaced two existing separate guidelines on CSR and sustainable development, issued in 2010 and 2011 respectively, state the following:

> Since corporate social responsibility and sustainability are so closely entwined, it can be said that corporate social responsibility and sustainability is a company's commitment to its stakeholders to conduct business in an economically, socially and environmentally sustainable manner that is transparent and ethical.

Corporate Social Responsibility and Small and Medium Enterprises

MSMEs (micro, small and medium enterprises) sector has surface as an extremely vibrant and dynamic sector of the Indian economy over the last five decades. MSMEs not only play vital role in providing large employment opportunities at reasonably low capital cost than large industries but also assist in industrialisation of rural and backward areas, thereby, reducing regional imbalances, assuring more equitable distribution of national income and wealth. MSMEs are harmonising to large industries as ancillary units and this sector contributes to a great deal to the socio-economic development of the country. The sector consisting of 36 million units, as of today, provides employment to over 80 million persons. The sector through more than 6,000 products contributes about 8 per cent to GDP besides 45 per cent to the total manufacturing output and 40 per cent to the exports from the country. The MSME sector has the prospective to spread industrial growth across the country and can be a key partner in the course of inclusive growth.

What are Small and Medium Enterprises?

SMEs (small and medium enterprises) notably contribute towards India's economic growth. These operate independently and also as ancillary to larger units and help generate employment and industrialise the rural and backward regions of India. They employ nearly 40 per cent of India's workforce and contribute around 45 per cent to India's manufacturing output.

What do they do?

The business operations of SMEs are executed in proximity to the locals. This enables them to be responsive of community needs, manage potential and develop CSR programmes suitably. The CSR clause in the Companies Act, 2013 covers companies that have a net profit of five crore INR and above, it is expected that while micro-enterprises will not qualify, many SMEs will. The CSR activities of these enterprises are determined by the individual interests of promoters who hold a majority of financial stake in the business. They tend to be in group and engaged in similar business activities. While the quantum of revenue accessible for CSR with individual SMEs is expected to be small, all eligible companies in a specific geographical cluster, who single handed as well as jointly impact the same community, can team their resources to generate a generous CSR fund.

How can SMEs Contribute to CSR Initiatives?

This area gives the opportunity to analyse the alternative of undertaking joint CSR activities by SMEs. This collaboration can also be utilised by other companies to take full advantage of the impact of their CSR initiatives while reducing the operational costs for fund management.

Why Collaborate for CSR Initiatives?

CSR pertains to all companies. SMEs in India have contributed in CSR activities but these efforts have not given the best results. One probable reason can be the fact that CSR activities depend on the profits of an SME and any variation in profits can negatively affect their capacity to maintain their involvement in CSR. Second reason can be the inadequate human resources available to SMEs which may also result in the lack of a specialised approach.

SMEs tend to centre their attention on short-term projects involving lesser operational costs. A survey conducted by UNIDO in 2008 on five SME clusters in India, found that 31 per cent to 79 per cent of the SMEs in these clusters, chose charity donations rather than long-term programmes for local communities. With the inception of the new Companies Act, 2013, the SME's approach to CSR has to be customised while keeping operational costs low. One workable alternative is to pool resources with other SMEs in the cluster and create combined CSR programmes managed by a single entity. This partnership can be formed within the units in a cluster as they interrelate with the same communities and have already recognised associations that cater to the business needs of the units.

Collaboration has the following benefits:

- *Reduces operational cost*: Individual CSR activities by a company comprises of establishing a CSR department, reviewing the needs of local communities, taking responsibility of programmes directly or through an NGO (non-governmental organisation) and conducting usual impact assessment studies. A common organisation catering to a number of companies will carry out these activities jointly and thus reduce the operational cost of management.
- *Undertake long-term projects*: A major obstacle in developing long term projects is the ambiguity in the CSR budget. This is dependent on the financial performance of the company. An unpredictable performance implies that the CSR budget allocations can be unreliable and can endanger a programme initiated earlier. Pooling resources concentrates on this issue to a definite extent as the other partners can enhance their share in case there is discrepancy in allocation from a certain segment of the cluster. The long term programmes also have larger impact than the short-term projects. Communities are progressively realising the significance of the support offered by these programmes. Long-term programmes also lead to improved community relations and this will ensure evade situations of community unrest that slow down business activities.
- *Learning from experiences*: A common entity with several participants from the cluster will help evaluate community needs, undertake appropriate programmes based on past experiences and deal with greater number of community issues. Collaboration among the SMEs in a cluster also gives an opportunity to manage social and environmental issues and answer better to the pressure from customers. Collaborations can also be forged amongst bigger companies, possibly through industry associations, to facilitate them to address general issues plaguing a geographical region or an industry.

Ministry of MSMEs envisage a vivacious MSME sector by promoting growth and development of the MSME Sector, including Khadi, Village and Coir Industries, in cooperation with concerned Ministries or Departments, State governments and other stakeholders, through offering support to existing enterprises and encouraging establishment of new enterprises.

The Process for a Small and Medium Enterprises

The first step involved in collaborating is to create a coalition of concerned SMEs. This may begin by the cluster association in case of large-scale participation from the cluster. On the other hand, it can be initiated by an individual SME in case there are only a few units interested in undertaking CSR activities in collaboration. Participation of the cluster association will ensure that the local priorities are given due consideration while developing CSR programmes. In case an adequate number of SMEs in a cluster do not wish to contribute or are not required under the Companies Act, 2013 to spend on CSR activities, the border line may be extended to other clusters, though this increases complication.

The coalition should then form a steering committee with the representatives from each SME so as to democratically decide on concerns. The steering committee should study the institutional process of execution, i.e. undertaking activities through an established trust, society, company or forming a new entity or directly managing the funds. The steps other than the guidelines pointed out by the steering committee include the following:

- Fix on the premise from Schedule VII of the Companies Act, 2013, beneficiary groups and geographies that it will aim based on the contribution from participants.
- Expanding internal processes to follow individual contribution by affiliates and their exploitation in CSR activities, finalising long-term projects based on estimated contributions by members and addressing non-payment by participants.

The CSR policy of individual SMEs should be devised to permit for flexibility in case of a collaborative effort to undertake CSR. This will mean that the policy, over and above the guidelines mentioned in the section 'Step One: Develop CSR Strategy and Policy', should allow the following:

- Flexibility in deciding upon thematic areas from Schedule VII of Companies Act, 2013, beneficiary groups and geographies as per the priorities of the entire association.
- Sustain to initiate CSR programmes to the level possible, in case the association is abandoned.

The next steps involved in the implementation or the concept development are: a) project development, b) operationalising institutional mechanism, c) contracting, d) budgeting and payments, e) monitoring, and f) impact measurement.

In cases where the total CSR funds are insufficient to cover the cost of collaboration, SMEs can also contribute to the Prime Minister's National Relief Fund or any other fund set up by the Central government or the state governments as per activity (ix) of the Schedule VII of the Companies Act, 2013.

CSR and Sustainability in the SME Sector

The responsibility of the SME sector to a country's economic growth is well-known. India is house to 48 million SMEs (2013) and is next only to China. The country has a national developmental objective of a growth rate of over 8 per cent on a persistent basis for which speedy industrial sector growth is needed. Towards this, Government's policy initiatives such as The New Micro Small and Medium Enterprises Development Act (2006), reducing of reserved SSI (small scale industries) list, advising FIs (financial institutions) to enhance their flow of credit to the SME sector, are all attempts towards advancing entrepreneurship, investment and growth. Presently, SMEs contribute 35 per cent to national exports and help in employment creation, enhancing innovation and making possible competitiveness in the economy.

Research has restated the significance of collaboration and the role of SMEs in making easy the CSR domain in the country. It is believed that CSR shall be useful for the SMEs, which will not be a shortcut to business accomplishment, but an investment that would pay off in the long run. The new Companies Act, 2013 has opened path for the SME sector provided the government is able to address the current challenges effectively. The SMEs need to work towards an enhanced thoughtfulness of CSR, which would increase their competitive advantage, improve awareness and loyalty among stakeholders.

SMEs need to adopt the culture of CSR which would help build models of business excellence with a equilibrium between economic, social and environmental goals thereby ensuring business payback. This collaboration can be formed within the units in a come together as they interact with the same communities and have already established associations that cater to the business needs of the units.

SMEs are the backbone of industrial development. They always represent the socio-economic policies of the Government of India. SMEs must adopt CSR for innovation, creativity, and flexibility which enable them to take action more quickly to structural changes and to adapt to the dynamic demands of consumers. The government must follow policies and legislations for the advantage of SMEs adapting CSR and take up initiatives aimed at encouraging SME involvement in CSR. Moreover for SMEs to fully utilise its potential, it is essential that the entrepreneurs along with the government support take necessary steps for further development.

Thus, the banks and other agencies should play an instrumental role in the formation of SMEs who can be MNCs of tomorrow Thus, CSR is not just the responsibility of big giants but also of small and medium enterprises too.

The smaller enterprises need to not always spend financially for CSR. They have to first train themselves on CSR. The UN through its UNIDO programmes in developing countries has successfully defined a TBL (triple bottom line) approach, which has proven to be a successful tool for SMEs in the developing countries to assist them in meeting social and environmental standards without compromising their competitiveness. The TBL approach is used as a framework for measuring and reporting corporate performance against economic, social and environmental performance. SMEs need to realise that profit alone will not drive them to become successful. They have to successfully integrate environment and society with economics. UNIDO still continues to be very communicative that:

> A properly implemented CSR concept can bring along a variety of competitive advantages, such as enhanced access to capital and markets, increased sales and profits, operational cost savings, improved productivity and quality, efficient human resource base, improved brand image and reputation, enhanced customer loyalty, better decision-making and risk management processes.

India has the second largest number of SMEs in the world, after China. While SMEs are the principal form of enterprise in India, the compliance to CSR standards and reporting to the Government is also essential. The government should consider modification in the Companies Act to ensure at least a reporting by SMEs on what they have done. This will compel them to initiate to think on those standards and compliance.

More often than not, SMEs tend to ignore the environment within the company itself. They could even look at motivating and training employees on health, sanitation, skill development, environment—these would change the immediate environment and benefit their families which in turn benefit the company. CSR initiatives will begin to result in higher motivation and loyalty among employees. This in turn will lead to better production efficiencies, lower employee turnover, and eventually lower costs for companies. Very soon, organisations will see an increased sales turnover due to the competitive advantage derived from a good CSR policy.

Compliance to CSR will ensure that the bulk of SMEs undertake the following to help produce quality products and derive customer satisfaction, thereby improving the overall environmental and social surrounding of each one of them. Large corporations have significant impact on society and environment. They are concerned about their brand reputation too.

Therefore, they invest in CSR. However, it is pertinent to appreciate that social and environmental impacts are interconnected. The two are related and have to be treated by all, whether an individual, small enterprise or large enterprise. CSR has to evolve into individual social responsibility—eventually for India to become developed. Hence, it is imperative that SMEs take on this responsibility. It is the government's responsibility to enable such a revolution, by bringing in the SMEs into the CSR act in a careful and responsible manner. The rules have to be enablers and not irritants for the SMEs. It is a no brainer that in India SMEs have frequently abdicated their environmental and societal responsibilities. This statement in no way implies that large organisations have become sustainable and are responsible. However, it will be fair to say that more and more large organisations have taken or are taking steps to reduce their environmental impact and in the process giving back to society, which is the very reason for their existence.

To create the sweeping change in education, environment and society that India needs, the returns from focussing on large organisations are diminishing with time. The focus has to shift to enabling SMEs to make an impact on the society and environment. The changes they can bring about, as they have done in manufacturing and contribution to the GDP (gross domestic product), in turning India into a developed country through making an impact within their organisation and their immediate neighbourhood is enormous.

This, in no way is to imply that large organisations have become 'sustainable', or cannot do much to reduce their environmental or societal impacts. However, it is fair to say that a number of large companies have progressively undertaken steps and measures to improve their social and environmental performance.

It is also well known that the large organisations, being forced to disclose their wider sustainability impacts, have increasingly passed on the burden to the SMEs which form their supply chain. The significant environmental and social impacts of large organisations are hidden in their supply chains. This is because of increasing cost competitiveness. So, the government and auditors really need to get to the root of the problem. India along with other developing countries is known for unsustainable practices of suppliers of raw materials (e.g. in electronics manufacturing, electroplating, dyeing or polymer recycling) or the unethical labour practices of production which is outsourced (e.g. in retail and clothing). These companies do not garner the same scrutiny as their large customers. With a changing global economic landscape and the rising aspirations of the middle class in India, it is high time that SMEs begin to change themselves and factor in an attitudinal change towards the society and environment and do their bit in the progressive change required to turn India to a better place in the near future. SMEs should remember, if the society and environment around them fails, businesses will fail too. They should also consider CSR as minimising negative impact and creating positive impact in what they do every day of the week. If they begin documenting this, CSR will happen not just automatically, but within their existing resources!

Conclusion: CSR—An Equal Responsibility of SME

Over 8,000 large companies complying to CSR has been a remarkable policy adoption by the Indian Government. This shift has put India in union with countries like Sweden, Mauritius and Norway who have strong policies on CSR for industries. But where India lags behind these countries is that the Companies Act does not successfully bring CSR into the conventional. SMEs are equally responsible towards making living conditions better for their employees and their families. What SMEs do not realise is that CSR is the only way through which the company can achieve equilibrium between economic, environmental and social goals. As we move ahead in the 21st century—India can achieve its dreams, and turn its growing young population into an asset only if each company big or small takes on responsibility for social, educational and environmental upliftment at large. This will go a long way in creating harmonious relationship between workers and the management, while at the same time addressing the expectations of all stakeholders in business.

References

Confederation of Indian Industries (2013). *Handbook on Corporate Social Responsibility in India.*

Fox, T. (2005). "Small and Medium-Sized Enterprises (SME's) and Corporate Social Responsibility", *A Discussion Paper*. June.

Jain, S. (2014). "CSR: An Equal Responsibility of SMEs", *Business Standard*, 28 March.

Ministry of Micro, Small and Medium Enterprises (2016a). *Annual Report 2015-16*. Government of India.

———. (2016b) *MSME's at a Glance 2016*. Government of India.

Nair, N.K. and J.S. Sodhi (2012). "CSR Practices by SME's in India: Lessons from Five Case Studies", *Indian Journal of Industrial Relations* 47(4), April.

Sood, M. (2015). "Corporate Social Responsibility and the Role of SME's in India", *International Journal of Latest Trends in Engineering and Technology 5(1).*

9

A. SRIDHAR RAJ

Looking Beyond Corporate Social Responsibility

The Scope for Socially Oriented Enterprises

Introduction

The ascendancy of CSR (corporate social responsibility) in both the corporate and the social worlds has ushered a new era of people centric governance. The changes have not only led to the increasing emphasis on the social orientation of the business but also led to increasing awareness among the corporate leaders about the social dimensions of their businesses and their activities from time to time. Such an orientation got buttressed in the societal dimensions of business in the last couple of years with more corporate entities joining the bandwagon of CSR. The focus on CSR has enabled the corporate world to shoulder some responsibilities of the state and para-state agencies, although the state agencies still carry their burden of service delivery to the people.

Background of Philanthropic Activities

Although there are few murmurings about the obligation of societal responsibility from the business world as mandated by the New Companies Act 2013, a large section of the business world is favourable towards the idea of the CSR as gleaned from the media reports. Such an inclination is visible in the activities of the organisations where even the employees are encouraged to participate in various social and economic activities aimed at ameliorating the living conditions of the people. In fact, such activities have become a part of employee engagement practices. That apart, during natural crises and disasters, the business world extends its support in reaching out to the people.

The business world also extends its supporting arm in nation building activities through special funds which are aimed at the development of the country's infrastructure like roads, schools, hospitals. However, all such endeavours have been more in the nature of charity and philanthropy and the funding and activities were more uneven in spread and scale, leading to wastage of resources. The impact was cosmetic and transient and earlier existing conditions soon came to dominate the changes done as a part of CSR.

Long before the concept of CSR made its way into the management literature, the Tata Group under the visionary founders did seminal work towards the fulfilment of its social responsibility. The activities ranged from promotion of educational institutions of high quality to providing scholarships to the needy people of the society. In fact, the establishment of trusts to take care of the societal responsibilities of the Tata Group speaks volumes about the leaders of the group and their inclination towards social responsibility. Similarly, the concept of trusteeship was promoted by G.D. Birla wherein the focus was on making the lives of the people better by teaching them the skills needed for better living.

Deloitte celebrates Impact Day, wherein the employees reach out to different types of needy people—children, aged, adolescent girls, etc., and the effort is to create an impact in their lives at least for a day. The employees are encouraged to shoulder the responsibility of impacting the lives of at least a few for one day so that the organisation as a whole contributes to the society and also to enable the employees to get sensitised to their social responsibility.

Service Delivery of the Government

Given the philanthropic orientation of the corporate world, the service delivery of the government agencies suffered from the last mile glitch and despite numerous efforts by the Government of India to minimise the last minute hurdle, not much headway could be made due to institutional, structural and cultural constraints. The governance malaise diluted the ideals of the constitution and over a period of time, the state agencies failed to deliver the goods and services to the people in an efficient and effective manner. Efforts to fine-tune the delivery system through governance reforms have not yielded fruitful results which further hampered service delivery and nothing much could be done by the Government.

The Government found a smart way of improvising its delivery system by formalising and institutionalising CSR through the New Companies Act 2013. The Act mandated the business entities to spend a part of their profits towards societal amelioration. The Act further provided a detailed list of the focus areas of CSR and these areas more or less resembled and overlapped with the Millennium Development Goals (MDGs). The MDGs enunciated by the United Nations (UN) helped the Governments to strengthen their service delivery in entirety so as to reach out to the people. This approach led to inclusive approach towards accessing the services provided by the

Government. The Act is in sync with the MDGs as far as the focus areas of CSR are concerned. Some of the activities considered to be the focus areas of CSR are hunger, poverty, livelihood, malnutrition, environment, education, gender, infrastructure, art and culture, etc.

The focus areas of CSR as illustrated by the new Companies Act, 2013 overlap with the basic functions and responsibilities of any modern day government and more so in the case of Government of India. Although the corporate world has initiated various social oriented programmes as a part of their CSR activities, the efforts are disparate and tried to address a small problem limited to a geographic or organisational entity. For example, the construction of toilets is one such illustration wherein the corporate entities made an attempt to address the problem in schools, colleges, rural areas, etc. Although such efforts are indeed laudable, they are more or less splintered and incoherent given the magnitude of the problems faced by the people of the country, which is an indication of service delivery of the governance institutions and structures.

Technically speaking, CSR activities have started addressing the governance related problems in general and service delivery problems in specific and such activities need to be appreciated as they have given a new dimension to business, apart from profiteering. However, the question that needs to be answered from the larger dimension is to what extent the CSR activities can replace the role of the Government agencies in addressing the focus areas of CSR.

As the Government cannot transfer many of its functions under the label of CSR to the corporate entities, there is a need to reinvigorate the service delivery of its agencies, rather than leaving the ground for the corporate entities to take up socially relevant and structurally huge problems like sanitation, drinking water, hunger, etc. Service delivery of public services need to be on the top of the Government agenda which can, in fact, help the corporate entities to address other societal problems for a different perspective rather than caught in the delivery of basic functions, originally meant for the Government agencies.

Structural Flaws of Corporate Social Responsibility

The CSR is technically flawed right from the day it was envisaged but found a place in the new Companies Act 2013. The protagonists of CSR were bent upon making it mandatory for the corporate entities to part away some percentage of their profits, which is neither rationale nor logical. This is because of the fact that these entities pay taxes to the Government which could be utilised for fulfilling its functions rather than shifting the responsibility to the corporate world. The antagonists are equally convinced that the Government cannot absolve itself from its responsibilities and shy away from its basic functions. The very mandatory nature of CSR activities may make the corporate entities more vulnerable in terms of their existence and may impact their profitability in the long run.

There is no Impact Assessment Authority which evaluates the impact of the programmes and projects initiated by the business entities spending a larger amount of money. Although the details about the CSR activities are shown either in Annual Reports or on their websites, the overall evaluation of the impact of such programmes is still debatable. The assessment in terms of viability, quality and sustainability of the projects and programmes initiated under the CSR head is left unattended by the Government. The questions regarding the prioritising of the projects which need to be addressed are:

- On what projects/programmes the CSR money should be spent?
- In case of multiple projects/programmes, who should have the discretion of prioritising them?
- What should be the geographical limits under which CSR funds can be spent by the agencies if it has limited geographical reach?
- What should be the geographical limits under which CSR funds can be spent by the agencies if it has vast geographical reach, often crossing 6-7 states like mining?
- What is the viability of the projects/programmes undertaken by the corporate entities?

The scope, size, impact and expanse of issues like sanitation, rural development, drinking water, infrastructure, etc., make it difficult for the Government agencies alone to deliver the goods and services. However, all such functions are more or less overlap with those activities which are a part of the CSR activities. For example, rural development is one of the priority areas of the Government of India and the same rural development is one of the focus areas for the corporate entities as a part of their CSR activities. The duplication of functions may dilute the functioning of either the state or the corporate entity in terms of contributing to the overall goals enshrined in the Act.

Overcoming Flaws and Looking Beyond Corporate Social Responsibility

CSR is not a fad but a reality for all the corporate entities which are profitable and a part of their profits are diverted towards socially relevant and useful projects. Rather than focusing on areas suggested by the Government of India, the whole paradigm of CSR needs to be altered given the myriad problems existing within the country. Rather than spending the money in a disparate manner, the same money could be utilised for the real betterment of the people in the country by promoting SOEs (social oriented enterprises).

Figure 9.1

e-Choupal in Action

Source: http://www.itcabd.com/commodities-and-services.aspx

The SOEs are those entities which could be promoted by the corporate entities from the CSR spending towards addressing the social and economic malaise and thereby scale up the same to the level of an enterprise. The focus of the SOEs may be both social and economic. There needs to be a focused approach and emphasis towards the establishment of these SOEs so that they are built to serve the larger causes of the society. The building up of such institutions by the corporate entities help in reaching out to the societal challenges from an orientation of profit making in the long run by an inclusive approach of development.

For example, e-Choupal is such an initiative or business model built upon addressing the grievances of the farmers at the bottom of the pyramid. The MFIs (microfinance institutions) is another socially oriented business model designed to empower women and also ameliorate their living conditions. Both these models have been successful looking beyond CSR and have enabled millions of people to overcome their constraints and move up the socio-economic ladder. Both these models have enabled the people to access resources and get benefitted by reaching out to the larger market by growing and expanding their businesses.

e-Choupal has been one of the most successful initiatives taken up to add value not only to the farmers but to the supply chain management of agricultural products. Given the small land holdings in rural India, the farmers suffered from various handicaps like lack of knowledge of prices, lack of access to agricultural inputs, the profiteering middlemen, lack of storage facilities, etc., and given the vast spread of farmers in the remote locations of the country, a humongous endeavour was needed to bring all the stakeholders and ingredients on a single platform.

e-Choupal provided the much needed platform where a corporate business entity has proactively stepped out to reach out to the farmers and enable them to get integrated with the world economy. e-Choupal had freed the farmers from undertaking all those activities which were exploitative and less profitable and helped them to move up in the value chain by acting as a single point window for accessing information, accessing inputs and accessing markets in a more profitable manner. The internet linked computers in villages revolutionised the mind set of the villagers whereby they not only came to know the power of internet but also the benefits of reaching out to the global economy. Some of the distinct features of e-Choupal are as follows:

- There are 6,100 e-Choupals across the country.
- Provide services to around 4 million farmers.
- Reaching out to 35,000 villages.
- Comprises over 6.5 million sq ft of warehousing space.
- Presence in 20 states and 160 districts.
- Quality assurance.
- Sustainable agricultural practices.

- Latest information on agricultural prices to farmers.
- Transparent transactions.

The benefits of e-Choupal are not limited to just transactions of agricultural products but are much more than that given the access of internet and services to the farmers at their door steps. The farmers have become more aware of the movement and pricing of agricultural goods and are equipped with the latest developments in the field of agriculture. The benefits of such a change are immense given the dismal performance of the government agencies—information dissemination among farmers, storage facilities, ensuring grain quality, transparency in transactions, etc. Given the performance of e-Choupal in the last 15 years, it can be stated that this socially oriented entrepreneurial activity had helped millions of farmers to unshackle themselves from the vagaries of price fluctuation and helped them to move to the next level in the value chain of supply chain management and society as well.

Bandhan Bank is another successful story of a socially oriented enterprise which has grown from grass roots serving the marginalised sections of the society. Started as a MFI in the year 2001 to address the dual objective of poverty alleviation and women empowerment, has reached out to 22 states with 2,022 branches and 67,17,331 borrowers till June 2015. The MFIs have been successful in filling the critical gap unattended by the public and private sector banks considering the huge costs. This section of the society largely depended upon the money lenders who squeezed the borrowers through high interest rates. The vicious cycle sustained as the borrowers were forced to borrow further to repay their loans and interests still they were exhausted in all senses.

Given such a dismal scenario, the MFIs made their headway by giving small loans to the people, particularly the women groups, which later became the backbone of financial inclusion in the country. The loans were provided for the entrepreneurial purposes which helped the borrowers either to scale up their business or expand their business enterprise. Although the philosophy of microfinance came under the scanner as some MFIs in some parts of the country resorted to strong arm tactics, Bandhan Financial Services Private Limited (BFSPL) stood strong given its credibility as a SOE. The mission of BFSPL is as follows:

> To reduce socio-economic poverty substantially and create employment by targeting low-income households across the country through providing cost-effective sustainable financial and non-financial services emphasising on social securities.[1]

1. *http://www.bandhanmf.com/philosophy.aspx.*

Given the scope and spread of BFSPL, various public sectors have become lenders to reach out the unbanked sections of the society which in turn led financial inclusion of a larger number of people, particularly women, in both rural and urban areas. Some of the banks which lent money to BFSPL include the following:

Table 9.1

Banks that Lent Money to BFSPL

State Bank of India	Axis Bank
Allahabad Bank	HDFC Bank
Bank of Baroda	Kotak Mahindra Bank
Syndicate Bank	South Indian Bank

Source: http://www.bandhanmf.com/philosophy.aspx

The social consciousness of BFSPL convinced the Reserve Bank of India and provided a banking license, thus emerged Bandhan Bank after competing with 25 applicants that included some of the big business conglomerates in India. Bandhan Bank started its operations in the year 2015.

Implications of Socially Oriented Enterprises

CSR as a philosophy is undeniably laudable and socially acceptable in a country like India where service delivery of public goods and services has not been satisfactory. The reasons could be many and beyond the scope of this paper but CSR as a mandate by the new Companies Act, 2013 has opened new vistas for corporate entities to spend money on the focus areas and such efforts are found to be disparate. The possibility of CSR funds being spent on the basis of wrong prioritisation may lead dilution of the philosophy of CSR itself which may put 'benevolence and generosity' of philanthropists at stake. CSR is necessary, but there is a huge scope for business entities to promote socially oriented enterprises which can address more systemic problems of the country in an efficient and effective manner, the manner in which e-Choupal and Bandhan bank have focused the societal and economic issues. Some of the implications of SOEs include the following:

- *Systemic problems*: SOEs are effective in addressing systemic problems in a better manner, hence, corporate entities may need to focus on launching SOEs rather than building toilets and walls.
- *Long lasting solutions:* SOEs may come out with more long lasting solutions to address the problems of the country rather than

just philanthropic activities, which are more cosmetic natured in providing solutions.

- *Mindset change:* SOEs are more effective in changing the mind set of the people as it happened in the case of Bandhan as women became more active partners in the process of financial inclusion. They have become more confident and economically independent as well.
- *Public sector banks:* Given the number of people enrolled in availing the micro financial services by the micro financial institutions, it can be stated that even the public sector banks could not achieve those targets. Hence, SOEs are better placed to reach the targets associated with social and economic issues.
- *Integration with mainstream:* e-Choupal has helped the farmers to get integrated with the world economy which is highly beneficial in the long run as the benefits of better prices have helped the farmers which could not be done by government agencies, hence, SOEs may be preferred at least in addressing the social and economic issues.
- *Larger picture*: CSR spending is more a piecemeal approach as the larger issues like poverty, hunger, unemployment are not much focused and it is here that the SOEs can play in important role by looking at the larger socio-economic picture of the society.
- *Usage and maintenance*: The impact of CSR spending is difficult to assess given the usage of the infrastructural facilities like school buildings, renovation of school buildings, etc., given the lack of teachers in schools. That apart, regarding the construction of toilets, the next question is about their repairs and maintenance and once such infrastructural facilities are taken care properly, there is every possibility of they being just monuments. SOEs are better placed to address such problems are they are more inclined to bring mindset change rather than building infrastructure.
- *Lobbying:* CSR spending may become another entitlement for the people and there is every possibility that lobbying groups start lobby for more spending in their own geographic areas. For example, the enterprises which are limited to certain geographic zones may limit their CSR activities to their geographic zones due to lobbying. SOEs are not subjected to such lobbying given the very nature of their activities.

Conclusion

Given the benefits of some of the experiments carried out in India—e-Choupal and Bandhan Bank, it is asserted that there is a huge opportunity for the corporate entities to promote more SOEs to address the larger social and economic problems of the country. Rather than spending money on a piecemeal approach, there is huge scope for channelising the CSR funds in SOEs which may be an effective approach in addressing the systemic issues. That apart, given the scale and spread of the social and economic problems in the country, it can be safely asserted that apart from CSR, there is a need to develop another channel of societal issues.

CSR alone may not offer long lasting solutions as the philosophy of CSR as per the new norms is more oriented towards spending. Given the poor record of usage and maintenance of infrastructural facilities, CSR spending may go waste once these facilities are not used and maintained properly. The solution may not lie entirely in SOEs, but apart from CSR, SOEs too can be a channel for the corporate entities as they are better aligned with the business and the society, rather than just spending.

References

Economic Times (2016a). *"Demonetisation: Bandhan Bank Stops Micro-Credit Disbursement", Economic Times*, 15 November. Accessed on 18 December 2016.

———. (2016b). "Micro Finance Companies Get Funds from Banks", *Economic Times*, 25 March. Accessed on 10 December 2016.

———. (2016c). "Clicking on: Farmer Connect Made Easier Thru E-Choupal", *Economic Times*, 7 July. Accessed on 10 December 2016.

———. (2016d). "Bandhan Bank Targets 180 New Branches by March 2017", *Economic Times*, 17 June. Accessed on 12 November 2016.

———. (2012). "ITC's E-Choupal Boosting Company's FMCG Business", *Economic Times*, 25 July 2012.

Forbes India (2016). *Bandhan: The Making of a Bank Highlights Chandra Shekhar Ghosh's Focus, Vision.* 7 July. Accessed on 18 December 2016.

10

MANOSMITA MAHAPATRA

Corporate Social Performance and Sustainable Development

A Sociological Study of Corporate Social Responsibility in Healthcare in Odisha

Introduction

The term CSR (corporate social responsibility) is in popular use even though competing and overlapping concepts were widespread in the field. There have been many examples of well established and successful organisations losing public trust and market strength on account of negligence of social norms or even unethical practices. India today is at a stage where it can make a range of choices, including those that would ensure sustainability. The corporate sector must not only lead in this effort as its duty to Indian society, but also as a measure of enlightened self-interest, since future markets worldwide would favour products and services that sub serve the objectives of sustainability. Even though civil society and the non-government sector in India have a remarkable record of service to the country, it is unfortunate that while most of them very ably highlight and expose problems in the system they seldom work on providing solutions.

In many developed countries, CSR has taken on the character of strategically planned actions that benefit all levels of society, and it has grown from entrepreneurial initiatives to state policy. CSR now provides benefits for stakeholder communities as well as for government. It allows a business to respond quickly to the emerging needs of a society, whether they are economic, environmental or social problems. The government is a secondary beneficiary, as successful corporate responsibility practices reduce the government's burden for responding to a wide range of issues. CSR requires a multifaceted approach and the terms that provide intrinsic definitions.

The definition given by the World Business Council for Sustainable Development (WBCSD) states, "CSR is the continuing commitment by business to contribute to economic development while improving the quality of life of the workforce and their families as well as of the community and society at large." The intrinsic and extrinsic stakeholders of CSR show that the organisation sometimes focuses on the internal beneficiaries of the company like workplace safety, providing social insurance, developing human resources and similar issues, while external responsibilities would refer to the impact on the community in which the business operates. In this context, CSR defines as a company's voluntary action to improve social welfare, economic condition, and the environment through strategically planned projects that ensure sustainable benefits for stakeholders and the community. Hence, the corporate display of social responsibility has become widespread over the past two decades (Vogel 2006).

The concept of CSP (corporate social performance) in 1970s became an established umbrella term embracing both descriptive and normative aspects of the field (Carrol and Shabana 2010) focusing on socially responsible initiatives of corporations (Carrol 1979). Corporate social performance is a set of descriptive categorisations of business activity, focusing on the impact and outcome for society, stakeholders and the firm itself (Wood 1991). He argues that CSP is more compressive than CSR models since it involves the identification of domains of an organisation's social responsibility, the development of process to evaluate the stakeholder demand and the implementation of programmes to manage social issues (Thomas and Simerly 1995).

Hence, CSP concerns the benefits that result from a business organisation's interaction with the larger environment including social, cultural, legal and political and economic dimension. In order to show that, companies should work to increase the benefits and eliminate harm resulting from their activities and which shows that corporate social performance is a structural category which can be measured and evaluated (Wood 2010). CSP can be measured through social reports, environmental reports, annual reports on social or environmental disclosure. The present paper makes an attempt to examine the social performance of company towards sustainable community development through CSR. In the present context, sustainable community development highlights the fact that how the company helps to maintain the social issues like health, education, environment, women livelihood, etc. and provides services for the upliftment of the community.

Objectives and Methodology

CSR from a social perspective is defined as corporate commitment to ethical behaviour particularly in relation to social justice. Such an approach of CSR from a societal perspective is less focused in research because capitalist globalisation have been creating disturbances in two fundamental social justice where CSR has tried to solve the problems of social injustice by behaving in socially ethical terms (Sklair and Miller 2010).The research gap highlights that the literature on CSR was largely focused as a management concept which have neglected the societal aspects of CSR (Brammer et al. 2012). Moreover, corporates are found to be involved in community but basically from a philanthropic approach where the corporate community involvement forms the oldest form of CSR (Chapple and Moon 2005). Later, corporate community involvement is seen to gain importance for the social initiatives to meet the social and economic needs of the communities in which they operate (Muthurinet et al. 2009).

The present study is carried on to examine the impact of social initiatives undertaken by the multinational company of Tata Steel towards community development through CSR. In this context, the study focuses on Tata Steel as a case because Tata Steel is the only company in global terms which participates in all the four groups of GRI (global reporting initiative) i.e, SA8000, sustainable development world index, Millennium Development Goals (MDGs) and accounting. The CSR effort of Tata Steel is carried out in Jamshedpur, Odisha and Chhattisgarh. It deals with different social issues towards community development such as education, healthcare, women empowerment, livelihood sustenance etc. The present paper attempts to explore the healthcare services of Tata Steel in Odisha.

The study uses both secondary and primary data. The study therefore gathers knowledge from two sources, i.e. knowledge regarding social reporting from annual reports through content analysis and through interviews. The study uses structured interview schedule as the tool of research and interview as a technique. The study utilises exploratory research design and relates to probability sampling. The sampling is stratified random sampling where 5 villages of Ganjam district are chosen since the company adopts the peripheral villages nearby the plant and performs its healthcare practices in those areas. From among the 5 strata (villages), the study undertakes 40 per cent of the total reproductive age group women on a random basis from each village respectively with a total of 152 respondents. Keeping the background in context, the two objectives formed are:

- To study the practice of CSR on healthcare services for rural women in Odisha.
- To understand the association between CSP and community development.

Summary of Findings

There is a need of healthcare initiative in Odisha as it records higher infant mortality rates in comparison to the national average. The neonatal mortality rate is 42 in rural Odisha and post neonatal mortality rate is 23 which are much higher than the national average as has been reported by vital statistics division report on health. Table 10.1 shows the maternal health conditions with a lower status of women in terms of health condition.

Table 10.1

Maternal Health Condition of Women in Odisha

Maternal Healthcare	*Odisha*		
	Total	*Rural*	*Urban*
Marriage among females below legal age (%)	5.9	6.5	3.2
Women who received any antenatal care	95.6	95.3	97.4
Abortion taking place in institutions	56.5	56.1	60.0
Mother who did not receive any post natal checkup	19.6	21.1	10.4
Total unmet need for family planning	23.2	23.5	21.7
Women who are aware of HIV/AIDS	80.6	78.2	92.7
Neonatal Mortality Rate	40	42	28
Post neonatal Mortality Rate.	22	23	16

Source: *Annual Health Survey 2011-12*, Vital Statistics Division, Registrar General and Census Commissioner, India

Practice of Corporate Social Responsibility in Healthcare

Tata Steel adopts many villages of Ganjam District in Odisha to carry out its CSR practices. In this regard, the company focuses mainly on maternal healthcare practices. The company has health intervention on primary healthcare, maternal and child health, preventive, promotive, curative and rehabilitative health services and on safe drinking water and sanitation. Tata Steel Rural Development Society (TSRDS) through its community health and hygiene programme carry out its health intervention activities in the villages and the villages around the Gopalpur area (Odisha) are taken as the focus of this investigation. Since 2006, TSRDS is carrying out its CSR services on health and hygiene in 35 villages surrounding its operational area of Gopalpur comprising a population of more than 8000 households. It focuses its activities on primary healthcare and reproductive healthcare needs.

The beneficiaries of the programmes include women folk in their reproductive age group of 20 years to 40 years, pregnant women, women immediately after the child birth and young married women. TSRDS carries out its activities in villages with the help of Anganwadi workers called Asha Didis. A doctor appointed by the TSRDS along with usual medicines in a mobile van visits an Anganwadi centre periodically on a specified day and time. TSRDS health services presently are confined to temporary and periodical health centres, doctor's advices and provision of usual medicines in the villages. In case of specified needs, the doctor advices the beneficiaries to consult the specialists and to go to the Government established hospitals outside the operating area. However, TSRDS organises frequent training and awareness programmes, temporary clinics for diagnosis and treatment of special health problems.

In the developing countries like India, maternal health services are part of formal healthcare system which is a prime concern for government in terms of financing and delivering health services (Berman 1998). Hence, in India, despite the widespread public infrastructure, a higher proportion of health services are provided by the private sector than by government facilities (Chatterjee 1988). In rural areas, low utilisation of maternal healthcare services during pregnancy, at delivery and in the post natal period, contributes to high maternal mortality (Bulatao and Ross 2003). The company performs maternal healthcare services to the rural women in order to empower those women who were earlier neglected in relation to maternity care leading to an enhancement in maternal mortality which is higher in Odisha. The health issues of Tata Steel towards empowering women emphasises on antenatal care, age related to marriage and child birth, prenatal and postnatal checkups, kinds of delivery problems they face, nature of help in financial and transport facilities for delivery, postnatal about child spacing and child immunisation which all play an important role to reduce the maternal mortality.

The findings depict that under the influence of TSRDS, more than half of the respondents have given birth in the age group of 21 to 25 which is assumed to be neither high nor low age which would bring a danger to the maternal health. The frequency of visits of pregnant mothers for prenatal care has been increased. The TSRDS provides free medicines and an overwhelming percent of respondents are satisfied with the doctor's advice and counselling for the right kind of diet and amount of labour at home along with balancing the stress level. It is observed that 8 out of 10 respondents are assisted by the appointed nurse of the company for delivery assistance and neonatal care because high level of antenatal care is associated with higher health facility (Bloom et al. 1999)and reduces maternal mortality. It is observed that with regard to the providence of medicine, majority of respondents (98%) were given both calcium and iron and 13 per cent of respondents were given only iron tablets. Table 10.2 shows the respondent's satisfaction for the medicines.

Table 10.2

Percentage of Respondent's Satisfaction for Company Medicine

Opinion	*No of Respondents*	*Percentage*
Yes	112	73.7
No	40	26.3
Total	152	100.0

Source: Compiled by the author.

From the survey, it is seen that 7 out of 10 respondents were satisfied with the company medicine provided to them during the pregnancy. Whereas, only nearly one fourth of the respondents opined that they were not satisfied with the care provided by the company for maternity. These respondents expressed various reasons for not being satisfied. Table 10.3 provides doctor's advice to the respondent's towards prenatal care.

Table 10.3

Doctor's Advice to the Respondent's Towards Prenatal Care

Types of Advice Given	*Advised*		*Not advised*		*Total*
	No.	*%*	*No.*	*%*	
To walk in the morning for sometime	63	41.4	89	58.6	152
To walk in the evening for sometime	126	82.9	26	17.1	152
To take medicine regularly as per doctor's advice	125	82.2	27	17.8	152
To check blood pressure regularly	136	89.5	16	10.5	152
To take food with more protein content	109	71.7	43	28.3	152
To avoid tension and anxiety in mind	61	40.1	91	59.9	152
To consult the doctor all regular intervals	32	21.1	120	78.9	152

Source: Compiled by the author.

From the survey, it is found that majority of the respondents (98%) were given doctor's advice for prenatal care. From the table, the advices were separately taken into consideration from among the total 152 respondents. It is seen that out of 152 respondents, 63 respondents were given advice to walk in the morning for sometime. Out of 152 respondents, 126 respondents were adviced to walk in the evening for sometimes. Similarly 125 respondents out of 152 were adviced to take medicine regularly. Moreover, from the survey it is seen that 4 out of 10 respondents were satisfied with the care provided for reproductive health. Rather, nearly one fourth of the respondents said they were more satisfied. However, 33 per cent of the respondents said they were less satisfied followed by 5 per cent who were not satisfied and 7 per cent did not have any opinion regarding the performance of reproductive health services (Figure 10.1).

Figure 10.1

Respondents Satisfaction with Reproductive Health Services

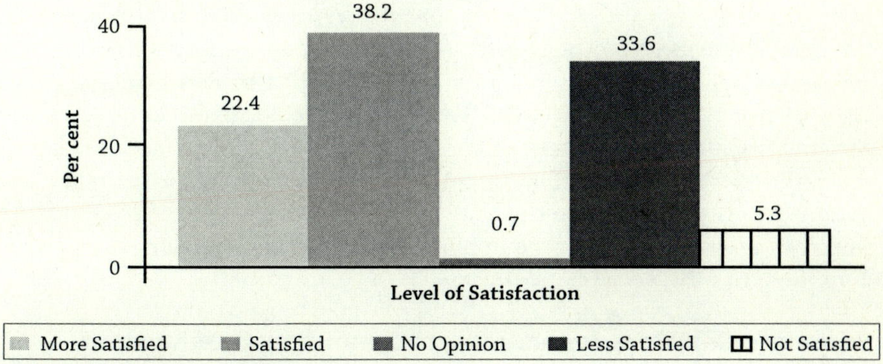

Source: Compiled by the author.

It is observed that more than half of the respondents (54%) are found to be satisfied with the knowledge of medicine, food habit and life style provided to the respondents. On the other hand, some respondents (43%) said that they are satisfied to some extent. However, very less (2%) respondents said that they are dissatisfied to some extent (Figure 10.2).

Figure 10.2

Respondent Satisfaction with the Knowledge of Medicine, Food Habits, and Lifestyle Condition to be taken during Pregnancy

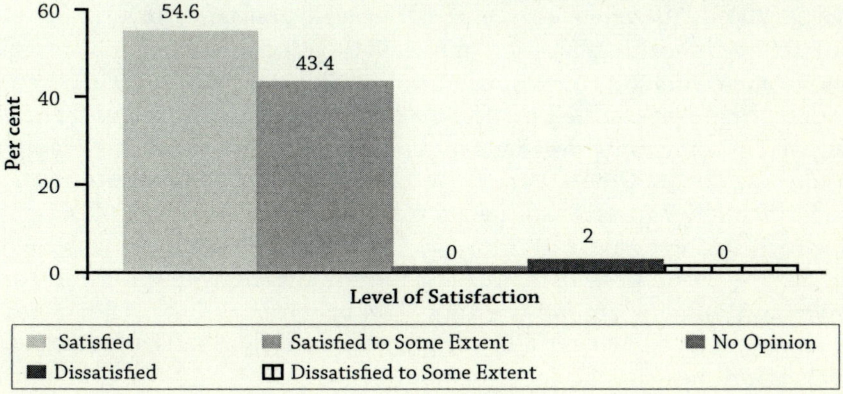

Source: Compiled by the author.

There are certain socio-economic determinants which link proximate causes of child death (Mosley and Chen 1984), which should be taken care of as postnatal care. It depends upon the care giver attributes such as mother's education and health related beliefs and practices which the company gives utmost attention. Child immunisation, breast feeding, guidance for food for the infant were given to the respondents. It is seen that 90 per cent of respondents were satisfied with the awareness given regarding child spacing and family planning. Besides reproductive health services, the company provides other health services of more general in nature like awareness services, training camps and public health and hygiene. More than half of the respondents (53.3%) opined their satisfaction over these services whereas 46.7 per cent of them showed their dissatisfaction. Half of the respondents were satisfied to get a chance to exchange ideas regarding healthcare once in a week in the health centre. Two-third of the respondents said they are satisfied with the opportunity given in the health camps that help them to form social networking.

Corporate Social Performance and Community Development

The corporate through their CSP are found to have corporate community involvement in order to gain importance for the social initiatives to meet the social and economic needs of the communities in which they operate (Muthurin et al. 2009). According to Hess et al. (2002), social initiatives include not only the traditional practice of corporate philanthropy but also encompass a variety of forms and points, ranging from corporate support for training and educating adults and youth in local communities to nationwide programme helping social welfare in developing countries. Thus, social initiatives in the business context are defined as any program, practice or policies undertaken by a business firm to benefit society (Bronn and Cohen 2009). Therefore, corporate activities increasingly involve activity in relation to health, education and welfare and even in relation to social justice and community development issues (Sklair and Miller 2010). Hence, for creating sustainable business in India, many instances of business engaged in community development are endured. One of the few examples is the case of Tata Group (Puranik and Mehta 2005).The corporate strategy undertaken by Tata is Tata Council for Community Initiative (TCCI). The business strategy taken by Tata Steel is TSRDS. The TSRDS is involved in various social development programmes aimed at helping the rural communities living around the Tata Steel operational units. TSRDS has 7 operating units and covers 600 villages. It is actively involved in livelihood generation, health and people empowerment. The CSP for community development is shown in Table 10.4 and Table 10.5.

Table 10.4

Corporate Sustainability Services of Tata Steel

Corporate Sustainability Services	*Initiatives*	*Activity*
Rural	Sustainable livelihood	Empowerment–shgs Environment
Tribal	Ethnicity and education	Promotion and preservation of ethnic identity Promotion of rural enterprises Education
Urban	Model bustee and vocational training	Vocational training Youth development/sports Volunteerism
Family health	Preventive, promotive and curative healthcare	Mother and child health Hiv/aids Communicable diseases

Table 10.5

Dimensions of Corporate Sustainability Services of Tata Steel

Areas of impact	*Key Interventions*
Sustainable livelihood	Focused approach in agriculture interventions.
Empowerment	Vocational training for employability.
Health	Focused approach on maternal and infant survival projects and HIV/AIDS interventions by engaging the communities.
Education	Providing scholarships to underprivileged children for higher education and assuring 100 per cent literacy in focused villages.
Preservation and promotion of tribal culture	Empowering diminishing tribes by promoting Rural enterprise and promotion of tribal dance and sports.
Environment	Addressing environmental concerns through renewable energy and plantation.
Promotion of sports in the community	Linkages through village and *bustee* sports, feeder centres and academies.

The national family planning health vision gives priority to the antenatal care where maternal mortality and negligence during the pregnancy leads to higher number of death of expectant mothers. It is seen that lack of postnatal care has been a danger to neonatal health and well being of the mother. The reason for high mortality rates could be accorded too many factors such as: (i) inadequate antenatal care, natal and postnatal care (ii) lack of awareness among the rural population regarding birth and child care and (iii) lack of professional advices and health facilities to the rural folk. Therefore, the company takes these family planning issues and antenatal and postnatal services. The community development assessment can be seen aptly linking CSP theory by taking the present study in context.

The CSP theory has been propagated by Garriga and Mele (2004) who say that corporate has a role to play for the welfare of society and its social initiatives brings forward community development. The basic propositions of CSP theory are: (i) Institutional principles of corporate social responsibility (ii) corporate social responsiveness, (iii) social impact of corporate behaviour. The present paper takes into account the first proposition as 'structural entity' of the company that is the principle of CSR, expressed on institutional, organisational and individual level. And the third proposition as 'community impact assessment' which mentions the ability to pursue goals that one has to reason value and that helps the women to empower themselves both by maternity health and enhanced social networking. The structural entity highlights the company has not only undertaken maternal health but other aspects as well to give an enhanced approach towards community health development. It includes healthcare services into three levels. Firstly, promotive healthcare which includes healthcare for mother and child AIDS awareness, health awareness and education, adolescent reproductive healthcare. Secondly, curative healthcare which includes clinical outreach units, village health providers, health camps, and eye camps, cleft lip and cleft palate procedure. Thirdly, preventive healthcare which includes immunisation, sanitation, safe drinking water, and protection against sexually transmitted diseases. The company performs many project based healthcare services covering a large number of beneficiaries.

The third proposition of the theory as the 'community impact assessment' shows the overall impact on the community development by empowering the rural women through theses healthcare initiatives of Tata Steel. The study highlights that an overwhelming percent of respondents are highly satisfied with the maternal healthcare. Majority of the respondents are of the opinion that they are highly satisfied towards the project based health services. The free camps, regular meetings, counselling by the doctor, regular health checkup and community meetings for health awareness of child spacing and family planning programmes has helped these women to exchange ideas regarding the health awareness and understand health rights. It has played a significant role to these rural women who never took an initiative to educate themselves regarding maternal and other health related issues. More than three fourth of the respondents are of the opinion that it also helped them to enhance their social networking by such gatherings and gain so much knowledge regarding maternity.

The project based health services like MANSI to reduce maternal and child mortality and morbidity, AASTHA benefitted 25,800 people from 4,600 households. It has benefitted 4,200 eligible couple; RISTHA improved the sexual and reproductive health along with adolescent wellbeing where 13,000 people have been benefited by periodic health camps. KAVACH created awareness of HIV among the floating truckers population benefiting 14,450 patients are treated. One of the significant impact is that it has brought a change in the approach of these rural women towards their health rights where they understand the benefits of family planning, the antenatal and prenatal health maintenance, their own sexual rights with spouse, the decision for conception and child bearing, sexual communication and negotiation with spouse. All these have brought a profound impact towards women empowerment and practicing to have a modern lifestyle.

Conclusion

The main characteristics of sustainability and citizenship is the value it allocates to companies for socially responsible behaviour, which undoubtedly contribute to social change, where the company functions as a social agent with corporate citizenship as strategies to social action (Albareda et al. 2007).The social initiatives undertaken by Tata Steel have brought a similar impact on the healthcare aspects of rural women. Maternity care of antenatal, neonatal and postnatal has helped to reduce maternal mortality in the area. Other healthcare such as primary and secondary health services of the company has benefitted the community. Also, 100 per cent immunisation has been found in the research place. Moreover, project based health services played a significant role to bring health awareness to the rural women. The health camps and meetings for counselling have increased the mobility and social networking related to health education for the women.

Reference

Albareda, L., M. Lozano, T. Ysa (2007). "Public Policies on Corporate Social Responsibility: The Role of Government in Europe", *Journal of Business Ethics* 74: 391-407.

Berman, P.A. (1998). "Rethinking Healthcare System: Private Healthcare Provision in India", *World Development* 26(8): 1463-79.

Bloom. S.S., T. Lippeveld and D. Wypi (1999). "Does Anetnatal Care Make Difference to Safe Delivery? A Study in Urban Uttar Prades, India", *Health Policy Plan* 14(1): 38-48.

Brammer, S., G. Jackson and D. Matten (2012). "Corporate Social Responsibility and Institutional Theory: New Perspectives on Private Governance", *Socio Economic Review* 10: 3-28.

Bronn, P.S. and D.V. Cohen (2009). "Corporate Motives for Social Initiatives: Legitimacy, Sustainability or the Bottom Line?" *Journal of Business Ethics* 87: 91-109.

Bulato, R.A. and J.A. Ross (2003). "Which Health Services Reduce Maternal Mortality? Evidences from Ratings of Maternal Health Services", *Tropical Medicine and International Health* 8: 710-721.

Carroll, A.B. (1979). "A Three-Dimensional Conceptual Model of Corporate Performance", *Academy of Management Review* 4(4): 497-505.

Carroll, A.B. and K.M. Shabana (2010). "The Business Case for Corporate Social Responsibility: A Review of Concepts, Research and Practice", *International Journal of Management Reviews* 12(1): 85-105

Chaterjee, M. (1988). *Implementing Health Policy*. New Delhi: The Centre for Policy Research.

Chapple, J. and J. Moon (2005). Corporate Social Responsibility in Asia: A Seven Country Study of CSR Web Site Reporting", *Business and Society* 44(4): 415-41.

Garriga. E and D. Mele (2004). "Corporate Social Responsibility Theories: Mapping the Territory", *Journal of Business Ethics* 53: 51-71.

Hess, D., N. Rogovsky and T. Dunfee: (2002). "The Next Wave of Corporate Community Involvement: Corporate Social Initiatives", *California Management Review* 44(2): 110–125.

Mosley, W.H and L.C. Chen (1984). "An Analytical Framework for the Study of Child Survival in Developing Countries", *Population and Development Review* 10: 25-45.

Muthuri, J.N, W. Chappel, J. Moon (2009). "An Integrated Approach to Implementing 'Community Participation' in Corporate Community Involvement: Lessons from Magadisoda Company in Kenya", *Journal of Busniess Ehics* 85: 431-44.

Puranik, R. and V. Mehta (2005). *Stakeholder Engagement Concept and Practice*, in C.V. Baxi and A. Prasad (eds.), *Corporate Social Responsibility*. New Delhi: Excell Books. pp.28-47.

Sklair, L. and D. Miller (2010). "Capitalist Globalisation, Corporate Social Responsibility and Social Policy", *Critical Social Policy* 30(4): 472-95.

Thomas, A.S. and R.L. Simerly. (1994). "The Chief Executive Officer and Corporate Social Performance: An Interdisciplinary Examination", *Journal of Business Ethics* 13: 959-68.

Vogel, D. (2006). *The Market for Virtue*. Washington, DC, Brookings Institute.

Wood, D.J. (1991). "Corporate Social Performance Revisited", *Academy of Management Review* 16(4): 691-718.

————. (2010). "Measuring Corporate Social Performance: A Review", *International Journal of Management Reviews* 12(1): 50-84.

Corporate Social Responsibility
The Emerging Discussions

11

PUNEETA GOEL and R.S. RAMESH

Linking Corporate Social Responsibility Reporting with Corporate Performance

Evidence from Selected Companies in India

Introduction

CSR (corporate social responsibility) defines the role of business which is beyond its objective of profitability and includes the concept of social and environment concerns for the community. As business is also a part of society and uses the resources equally, it is responsible for the protection of the society. The concept of CSR aims at making the process of maximising the wealth of shareholders more effective and taking care of the needs of the society as well. Business needs to manage its relationship with wider society, whether for reasons of commercial viability or to add value to society (Blowfield and Frynas 2005).

Archie Carroll in 1991 describes CSR as "a multilayered concept that can be differentiated into four interrelated aspects—economic, legal, ethical and philanthropic responsibilities." The World Business Council for Sustained Development (1992) defined CSR as: "The continuing commitment by business to behave ethically and contribute to economic development while improving the quality of life of the workforce and their families as well as of the local community and society at large".

Thus, CSR has two-fold objectives i.e. to behave ethically towards internal and external stakeholders and to be responsible towards environment and society at large. The appropriate socially responsible actions give the new avenues to the companies to do business innovatively and ethically and to achieve better outcomes from its performance (Nguyen 2011). Improved government regulations, market reputation and stakeholder's pressure are the main forces driving CSR.

CSR has acquired a significant role in business strategies, becoming an important issue of governance and organisational performance. Most of the literature has focused on importance of CSR (Biscaccianti 2003, Abbott and Monsen 1979, Foote et al. 2010, Kansal and Singh 2012, Dey and Sircar 2012, Padhiyar 2013, Das 2009) and its relationship with corporate performance (Mittal et al. 2008, Aupperle et al. 1985, Byus et al. 2010, Perera et al. 2011, Jackson and Hua 2009, Mc Guire et al. 1998), providing interesting but not unanimous findings. All these studies have been done in the pre-reform period especially in India. The Companies Act, 2013 made it mandatory for the companies having turnover of more than ₹1,000 crore and net worth of more than ₹500 crore to invest 2 per cent of the net profit in CSR activities. It would be interesting to do a pre and post-reform analysis of CSR by Indian companies and study its relationship with corporate financial performance.

Review of Literature

The review of literature has been divided into two parts where first part deals with CSR and corporate performance studied in India and the second part deals with the prior research on CSR and corporate performance done in other parts of the world.

CSR and Corporate Performance in the Indian Context

The increased realisation of CSR by companies in India is not only having a positive influence on society but also helping the companies to act in economically, socially and environmentally sustainable and responsible manner (Murthy and Pitty 2013). Nearly all leading companies in India are involved in CSR programmes in areas like education, health, livelihood creation, skill development, empowerment of weaker sections of the society, raising awareness on protecting and enhancing the environment (Jayakumar et al. 2012). CSR tries to keep a balance between economic and social goals of the organisation. CSR strategy can be used as an important tool for competitive advantage that may lead to sustainable development (Padhiyar 2013, Das 2009).

CSR has become an integral part of their business strategy in India (Shanmugam and Mohamed 2011). Business world in India has been practicing CSR since its inception. CSR reporting is used as an important instrument to improve its ratings (Guha 2011). When CSR initiative are strategically integrated in the operations of the business, it not only benefits the stakeholders but helps the organisation to build reputation, customer confidence, employee satisfaction and better market conditions (Kansal and Singh 2012, Dey and Sircar 2012). However, Arevalo and Aravind (2011) found that in India, the liberal mode of social responsibility is mostly adopted as it focuses on social responsibility but is limited to private owners only. CSR in India is not practiced to serve the society but to save taxes and take benefit of other government schemes. Although now some companies have started voluntary efforts toward CSR but still it has not become a strategic part of their planning as compared to the companies in developed countries.

Mittal et al. (2008) stressed that immense pressure from the stakeholders has forced Indian companies to embrace CSR activities. Their study reveals an insignificant relation between CSR and EVA (economic value added) but CSR and MVA (market value added) are positively correlated. CSR has evolved over a period of time in India but there is no enough evidence available to link it with improved financial performance. An analysis of CSR reporting by Indian companies against MNC reveal that MNC give importance to quality of work life of employee and product quality where as Indian companies give importance to fair remuneration to employees and product pricing (Tewari 2011). CSR has grown in India but the lack of awareness and legal norms raise a doubt in the minds of the investors to value CSR at the time of investment or not. Very few investors in India give weightage to CSR initiatives undertaken by the companies as they think it to be a constraint on their profitability which may have negative impact on their returns (Verma 2011).

CSR and Corporate Performance in the International Context

CSR programmes have to be institutionalised within the strategic framework to take their benefit in the long run (Biscaccianti 2003). Following CSR as part of corporate strategy does not result into increased returns but at the same time this is positively valued by the investors (Abbott and Monsen 1979). CSR should be adopted strategically by the organisation as it helps to meet the expectation of the shareholders which may have positive influence on the financial results of the company as well (Foote et al. 2010). Adopting innovative practices and making philanthropic efforts can result into improved financial performance in the long run (Lim 2010).

Aupperle et al. (1985) found that non-economic components got more weightage than economic components showing that social concerns are important issues for executives. But giving more consideration to CSR does not have higher return on assets. Even the study done by Alepander and Buchholz (1978), Brine et al. (2007) did not find any significant relationship between social responsibility and stock market performance. Byus et al. (2010) and Perera et al. (2011) did not find any significant difference in financial performance of the companies after being indexed in the list of sustainable companies.

In contrast to this finding, Jackson and Hua (2009), Mc Guire et al. (1998) found that CSR have an impact on financial performance and reduce the firm risk. Ziegler and Arx (2008) provide evidence from USA and Europe confirming that CSR has positive impact on the financial outcomes. Connell and Sullivan (n.d) found that CSR can be positively related to financial performance as their research supports that bond ratings have improved for the companies which embrace CSR.

Objectives of the Paper

The review of literature gives diverse relationship between CSR and financial performance. Indian studies have stressed on the CSR performance of Indian companies in the pre-reform period and only a few studies have been done to establish the relationship between CSR and financial performance of the companies. India is among the first country to implement mandatory CSR spending and the businesses world across are watching this Indian model for strategic implementation of CSR policies. Thus, this paper aims to explore and study the extent of CSR practices adopted by Indian companies and correlate the CSR performance with financial performance in pre and post reform period. The broad objectives of the paper are:

1. To understand the extent of CSR being followed and reported by the selected companies on the defined parameters.
2. To do a pre and post-reform period comparison of the CSR performance of selected companies.
3. To study the relationship between CSR and CFP (corporate financial performance).

Hypothesis

H0: There is no significant difference in corporate social performance during pre and post reform period.

H1: There is a significant difference in corporate social performance during pre and post reform period.

H0: There is no significant relationship between corporate social performance and financial performance.

H2: There is a significant relationship between corporate social performance and financial performance.

Methodology

Sample Size

A sample of top 30 manufacturing companies has been taken from the list of *ET 500, 2012* excluding the companies involved in communications, banking and financial services. Same companies have been taken for 2016 and their ranking as per *ET 500, 2015* has also been given.

Data Collection

Data regarding CSR and financial performance has been collected using the annual reports, sustainability reports and business responsibility reports available at the websites of the selected companies for the year 2012-13 and 2015-16.

Data Analysis

To address hypothesis 1, paired t-test has been applied to check the significant difference in the CSR performance of the selected companies during the pre-reform period of 2012-13 and during the post reform period of 2015-16.

To address hypothesis 2, correlation analysis has been done to study the relationship between corporate social responsibility score based on selected parameters and financial performance based on financial ratios of ROS (return on sales) and ROA (return on assets).

Parameters of Corporate Social Responsibility

- *Employees Grievance Redressal*: The companies redressing more than 90 per cent of the employee's complaints received during the year get a score of 3, if 70-90 per cent of the complaints are redressed, a score of 2 is given and if less than 70 per cent complaints are redressed or it is not reported by the company, then a score of only 1 is given.
- *Customer Grievance Redressal*: The companies redressing more than 90 per cent of the consumer's complaints received during the year get a score of 3, if 70-90 per cent of the complaints are redressed, a score of 2 is given and if less than 70 per cent complaints are redressed or it is not reported by the company, then a score of only 1 is given.
- *Social Initiatives*: More the initiatives undertaken for society and local community, higher is the score allotted to them. The score ranges from 1-3 depending upon the steps taken for social development and community care ranging from healthcare, education, empowerment of women, skill development, technology support, encouragement of sports etc.
- *Percentage profit spent on CSR*: Companies spending more than 2 per cent on CSR get a score of 3; those spending between 1-2 per

cent get a score of 2 and if the companies are spending less than 1 per cent of their net profits on CSR activities get a score of only 1.

- *Environment Conservation*: More the initiatives undertaken for conservation of environment, higher is the score allotted to them. The score ranges from 1-4 depending upon the steps taken for environment protection ranging from waste management, water management, use of renewable resources, recycling, efficient use of resources, carbon footprint accounting etc.

Analysis and Discussion

Figure 11.1 shows the CSR performance of the 30 selected companies based on 5 parameters identified to calculate the total CSR score. The light grey bar shows the CSR performance in 2012-13 that is before the mandatory CSR requirements as stated by Companies Act, 2013. The dark grey bar shows the CSR performance in 2015-16 which is after the implementation of the new reforms for CSR. It has been observed that CSR performance has improved over the period of time and there is a positive influence of the reforms introduced by Ministry of Corporate Affairs in India. Only 5 companies out of 30 have less CSR score in post reform period and 4 companies have performed at same level. This indicates that 70 per cent of the selected companies have improved CSR performance post reforms in India.

Figure 11.1

CSR Performance of Selected Companies during 2012-13 and 2015-16

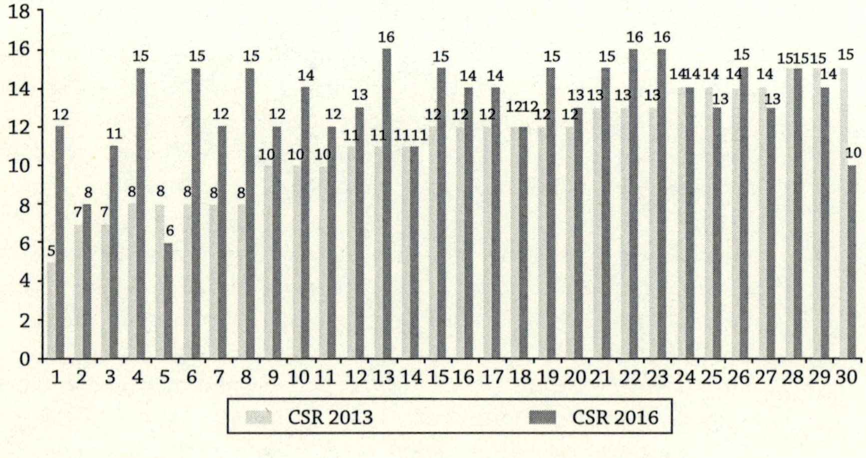

Table 11.1 shows the results of the paired sample test for CSR performance in 2012-13 and 2015-16. The mean score of CSR has increased from 11.133 to 13.2 which indicate increase in CSR performance of the selected companies after the introduction of the reforms. The standard deviation has also decreased which shows less variation in CSR performance of the selected companies.

Table 11.1

Paired Samples Statistics

		Mean	*N*	*Std. Deviation*	*Std. Error Mean*
Pair 1	CSR2013	11.133	30.000	2.738	0.499
	CSR2016	13.200	30.000	2.340	0.427

Table 11.2

Paired Samples Correlations

		N	*Correlation*	*Sig. (p)*
Pair 1	CSR2013 & CSR2016	30.000	0.378	0.040

Table 11.2 shows the correlation between the total CSR score of 2012-13 and 2015-16. There is a positive but moderate correlation (r=0.378) between the CSR performance in 2012-13 and 2015-16. As the p value is 0.04 which is less than 5 per cent, there is a significant correlation between CSR performances of the two periods. This shows the companies doing CSR in pre-reform period have done better CSR performance in post reform period. Thus, there is a positive influence of CSR reforms on the CSP (corporate social performance) of Indian companies.

Table 11.3

Paired Samples Test

		Paired Differences					*T*	*Df*	*Sig. (p) (2-tailed)*
					Lower	*Upper*			
Pair 1	CSR 2013-CSR 2016	-2.067	2.852	0.521	-3.132	-1.002	-3.969	29.000	0.000

Table 11.3 shows the result of paired t-test between CSR performance in 2012-13 and 2015-16. The p value is 0.00 which indicates a statistically significant difference between the CSR performance of companies in the pre reform and post reform period. The negative value of t-test indicates

improvement in CSR performance in the post reform period. This leads to rejecting the null hypothesis and accepting alternate hypothesis 1 i.e. is CSR performance has significantly improved after the introduction of reforms related to CSR and there is a significant difference between CSPe during pre and post reform periods.

We further need to check if this has any relationship with the financial performance of the companies as well. This is dealt in the next section of the paper.

Table 11.4

Correlations

		ROS13	*ROA13*	*ROS16*	*ROA16*
CSR2013	Pearson Correlation	0.221	0.289		
	Sig. (2-tailed)	0.242	0.122		
CSR2016	Pearson Correlation			0.167	0.393
	Sig. (2-tailed)			0.377	0.032
	N	30	30	30.000	30.000

Table 11.4 highlight the correlation between CSR score and financial performance indicated by ROS and ROA. In 2012-13, CSR shows a correlation of r=0.221 with ROS and r=0.289 with ROA. Correlation of CSR score with financial performance in 2016 show a decrease in r (0.167) for ROS but an increase in r (0.393) for ROA. As the p value is more than 0.05 in all cases except for the correlation between CSR 16 and ROA16, CSR performance is not significantly related to operating performance but the improved CSR score is significantly related to ROA of the company. Overall we can conclude that CSR score in 2012 and 2016 is not significantly correlated to financial performance. Thus the null hypothesis 2 is accepted and alternate hypothesis 2 i.e. CSR is significantly correlated to financial performance is rejected.

Discussion

All the companies under study have undertaken CSR initiatives and recognised the responsibility towards different stakeholders' employees, customers and communities at large. CSR implementation helps in fostering long term relationship with stakeholders (Chaudhri and Wang 2007). Indian Companies are trying to match the mandatory requirement of spending 2 per cent of their profit on CSR initiatives (Sharma 2013) as most of the companies under study have a score of 2 or 3 in spending the requisite amount on CSR.

The score for social initiatives is fairly high for all the companies which suggest that Indian companies stress more on community welfare in their social initiatives (Shanmugam and Mohamed 2011; Kansal and Singh 2012). It has been observed that most of the companies are taking care of grievances of the employees and the customers but some of them are not reporting the same as per the guidelines. This study highlights that business and social responsibility can go hand in hand where the corporate world would recognise these practices as an integral part of their strategy for competitive advantage rather than treating social responsibility as a burden on corporate performance. Being responsible towards employees and customers brings loyalty, customer goodwill and resultant market share (Chatterjee 2007).

This is an undeniable fact that CSR is beneficial for the stakeholders by way of more satisfied employees and customers whose complaints are redressed properly, social initiatives are adopted through charity foundation, NGOs and community welfare (Fadun 2014, Noamene and Elouadi 2015).

The results of the study show that there is positive and significant correlation between CSR performance of Indian companies in pre reform and post reform periods. At the same time, it was found that CSR is positively correlated to ROS and ROA in both the periods under study which means increase in CSR investment would have a direct impact on profitability but the statistical analysis reveal that there is no significant impact of CSR performance on profitability of the business. The results are consistent with Izzo and Magnanelli (n.d.) who have denied the existence of a particular role of CSP in defining the cost of debt of the company. Even (Brine et al. 2007) did not find any statistically significant relationship between adopting CSR and financial performance of Australian companies. Griffin and Mahon (1997) could not find any significant relationship between CSR and financial performance. The results of the study by Goukasian and Whitney (2007) also reveal that operating performance of the companies has worsened compared to their performance prior to the identification of CSR activities in the business organisation.

The results are inconsistent with Rais and Goedegebuurre (2009) where they have reported that CSP leads to better financial performance in term of revenue and growth. Even though the investors are not valuing the social responsibility and disclosure but still it has impact on corporate performance through increased reputation, product image and other non-financial indicators. The present study confirms the result of the study by Tripathi and Seth (2014) in which the researchers did not find any significant relationship between CSP and CFP for the selected Indian companies. It seems that Indian companies have a lopsided approach towards CSR initiatives as more stress is on social initiatives and other stakeholders have been ignored by most of the companies. The low level of CSR performance against the expected score may be due to the lack of integrated and rational CSR policy and governing standards (Kansal and Singh 2011).

Conclusion

No doubt the things are changing and companies and managers are becoming proactive in adopting social initiatives as integral part of their operations but Indian corporate world has to go a long way to sincerely implement the regulation as per new Companies Act, 2013. As we are moving from voluntary disclosure to mandatory disclosures, many new challenges will come to the forefront. It is still the infant stage for Indian companies to adopt these changes and make CSR an integral part of their corporate agenda. Further analysis using different sectors and industries would give a clear picture of the impact of CSR on financial performance of the companies in India.

The study recommends that Indian companies should adopt a balanced approach towards its responsibility for different stakeholders and form separate committees for proper planning, implementation and disclosure of CSR initiatives. The need of the hour is to formulate effective strategic practices according to the type of industry and then relationship with its stakeholders so that CSR initiatives can be implemented to attain its goal of sustainability with social and economic growth. The findings are useful for the stakeholders as the shareholders would be benefited by the increase in profitability and efficiency of the company and the employees, customers and society at large would be at advantage when companies fulfil their social responsibility and follow sustainable business practices.

References

Abbott, W.F. and R.J. Monsen (1979). "On the Measurement of Corporate Social Responsibility: Self-Reported Disclosures as a Method of Measuring Corporate Social Involvement", *Academy of Management Journal* 22(3): 501-15. DOI:10.2307/255740

Arevalo, J.A. and D. Aravind (2011). "Corporate Social Responsibility Practices in India: Approach, Drivers, and Barriers", *Corporate Governance* 11(4): 399-414.

Aupperle, K.E., A.B. Carroll and J.D. Hatfield (1985). "An Empirical Examination of the Relationship between Corporate Social Responsibility and Profitability", *Academy of Management Journal* 28(2): 446-63.

Biscaccianti, A. (2003). "Business Ethics and Profit: The Impact of Corporate Social Responsibility Programs on Corporate Strategic Planning", *Cahiers du CEREN* 14-27.

Blowfield, M., and J.G. Frynas (2005). "Setting New Agendas: Critical Perspectives on Corporate Social Responsibility in the Developing World", *International Affairs* 81: 499–513.

Brine, M., R. Brown and G. Hackett (2007). "Corporate Social Responsibility and Financial Performance in the Australian Context" [online]. *Economic Round-up:* 47-58. *http://search.informit.com.au/documentSummary;dn=254072917099846;*

Byus, K., D. Deis and B. Ouyang (2010). "Doing Well by Doing Good: Corporate Social Responsibility and Profitability", *SAM Advanced Management Journal* 75(1): 44-55.

Carroll, A.B. (1991). "'The Pyramid of Corporate Social Responsibility: Toward the Moral Management of Organisational Stakeholders", *Business Horizons* 39-48.

Chatterjee, S. (2007). *Do Successful Companies Value Social Responsibility and Ethics in Marketing in India? International Marketing Conference on Marketing & Society.* 8-10 April. IIMK. pp.29-37.

Chaudhri, V., and J. Wang (2007). "Communicating Corporate Social Responsibility on the Internet: A Case Study of the Top 100 Information Technology Companies in India", *Management Communication Quarterly* 21(2): 232-47. Retrieved from *http://search.proquest.com/docview/216308596?accountid=164287*

Das, S.C. (2009). "Status and Direction of Corporate Social Responsibility in Indian Perspective: An Exploratory Study", *Social Responsibility Journal* 5(1): 34-47. *doi:http://dx.doi.org/10.1108/17471110910939980*

Dey, M., and S. Sircar (2012). "Integrating Corporate Social Responsibility Initiatives with Business Strategy: A Study of Some Indian Companies", *IUP Journal of Corporate Governance* 11(1): 36-51. Retrieved from *http://search.proquest.com/docview/1019963106?accountid=164287*

Fadus, S.O. (2014). "Corporate Social Responsibility (CSR) Practices and Stakeholder Expectations: The Nigerian Perspective", *Research in Business and Management* 1(2): 13-31.

Foote, J., N. Gaffney and J.R. Evans (2010). "Corporate Social Responsibility: Implications for Performance Excellence", *Total Quality Management* 799-812. Routledge.

Gautam, R., and A. Singh (2010). "Corporate Social Responsibility Practices in India: A Study of Top 500 Companies", *Global Business and Management Research* 2(1): 41-56. Retrieved from *http://search.proquest.com/docview/917181577?accountid=164287*

Goukasian, L., and L.K. Whitney (2008). *Corporate Socially Responsible Firms Perform Well! Evidence from Financial and Operating Performances.* DOI: 10.2139/ssrn.972649.

Griffin, J.J. and J.F. Mahon (1997). "The Corporate Social Performance and Corporate Financial Performance Debate: Twenty Five Years of Incomparable Research", *Business and Society* 36(1): 5-31. Sage Publications.

Guha, L. (2011). "Corporate Social Responsibility Rating: India Focus", *IUP Journal of Management Research* 10(3): 28-41. Retrieved from *http://search.proquest.com/docview/917430401?accountid=164287*

Izzo, M.F. and B.S. Magnanelli (n.d.). *Does it Pay or Does Firm Pay?* Retrieved from: *http://ssrn.com/abstract=1986131*

Jackson, L., and N. Hua (2009). "Corporate Social Responsibility and Financial Performance: A Snapshot from the Lodging and Gaming Industries", *Journal of Hospitality Financial Management* 63-78.

Jayakumar, A., G. Anbalagan and L. Kannan (2012). *CSR in India: A Vision for the Future*. Retrieved from *http://search.proquest.com/docview/1328550086?accountid=164287*

Kansal, M., and S. Singh (2012). "Measurement of Corporate Social Performance: An Indian Perspective", *Social Responsibility Journal* 8(4): 527-46. *doi:http://dx.doi.org/10.1108/17471111211272101*.

Lim, T. (2010). *Measuring the Value of Corporate Philanthropy-Social Impacts, Business Benefits and Investors Returns*. New York: Committee Encouraging Corporate Philanthropy.

McGuire, J., A. Sundgren and T. Schneeweis (1988). "Corporate Social Responsibility and Firm Financial Performance", *Academy of Management Journal* 31(4): 854-72.

Mittal, R.K., N. Sinha and A. Singh (2008). "An Analysis of Linkage Between Economic Value Added and Corporate Social Responsibility", *Management Decision* 46(9): 1437-43. *doi:http://dx.doi.org/10.1108/00251740810912037.*

Murthy, M.K., and N. Pitty (2013). *Corporate Social Responsibilities of Indian Public Sector Enterprises—A Case Study of Bharat Heavy Electricals Limited (BHEL).* Paper presented at the 194-XI. Retrieved from *http://search.proquest.com/docview/1326319272?accountid=164287.*

Nguyen, T.H.N. (2011). "Being Socially Responsible and Environmentally Friendly Improves the Corporate Competitiveness and Profitability?" *Advances in Management* 4 (3): 21-25. *doi:http://dx.doi.org/10.1108/14720701111159244.*

Noamene, T.B. and S. Elouadi (2015). "The Pyramid of Corporate Social Responsibility (CSR): An Empirical Examination in Tunisian Context", *International Business Review* 8(10): 117-25

O'Connell, V. and D. O'Sullivan (n.d.). *Performance Measurement, Firm Risk and Corporate Social Responsibility.*

O'Connell, V. And D. O'Sullivan (n.d.) "Performance Measurement, Firm Risk and Corporate Social Responsibility", Retrieved from *http://files.journalofregionaldevelopment.webnode.cz/200000035-df5bbe055d/Oconnel.pdf*

Padhiyar, S. (2013). "A Case Study on Holistic View of CSR Activities at Indian Oil Corporation (IOC)", *Asia Pacific Journal of Management & Entrepreneurship Research* 2(4): 28-38. Retrieved from *http://search.proquest.com/docview/1446932869?accountid=164287.*

Perera, L.C.J., R. Gonçalves, M.T.P. Antunes and J.O. Imoniana (2011). "Sustainable Practice and Business Profitability in Brazil", *Journal of International Business and Economics* 11(3): 14-24.

Rais, S., and R.V. Goedegebuurre (2009). "Corporate Social Performance and Financial Performance. The Case of Indonesian Firms in the Manufacturing Industry", *Problems and Perspectives in Management* 224-38.

Sandhu, H.S. and S. Kapoor (2010). "Corporate Social Responsibility Initiatives: An Analysis of Voluntary Corporate Disclosure", *South Asian Journal of Management* 17(2): 47-80. Retrieved from *http://search.proquest.com/docview/748831625?accountid=164287.*

Shanmugam, K. and N.S. Mohamed (2011). "A Study on CSR Initiatives in Indian Automobile Industry", *Interdisciplinary Journal of Contemporary Research in Business* 3(6): 85-100. Retrieved from *http://search.proquest.com/docview/907119240?accountid=164287.*

Sharma, B. (2013). "India Inc's Evolving Corporate Social Responsibility Landscape—From Voluntary to Mandatory", *The Chartered Accountant:* 73-76, May.

Tewari, R. (2011). "Communicating Corporate Social Responsibility in Annual Reports: A Comparative Study of Indian Companies & Multi-national Corporations", *Journal of Management and Public Policy* 2(2): 22-51. Retrieved from *http://search.proquest.com/docview/1018682384?accountid=164287.*

Tripathi, V. and S. Seth (2014). "The Link Between Corporate Social and Financial Performance of Nifty 50 Companies in India", *Aspirare:* 48-70. [In the text citation: Tripathi and Seth 2014].

Verma, S. (2011). "Why Indian Companies Indulge in CSR?", *Journal of Management and Public Policy* 2(2): 52-69. Retrieved from *http://search.proquest.com/docview/1018682370?accountid=164287.*

Ziegler, A. and V.U. Arx (2008). *The Effect of CSR on Stock Performance: New Evidence for the USA and Europe.* Zurich: Center of Economic Research at ETH Zurich. Retrieved from: *http://www.cer.ethz.ch/research/wp_08_85.pdf.*

12

ANUP KUMAR

Relationship among Sustainable Development Goals, Sustainable Supply Chain Management, and Corporate Social Responsibility

A Case of India

Introduction

Sustainable growth is a concept which focuses on integrating economic activity with environmental protection and social concerns. GSCM (green supply chain management) as of now is mainly focused on environmental concerns however, there is a need to address social and economic concerns of the supply chain also. SSCM (sustainable supply chain management) concept has evolved to integrate the social, environmental and economic concerns of the supply chain (Beske and Seuring 2014). A systemic review had been conducted for the development of SSCM and to set future research agenda by many researchers (Carter and Rogers 2008, Seuring and Müller 2008); The concept of these reviews have established the foundational theory of SSCM for building the applicable frameworks. How to measure progress towards achieving sustainable development and growth has emerged as one of the key issues on the sustainability agenda. In recent years, intensive efforts have been put on a wide range of actors, such as international agencies, governments, non-governmental organisations, communities, and business organisations to develop measurement systems and indicators that characterise progress towards sustainable development, or at least, some of the dimensions of sustainability. An effort has been made in this study to present an overview of some of the most prominent initiatives that have been taken to manage sustainability at the international, national, local and corporate levels.

The term 'sustainability' is defined as one which meets the needs of the present generation without compromising the ability of future generations to meet their needs (WCED 1987). Many authors had tried to instil the concept of sustainability and sustainability performance into product chains which leads to the definition of SSCM (Kremer et al. 2015, Lee and Wu 2014). SSCM is defined as the management of material and information flows as well as cooperation amongst companies along the supply chain while taking goals from all three dimensions of sustainable development, i.e. economic, environmental and social into account (Seuring and Müller 2008), whereas GSCM has mainly focused on environmental concerns.

There are many logics that highlight the importance of sustainability, but some of the important facts are: (i) human constitute 0.5 per cent of the biomass on planet earth but consume approximately 20 per cent of the world primary production, and (ii) projections indicate that human population is likely to reach 9.2 billion by 2050. This clearly indicates that we are going to face some tough challenges in coming future. The science and technology have given immense power to human race, imagine if in 16th century some community had wireless mobiles, it may have been viewed as a superhuman community. The knowledge about the cosmos had been sighted in ancient articles of secret *Vedas*, where the ancient humans knew about the power of nature and its effect on the human life, the special orientation of solar system in time and space and, the uniqueness of the earth, long before 1500 BC. Now after all the progress made over the years, researchers are trying to establish a trade-off between consumption and generation for sustainable development. Starting from Maslow's hierarchy of needs to supply chain management and even in economics, the activities of a social system are mainly linked to satisfying needs of stakeholders in the society. A supply chain network is defined by fulfilment of needs of the customers; therefore for addressing the sustainable development issue, it is essential to have a relook at the policies that measure the sustainability of the societies in a supply chain perspective.

The human race has evolved from water to land and is now trying to mark its presence in space. With so much of progress and empowerment in the 21st century, the social scientists are busy in finding the way to sustain the progress of human race. A debate is going on worldwide about the type of progress human race has achieved and whether the way the race is moving is sustainable? Are we moving in right direction? Excess consumption and social imbalance have forced the society to rethink about the way the world is moving. According to Millennium Development Goals (MDGs) 2015 report, the number of people living in slums conditions are growing all over the world. The *World Social Situation Report* by United Nations (UN) reveals more than 40 per cent of the world population is forced to live in less than 1.25 dollar per day. The report has also presented the dark side of the world development by giving the percentage increase that has taken place in pollution, degradation of the quality of river water, scarcity of drinking water, and many such alarming events.

Data presented in the later part regarding world development highlights that the way the human race is moving forward is not the right way; scientists and researchers must devise the format of sustainable development so that the story of development becomes acceptable to all the stakeholders on the earth, including human and nature. Sustainability has been defined in a different perspective and at different point of time, it needs to be conceptualised in totality. An extensive review of articles have been undertaken in the study to addresses the sustainability management issues in different perspective of a supply chain and sustainable development for finding evidence or associations to answer following research questions and to set future research direction:

- Whether Sustainable Development Goals (SDGs) could be achieved with sustainable supply chain management?
- Is encouraging CSR amongst supply chain, an initiative towards achieving sustainable development goals?

Methodology

Content analysis has been widely used in medical science for getting intelligence from published work (Crum et al. 2011, Meyer 1993). Crowther and Cook (2007) have lightened how to plan content analysis in medical sciences. Application of content analysis in business and management takes a high level of meta-analysis combined with manual reading. The method proposed by above researchers should not be used blindly for making conclusions. Extreme care has been taken in this research for using content analysis, authors have taken the views of Crowther and Cook 2007, and Schmidt and Hunter 2014 and also did manual readings of selected articles for making conclusions. To establish the association between SSCM and sustainable development, a systemic review has been conducted and research articles have been searched using keywords: sustainable development, measurement of sustainability and sustainable supply chain management on three major publishers' portal namely *sciencedirect.com*, Emerald insight and Taylor & Francis. Search has been narrowed by combined keyword 'frameworks for sustainable supply chain management and sustainable developed.' Approximately 50 papers from each of the said publishers have been randomly selected, out of which a total of 145 articles are reviewed. Reliability test for content analysis has been carried out using the method proposed by (Hayes and Krippendorff 2007) in SPSS and the alpha value of test result was 0.83 which is acceptable. A conceptual framework has been proposed to accomplish the SDGs. The framework is compared with traditional practices and sustainable practices using a case study of evidence and informed management knowledge (Tranfield et al. 2003).

Descriptive Statistics of the Reviewed Papers

Top contributions in this area are from *Journal of Cleaner Production* (16), *Journal of Production Economics* (11), *Supply Chain Management: An International Journal* (25), *International Journal of Productivity and Performance Measurement* (9), *International Journal of Production Research* (14) and *Production Planning and Control* (9), which shows that there is a sudden (almost a double) increase in the articles getting published in this area from 2013 to 2014. This clearly indicates that the topic has gained paramount importance in the past few years. The environmental dimension of the sustainability has got more weight (74.48%), followed by economic (71%) and social (60%) dimensions. Perhaps the cause for higher weight of environmental dimensions may be stringent government policies and the emergence of environmental engineering as a special branch of research.

Inferential Statistics

Content analysis has been done by 145 reviewed articles to verify the hypothesis stated in research question 1, that SSCM positively supports sustainable development.

Content analysis reveals that 48.96 per cent of reviewed articles have taken all three dimensions of sustainability; therefore, it is legitimate to test the stated hypothesis among 48.96 per cent of articles. Out of 71 articles which had all dimensions of sustainability 43 articles stated positive association between sustainable development and SSCM while 10 stated negative and 18 did not say anything about sustainable development. Out of 145 articles which have at least one sustainability dimension, 73 articles have endorsed positive association between sustainable development and SSCM. The majority of the reviewed articles have endorsed the positive association between sustainable development and SSCM. The reviewed articles have also indicated an increased growth in citations on sustainability science.

Sustainable Development and Supply Chain Management

Majority of sustainable development indicators are same as SSCM. The conceptual theory building in the area of SSCM and sustainable development is still in premature phase, although a handful theoretical framework for sustainable development have been proposed by researchers (Azapagic 2004, Azapagic and Perdan 2000, Boron and Murray 2004, Hezri and Hasan 2004, Jabareen 2008, Loorbach 2010; Mitchell et al. 1995, Rao 2000, Svensson 2007), but they are unable to explain how to achieve sustainable development. Authors have argued in this paper to link SSCM to Sustainable Development to achieve SDG. The very purpose of a supply chain is to create value for the consumer through cooperative structured shared interest. Many of the researchers have misunderstood the concept and the intricacies of supply chain management. The macroeconomic parameters of a country have an intense relationship with supply chain management. The mismanagement of a particular supply chain could be a catastrophe for a country.

Through this paper, a structured (manual as well as key work search) review has been conducted to find out whether the above set of SDG goals could be achieved through SSCM. Hall et al. (2011) have analysed why a company should invest in SSCM using a complexity approach and they found that focusing on individual sustainable development elements independently are not going to help significantly with their SSCM practices. Therefore, it is essential to establish an integrative framework to accomplish SDGs through SSCM practices. The word sustainable development indicates the participation of each and every member of the society in economic activity. Gobattoni et al. (2015) have advocated traditional farming systems and other activities such as craftsmanship, manufacturing activities and local food production), that essentially leads to human integration with nature. The Common Agricultural Policy (CAP), formulated by Europe has challenges regarding participatory planning and people's attitude to traditional work. Participatory economic activity and collaboration are major indicators of SSCM, a few examples like Amul and Gopaljee dairy supply chain from India could be stated in support of the argument. The human race has endless needs therefore for the satisfaction of needs a system has been developed and defined as supply chain management that has linkages (network) for different human activities. Therefore essentially for sustainable development theory, researchers have to think how to address those endless needs legitimately. A system view of supply chain management takes a holistic approach (Figure 12.1), which links fundamental human needs, to SSCM and Sustainable Development. The core theme of a sustainable economy is to satisfy human's needs legitimately with an inclusive participation of the members.

The objective of a supply chain is to maximise supply chain surplus that is defined by Chopra and Meindl 2007 as:

Supply chain surplus = Customer value – Supply chain cost

The value of the product or service fulfilled by a supply chain may vary according to the need of the product and services but for sustainable supply chain management, the cost should be minimised, acoording to the function of environmental, social and economical concerns of the supply chain, which includes waste produced, carbon emission, etc.

Table 12.1

List of Sustainability Indices

No	*Index*	*Acronym/Institution*
1	EPI	Environmental Performance Index
2	NRMI	Natural Resource Management Index
3	HF	Human Footprint
4	GRI	Global Reporting Initiatives
5	GPI	Genuine Progress Index
6	DJSI	Dow Jones Sustainability Index
7	CSD	Commission on Sustainable Development
8	Dashboard	Developed by Consultive Group of Sustainable Development Indicators
9	Barometer	Developed by World Conservation Institute
10	TBL	Triple Bottom Line Index
11	Ethos	Corporate Social Responsibility Indicators
12	IChemE	Institute of Chemical Engineers

Table 12.1 shows the different measurement indices used for measurement of sustainability (Beske and Seuring 2014). These indices are being used by a majority of the companies for their sustainability initiatives. Afful-Dadzie et al. (2016) argued that these indices have failed to provide a minimum acceptable level of indicators. How to use these indices in the deployment of sustainability indicators is also not very clear.

Figure 12.1

Process View of Attaining Sustainable Development through SSCM

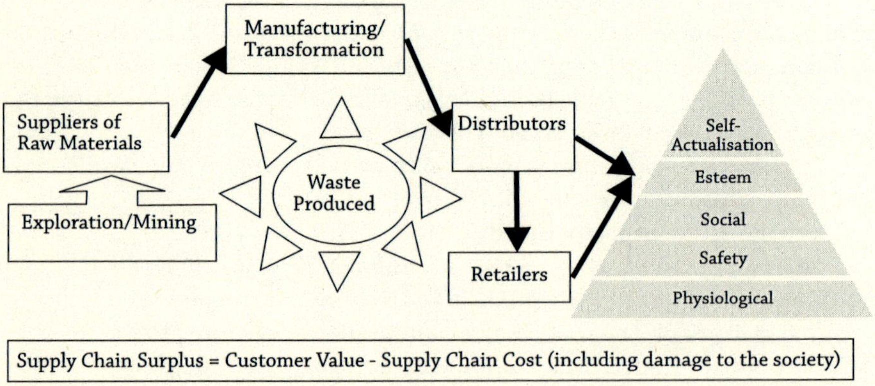

Source: Drafted by authors.

Authors have conducted a survey on sustainability initiatives of top 10 Fortune 500 companies, which reveal that companies are practicing GRI's global sustainability reporting. The sustainability reporting initiatives contain CSR as well. CSR initiatives are now reported and designed as sustainability programmes for companies. The shift from CSR to sustainability reporting is evident from the fact that top fortune 500 companies have adopted the sustainability reporting framework. Sustainability reporting practices are unstructured; they should be structured and must contain concrete evidence of sustainability initiatives.

Management of Sustainability and its Indicators

Sustainable development and inclusive growth hold a lot of importance in today's time. As stated in research question, authors are trying to find evidence and association between SSCM and sustainable development. UN General Assembly proposed a set of global SDGs which comprises 17 goals and 169 targets. The SDGs are:

> GOAL 1: End poverty in all its forms everywhere, GOAL 2: End hunger, achieve food security and improved nutrition and promote sustainable agriculture, GOAL 3: Ensure healthy lives and promote well-being for all at all ages, GOAL 4: Ensure inclusive and equitable quality education and promote lifelong learning opportunities for all, GOAL 5: Achieve gender equality and empower all women and girls, GOAL 6: Ensure availability and sustainable management of water and sanitation for all, GOAL 7: Ensure access to affordable, reliable, sustainable and modern energy for all, GOAL 8: Promote sustained, inclusive and sustainable economic growth, full and productive employment and decent work for all, GOAL 9: Build resilient infrastructure, promote inclusive and sustainable industrialisation and foster innovation, GOAL 10: Reduce inequality within and among countries, GOAL 11: Make cities and human settlements inclusive, safe, resilient and sustainable, GOAL 12: Ensure sustainable consumption and production patterns, GOAL 13: Take urgent action to combat climate change and its impacts, GOAL 14: Conserve and sustainably use the oceans, seas and marine resources for sustainable development, GOAL 15: Protect, restore and promote sustainable use of terrestrial ecosystems, sustainably manage forests, combat desertification, and halt and reverse land degradation and halt biodiversity loss, GOAL 16: Promote peaceful and inclusive societies for sustainable development, provide access to justice for all and build effective, accountable and inclusive institutions at all levels,

GOAL 17: Strengthen the means of implementation and revitalise the global partnership for sustainable development.[1]

Further to that, a preliminary set of 330 indicators was introduced in March 2015. Some SDGs are built on preceding MDGs while others incorporated new ideas, a critical review of these indicators has been carried out by (Hák et al. 2016) . Many researchers have indicated the sustainability of energy supply chain, infrastructure need, road and transports mechanism to enhance inclusive growth (Emodi and Boo 2015, Gaigaliset al. 2015, García-Álvarez et al. 2016, Salvi and Subramanian 2015, Zhanget al. 2015), whereas a few types of research have tried to find the way of capturing sustainability matrices for measurement (Hák et al. 2016, Horlings and Kanemasu 2015, Qin et al. 2015). (Delai and Takahashi 2011) have personated a well-structured review of different sustainability measurement indices and frameworks like GRI, IChemE, DJSI, CSD, dashboard, barometer, TBL, and Ethos. Beske-Janssen et al. (2015) have discussed performance measurement and management tools in SSCM.

Social Indicators

A reference model for social sustainability measurement has been proposed by Delai and Takahashi (2011) that indicates the dimensions and level of sustainability measurement. The reference model proposed could be linked to SSCM reference model as proposed in Figure 12.2.

Environmental Indicators

GSCM concept was introduced to include environmental concerns of the supply chain. Plenty of scholarly study and formulations have been carved out in this area. Major concepts that came out from these studies are remanufacturing, recycling, green production, waste management, green energy, reverse logistics, etc. (Arif-Uz-Zaman and Ahsan 2014). A sustainability reporting framework is being proposed (Figure 12.3), which is based on the content analysis of the reviewed papers.

Economic Indicators

Economic efficiency had been the major performance criteria for a supply chain that includes financial, cost, service and operational efficiencies of a supply chain till the emergence of SCM (supply chain management), GCCs (global commodity chains), GVCs (global value chains) and GPNs (global production networks) (Bush et al. 2015).

---

1. *https://sustainabledevelopment.un.org/content/documents/1579SDGs%20Proposal.pdf*

After 2000, a sudden increase of articles on sustainability and a worldwide debate on sustainability has forced the supply chain planners and designers to design holistic performance criterion in sync with economic performance, a social performance, and environmental performance. Economic indicators alone have been used for performance measurement by about 40 per cent of the reviewed articles while the rest of the reviewed articles have suggested the combination of three dimensions of sustainability. After a rigorous review of the 145 stated articles, a list of economic indicators has been compiled and shown in Table 12.2. A conceptual framework for management of economic sustainability has also been proposed and shown in Figure 12.5.

Figure 12.2

Social Framework of Sustainable Development Using SSCM

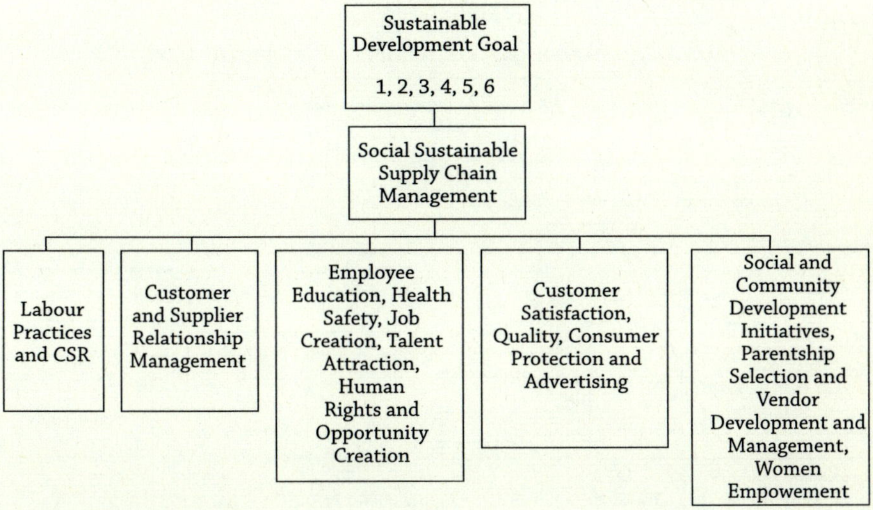

Source: Drafted by authors.

SSCM Framework to Achieve Sustainable Development

Authors are arguing for an orientation which could enable SSCM to create conditions for a new praxis based on sustainable human development. Such development is founded on the satisfaction of fundamental human needs, generation of growing level of self-reliance, and on the legitimate use of nature and technology to attain global standards with the inclusion of local activity, persons, civil society, and the state. Human needs, self-reliance and organic articulation are the foundations which support sustainable development (Max-Neef et al. 1992). SSCM could become the engine to

Figure 12.3

Proposed Sustainability Reporting Framework

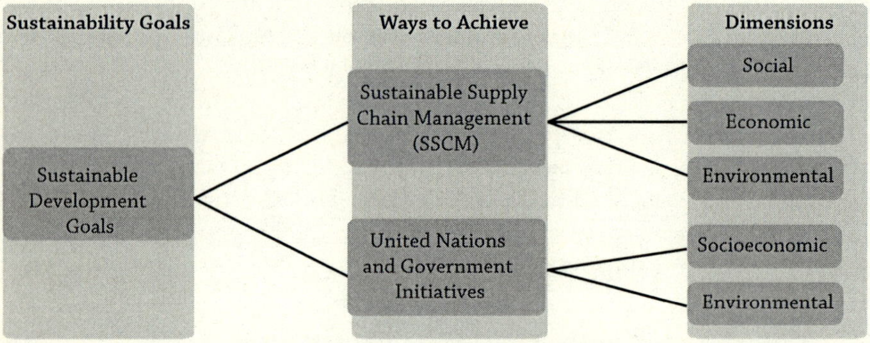

Figure 12.4

Environmental Framework of Sustainable Development Using SSCM

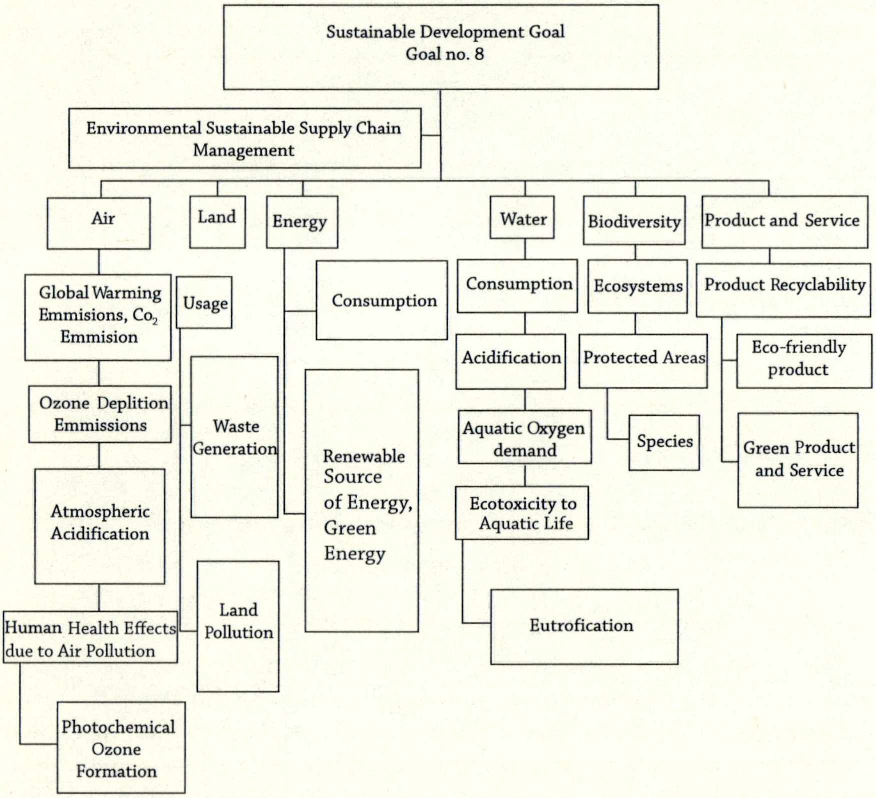

Source: Drafted by authors.

Figure 12.5

Economic Framework for Sustainable Development

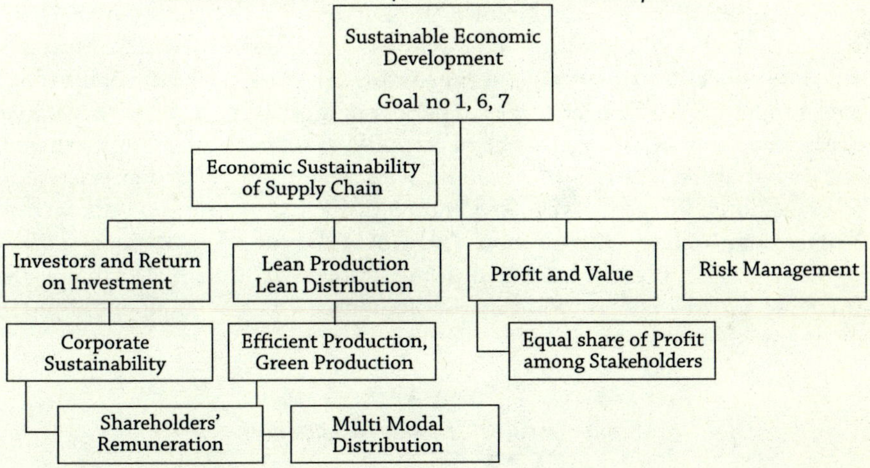

Source: Drafted by authors.

Table 12.2

Economic Indicators of SSCM

S.No.	*Component*	*Indicator*
1	Cost	Inventory
2		Transportation
3		Facilities and handling
4		Information
5		Productivity
6	Service	Response time
7		Product variety
8		Product availability
9		Customer experience
10		Time to market
11		Order visibility
12		Return ability
13	Financial	Return on investment
14		Return on equity
15		Return on assets
16		Accounts payable turnover

pull the wheel (see Figure 12.6) of fundamental needs of the human. The traditional supply chain management follows top-down approach while proposed SSCM framework follows the bottom-up approach which is the foundation of sustainability. The proposed framework for SSCM starts with the objective to satisfy the needs of the consumer through village level cooperatives, district level cooperatives, and state level cooperatives. These cooperatives may consist of suppliers, financiers, manufacturers, and distributors. Trained professionals manage the flow of materials and money among different levels (see Figure 12.7). The bottom-up approach to manage supply chains has an inbuilt advantage of the adequate local market to sustain. The SSCM social, economic, and environmental frameworks discussed in previous sections are implemented at each stage of proposed SSCM framework for Sustainable Development.

Figure 12.6

Fundamental Human Need Wheel

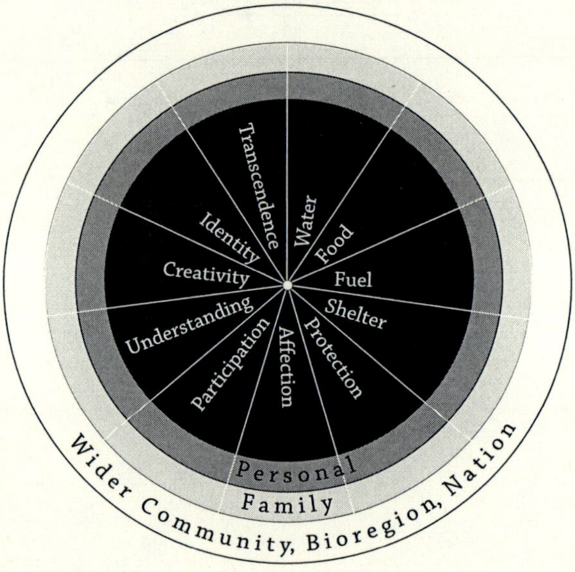

Source: Max-Neef et al. 1992.

Real Case of SSCM

In the 21st century, it is essential for a democratic country to develop systems and methods for the people and by the people for sustainability. This case is developed by interviewing executives of three dairy sector company located in India; no data is used from these companies. Authors have taken three exemplars of the dairy sector (Amul, Gopaljee, and Mother

Dairy) of proposed SSCM framework from India. These companies have followed proposed bottom-up approach to sustaining the growth. They are using the cooperative model of the supply chain to include the larger participation of individuals with high level of transparency. The Amul model has helped India to emerge as the largest milk producer in the world. More than 15 million milk producers pour their milk in 1,44,500 dairy cooperative societies across the country. Their milk is processed in 184 District Co-operative Unions and marketed by 22 State Marketing Federations, ensuring a better life for millions. All the three examplans use the SSCM framework as proposed to ensure sustainable development in India. The same framework may be imitated in other food supply chain for sustainable development. They have vertical integration for implementation and control of their process to manage their value chain (Figure 12.7). They follow three different levels for sustainable planning which gives them better control and flexibility to deploy sustainability requirements. First level consist

Figure 12.7

Sustainable Development and SSCM

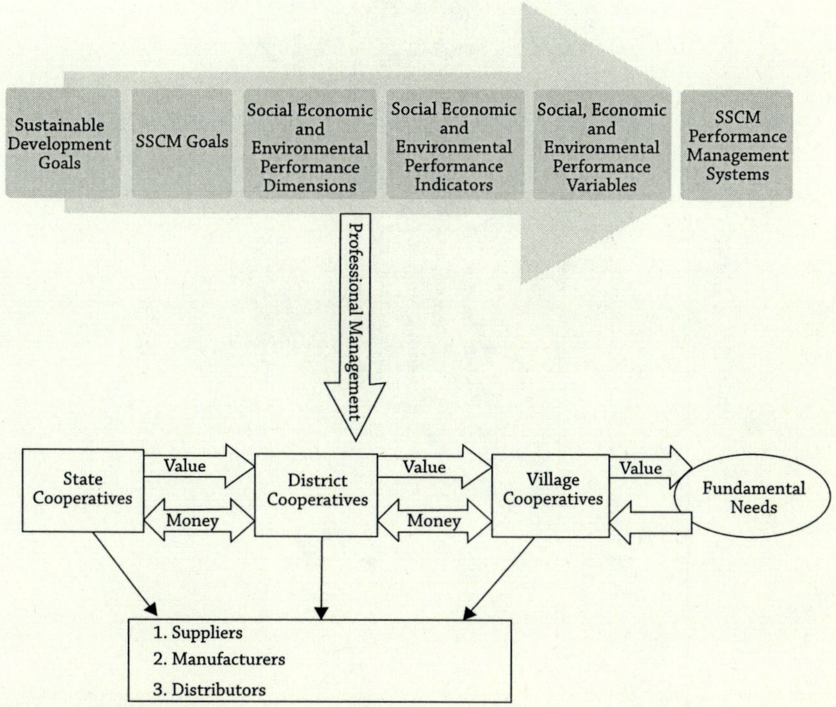

Source: Drafted by authors.

Table 12.3

Sustainability Initiatives used by Top 10 Fortune 500 Companies

Rank	Company	Website	Sustainability Initiatives		
			Social	Environmental	Economic
1	Wal-Mart Stores	www.corporate.walmart.com	The Walmart Foundation meets the needs of the under-served by directing charitable giving towards the core areas of focus: opportunity, sustainability and community.		
2	Exxon Mobil	www.exxonmobil.com	Malaria, corporate citizenship, human rights, local economic development, indigenous peoples, cultural heritage and diversity, land use and resettlement, transparency and corruption, community relations	Air emissions reductions, ecosystem services, environmental drilling initiatives, environmental stewardship, freshwater management, managing arctic resources, site remediation, spill performance	Environment and safety, operations, policy, technology, flexibility, energy efficiency
3	Chevron	www.chevron.com	Health, education, volunteerism, fresh water	Fresh water, biodiversity	Energy efficiency, land management, IPIECA/API/OGP reporting standard
4	Berkshire Hathaway	www.berkshirehathaway.com	Investors health		

5	Apple	www.apple.com	Environment, supplier responsibility, accessibility, privacy, inclusion and diversity, education, reuse and recycling		
6	Phillips 66	www.phillips66.com	Operating excellence, people, transparency & accountability, community investments, supplier diversity, governance & ethics, environmental metrics.		
7	General Motors	www.gm.com	Sustainability takes into consideration environmental, social and economic opportunities and supports the long-term success of our company. value is created through top-line growth opportunities, bottom-line improvements and risk mitigation. how much value created is driven by our customers — everything starts and ends with our customers. at gm, we view sustainability as a business approach that creates long-term stakeholder value. it is an approach that is executed by every function at every level of our company.		
8	Ford Motor	www.ford.com	Investor's health		
9	General Electric	www.ge.com	At GE, sustainability means aligning our business strategy to meet societal needs, while minimizing environmental impact and advancing social development. This commitment is embedded at every level of our company.		
10	Valero Energy	www.valero.com	Social health and safety, community, benefit of children, volunteerism, employee benefit	Environmental matrices, environmental awards	Investors, financial reports, filings & statements, industry fundamentals, investor FAQs

of sustainable enterprise planning, second level consist of sustainable collaboration and communication while third level consist of sustainable operational planning (See Figure 12.7). The sustainability initiatives shown in Table 12.3 which is used by Top 10 Fortune 500 companies follows top-down approach while these three exemplars of SSCM companies from India follows the bottom-up approach. Bottom-up approach for SSCM practices is the key difference between traditional SCM and SSCM.

The framework proposed by the authors in this paper is similar to these companies. They are contributing to enhancing the livelihood of millions. These real exemplars are a germane application of the proposed framework.

While analysing the Amul case and other related structures, it is evident that SSCM has encouraging CSR amongst supply chain, an initiative towards achieving sustainable development goals. The CSR initiatives that relates to the social dimensions of the sustainability have been embedded in the framework that Amul has adopted. Amul has witnessed continuous growth since its inception and the organisation actively participates in CSR. Therefore this germane case indicates that SSCM framework has embedded CSR activities that come under its social dimension of sustainability.

Amul Dairy has launched a novel scheme for total rural sanitation and has set a target for itself whereby not a single milk producer will attend to nature's call in the open. The Dairy with the support of District Rural Development Agency (DRDA) will provide interest-free loans to its milk producers in Anand and Kheda districts to set up *pucca* toilet blocks, which will not only help women milk producers avoid embarrassment but will also ensure hygiene.

The mission is not just about bringing a cultural change by imbibing good habits among milk producers but is also targeted towards encouraging hygienic practices in the milk supply chain. Amul through their CSR activity has prepared a model low-cost toilet block that costs ₹11,500 per unit. While DRDA will support this initiative through subsidy ranging between ₹4,500 and ₹4,600 for BPL/APL families, Amul will provide its members an interest-free loan worth ₹4,300 returnable in 4 years' time. A member can pay up this loan by getting ₹100 per month, deducted from his/her bill.

Conclusion and Future Direction for Research

Proposed conceptual framework for SSCM is compared with existing models of the sustainable supply chain in India. It is evident from the articles that GSCM is a subset of SSCM, as SSCM covers all dimensions of sustainability. Forty-eight (48) per cent of the reviewed articles have endorsed that SSCM could achieve sustainability goals as proposed by UNs SDGs report.

Figure 12.8

Exemplars from India of SSCM Framework for Sustainable Development

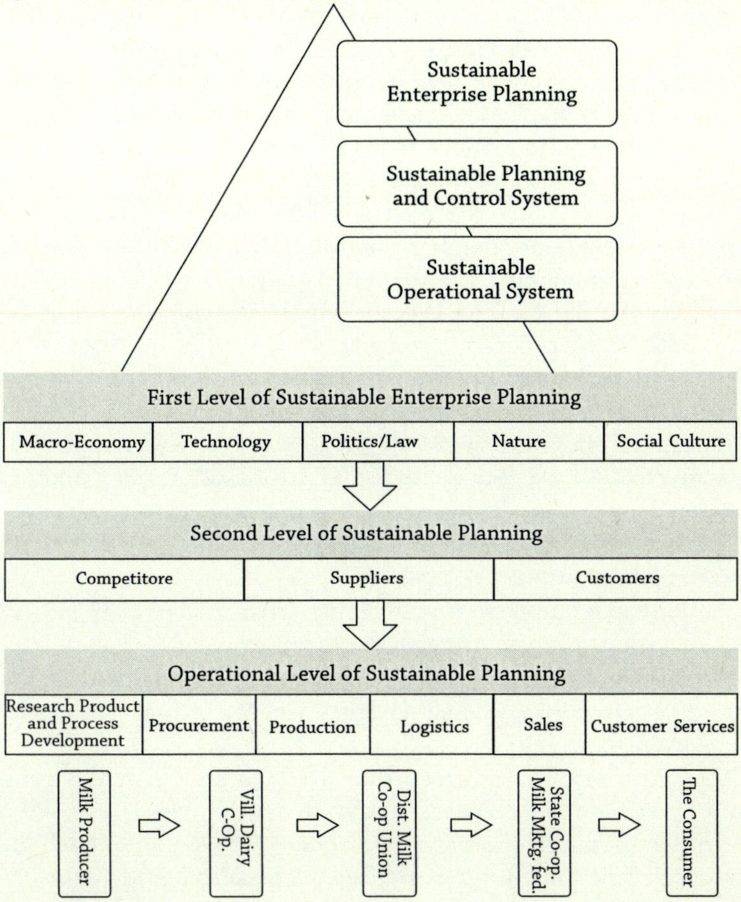

Source: Drafted by authors.

The research questions set has been answered through content analysis of reviewed articles. Most of the articles that address the SSCM have mentioned that sustainable development could be achieved through SSCM (80%). The impact of sustainability initiatives on other functions and capabilities of a supply chain have been studied and concluded with a positive with some lag, while some authors have shown negative impact. Social, environmental and economic indicators and variables for SSCM are the subsets of 300 indicators of sustainable development mentioned in the UN SDG's Report 2015. Overall the data and content analysis reveal that through SSCM alongwith government and NGO's initiatives, sustainable development could be achieved, a framework for the achievement of sustainable development is shown in Figure 12.7. Moreover, for the management of SSCM, a systemic management and control process could be adopted as shown in Figure 12.8. An SSCM management system may contain the performance measurement methods, matrices, and indices for different dimensions of social, economic, and environmental sustainability development. It is also evident that CSR activities are embedded into the social dimension of the SSCM framework (Figure 12.2).

Content analysis of articles reviewed has shown a positive association between sustainable development and SSCM. Reviewed articles have also indicated sharp growth of research on sustainability science that is clearly associated with SSCM. The UN sustainability goals could be achieved through SSCM, hence, SSCM is going to set directions for future research.

House of sustainability framework is proposed for deployment of sustainability. A report conducted by Elsevier in collaboration with SciDev (2015) examine six key themes—dignity, people, prosperity, planet, justice, and partnership—that encompass the 17 UN SDGs. The key findings of the report are:

- Sustainability science is a field with a high growth rate (7.6%) in research output.
- Research output in sustainability science attracts 30 per cent more citations than an average research paper.
- Research in sustainability science is highly collaborative.
- Sustainability science is less interdisciplinary than the world average.

The report has also indicated that the high growth rate is contributed mainly by developed countries, but it also shows the collaboration between northern and southern hemisphere. The key findings indicate the importance of the topic as a research agenda. It also points that till now it is less interdisciplinary therefore it has the potential to expand.

References

Afful-Dadzie, A., E. Afful-Dadzie and C. Turkson (2016). "A TOPSIS Extension Framework for Re-Conceptualizing Sustainability Measurement", *Kybernetes* 45(1), null.

Arif-Uz-Zaman, K. and A.M.M.N. Ahsan (2014). "Lean Supply Chain Performance Measurement", *International Journal of Productivity and Performance Management* 63(5): 588-612.

Azapagic, A. (2004). "Developing a Framework for Sustainable Development Indicators for the Mining and Minerals Industry", *Journal of Cleaner Production* 12(6): 639-62.

Azapagic, A. and S. Perdan (2000). "Indicators of Sustainable Development for Industry: A General Framework", *Process Safety and Environmental Protection* 78(4): 243-61.

Beske-Janssen, P., M.P. Johnson and S. Schaltegger (2015). "20 Years of Performance Measurement in Sustainable Supply Chain Management—What has been Achieved?" *Supply Chain Management: An International Journal* 20(6), null.

Beske, P., and S. Seuring (2014). "Putting Sustainability into Supply Chain Management", *Supply Chain Management: An International Journal* 19(3): 322-31.

Boron, S., and K. Murray (2004). "Bridging the Unsustainability Gap: A Framework for Sustainable Development", *Sustainable Development* 12(2): 65-73.

Bush, S.R., P. Oosterveer, M. Bailey and A.P.J. Mol (2015). "Sustainability Governance of Chains and Networks: A Review and Future Outlook", *Journal of Cleaner Production* 107: 8-19.

Carter, C.R., and D.S. Rogers (2008). "A Framework of Sustainable Supply Chain Management: Moving Toward New Theory", *International Journal of Physical Distribution and Logistics Management* 38(5): 360-87.

Chopra, S., and P. Meindl (2007). Supply Chain Management. Strategy, Planning and Operation: Springer.

Crowther, M.A. and D.J. Cook (2007). "Trials and Tribulations of Systematic Reviews and Meta-analyses", *ASH Education Program Book* 2007(1): 493-97.

Crum, M., R. Poist, C.R. Carter and P. Liane Easton (2011). "Sustainable Supply Chain Management: Evolution and Future Directions", *International Journal of Physical Distribution and Logistics Management* 41(1): 46-62.

Delai, I. and S. Takahashi (2011). "Sustainability Measurement System: A Reference Model Proposal", *Social Responsibility Journal* 7(3): 438-71.

Emodi, N.V., and K.J. Boo (2015). "Sustainable Energy Development in Nigeria: Current Status and Policy Options", *Renewable and Sustainable Energy Reviews* 51: 356-81.

Gaigalis, V., A. Markevicius, R. Skema and J. Savickas (2015). "Sustainable Energy Strategy of Lithuanian Ignalina Nuclear Power Plant Region for 2012–2035 as a Chance for Regional Development", *Renewable and Sustainable Energy Reviews* 51: 1680-96.

García-Álvarez, M. T., B. Moreno and I. Soares (2016). "Analyzing the Sustainable Energy Development in the EU-15 by an Aggregated Synthetic Index", *Ecological Indicators* 60: 996-1007.

Gobattoni, F., R. Pelorosso, A. Leone and M.N. Ripa (2015). "Sustainable Rural Development: The Role of Traditional Activities in Central Italy", *Land Use Policy* 48: 412-27.

Hák, T., S. Janoušková and B. Moldan (2016). "Sustainable Development Goals: A Need for Relevant Indicators", *Ecological Indicators* 60: 565-73.

Hall, J., S. Matos and B. Silvestre (2011). "Understanding Why Firms should Invest in Sustainable Supply Chains: A complexity approach. [doi: 10.1080/00207543.2011.571930]. *International Journal of Production Research* 50(5): 1332-48.

Hayes, A.F. and K. Krippendorff (2007). "Answering the Call for a Standard Reliability Measure for Coding Data", *Communication Methods and Measures* 1(1): 77-89.

Hezri, A.A. and M.N. Hasan (2004). "Management Framework for Sustainable Development Indicators in the State of Selangor, Malaysia", *Ecological Indicators* 4(4): 287-304.

Horlings, L.G. and Y. Kanemasu (2015). "Sustainable Development and Policies in Rural Regions; Insights from the Shetland Islands", *Land Use Policy* 49: 310-21.

Jabareen, Y. (2008). "A New Conceptual Framework for Sustainable Development", *Environment, Development and Sustainability* 10(2): 179-92.

Kremer, G.E., K. Haapala, A. Murat, R.B. Chinnam, K.Y. Kim, L. Monplaisir *et al.* (2015). "Directions for Instilling Economic and Environmental Sustainability Across Product Supply Chains", *Journal of Cleaner Production*.

Lee, K.-H. and Y. Wu (2014). "Integrating Sustainability Performance Measurement into Logistics and Supply Networks: A Multi-methodological Approach", *The British Accounting Review* 46(4): 361-78.

Loorbach, D. (2010). "Transition Management for Sustainable Development: A Prescriptive, Complexity-based Governance Framework", *Governance* 23(1): 161-83.

Max-Neef, M., A. Elizalde and M. Hopenhayn (1992). "Development and Human Needs", *Real-life Economics: Understanding Wealth Creation*, 197-213.

Meyer, J. E. (1993). "New Paradigm Research in Practice: The Trials and Tribulations of Action Research", *Journal of Advanced Nursing* 18(7): 1066-72.

Mitchell, G., A. May and A. McDonald (1995). "PICABUE: a Methodological Framework for the Development of Indicators of Sustainable Development", *The International Journal of Sustainable Development and World Ecology* 2(2): 104-23.

Qin, X., C. Sun and W. Zou (2015). "Quantitative Models for Assessing the Human-ocean System's Sustainable Development in Coastal Acities: The Perspective of Metabolic-Recycling in the Bohai Sea Ring Area, China", *Ocean & Coastal Management* 107: 46-58.

Rao, P. K. (2000). *Sustainable Development: Economics and Policy.* Blackwell Publishers.

Salvi, B.L. and K. A. Subramanian (2015). "Sustainable Development of Road Transportation Sector Using Hydrogen Energy System", *Renewable and Sustainable Energy Reviews* 51: 1132-155.

Seuring, S. and M. Müller (2008). "From a Articles Review to a Conceptual Framework for Sustainable Supply Chain Management", *Journal of Cleaner Production* 16(15): 1699-710.

Svensson, G. (2007). "Aspects of Sustainable Supply Chain Management (SSCM): Conceptual Framework and Empirical Example", *Supply Chain Management: An International Journal* 12(4): 262-66.

Tranfield, D., D. Denyer and P. Smart (2003). "Towards a Methodology for Developing Evidence-informed Management Knowledge by Means of Systematic Review", *British Journal of Management* 14(3): 207-22.

WCED, U. (1987). Our Common Future. World Commission on Environment and DevelopmentOxford University Press.

Zhang, X., Y. Wu, M. Skitmore and S. Jiang (2015). "Sustainable Infrastructure Projects in Balancing Urban–rural Development: Towards the Goal of Efficiency and Equity", *Journal of Cleaner Production* 107: 445-54.

13

KHANDOKER ASEF SAFA KABIR UPAL

Role of Corporate Social Responsibility and Business Ethics Courses in Developing Distinctive Skills in Students

A Case Study of Bangladeshi Business Schools

Introduction

A significant number of business schools worldwide have introduced business ethics and CSR (corporate social responsibility) courses (Christensen et al. 2007). Several factors have been identified as catalysts behind adoption of these courses, including globalisation, financial scandals, and expansion of civil society (Crane and Matten 2004). The underlying theory of this study stems from the new perspectives on business ethics and CSR education that emphasise its broader focus on improving students' effectiveness and competitive abilities (Cornelius et al. 2007). The study aims to investigate this issue in a selected context.

The objective of the study is to investigate specific skills that these courses aim to equip students with, mainly from the perspective of individuals who design and teach these courses. As empirical study, 11 course instructors of business ethics and/or CSR from 4 universities in Bangladesh have been interviewed and course outlines of 8 business ethics and CSR courses have been analysed.

The study focuses on related questions such as: Why teach business ethics and CSR in business schools? What is the importance of these courses in a country like Bangladesh? What skills do these courses aim to offer? How the instructors of these courses are addressing these issues and delivering these skills through their teaching methodologies?

Most studies on business ethics and CSR courses investigated importance, methodologies, and justifications of these courses (Ritter 2006). In contrast, this research aims to assess the scope of skill building of these courses from the viewpoint of a group of academics who teach and design these courses.

Moreover, most studies on these courses were based on Western business schools, in Europe and North America (Srinivasan et al. 2012). However, prominent business schools worldwide have adopted these courses that address similar ethical issues (Srinivasan et al. 2012). By focusing on four Bangladeshi business schools and their courses, this study aims to contribute into studies conducted on South Asian business ethics education (Srinivasan 2012).

Today 'business ethics' is a relatively broad expression and these courses worldwide have been labelled by using various pertinent terms (Gorenak 2011). For this study, those courses have been considered, which predominantly address business ethics, CSR, sustainability, business and environment, and stakeholders' management (Appendix A-13.1). In Bangladeshi business schools, many of these courses are being taught in conjunction with relevant topics, such as *business law and leadership* (Appendix A).

Bangladesh is a developing country in South Asia (Shill 2008). The country has a vibrant corporate sector dominated by family-run private firms (Haque et al. 2007). Lack of business ethics is a major predicament in Bangladesh's corporate landscape (Khan 2009). Bangladesh has a volatile stock market, and underdeveloped corporate laws, which are inadequately enforced (Khan 2009). Moreover, it has a feeble governance infrastructure (Shill 2008). From that contextual perspective, Bangladesh provides an excellent backdrop for this study.

Literature Review

According to Bixby et al. (2012: 12), 'business ethics is a form of applied ethics that examines ethical principles within a commercial context; the various moral or ethical problems that can arise in a business setting.' Similarly, Carroll (1979: 497) defined CSR as 'the economic, legal, ethical, and discretionary expectations that society has of organisations'. Matten and Moon (2004) suggested that CSR is a composite concept that overlaps with business ethics, corporate citizenship, sustainability and environmental responsibility.

Essentially, business ethics is a comprehensive term, which is used to discuss CSR and sustainability (Crane et al. 2008). Most studies highlighted significant overlaps between courses labelled as business ethics and CSR (Christensen et al. 2007). Academically, business ethics is a relatively recent discipline (De George 1987). In the 1970s, it was originated by United States (US) academics, who started to study business from viewpoint of ethical theories (Freeman et al. 2009). During revolutionary epoch of 1970s another group of scholars started to talk about CSR (Freeman et al. 2009). Subsequently, typical concepts emerged, such as Stakeholders' Sustainability and Social Reporting (De George 1987).

Initially, adoption of business ethics and CSR courses was debatable (McDonald and Donleavy 1995). In recent years, corporate scandals, triggered by lack of ethical considerations, redefined the necessity of these courses (Gorenak 2011). Consequently, these courses have been adopted by renowned business schools worldwide (Christensen et al. 2007).

Figure 13.1

Forces Shaping the Domain of Business Ethics Curriculum

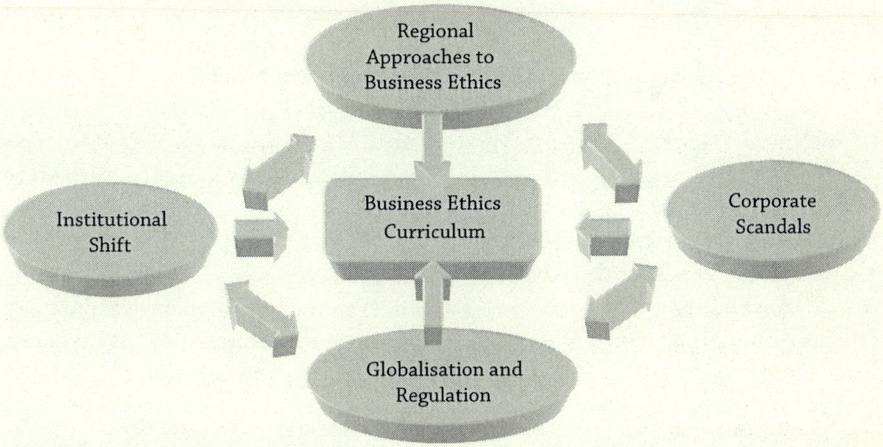

Source: Crane and Matten, 2004: 360.

Crane and Matten's (2004) investigation of business ethics curriculum emphasised four driving forces: globalisation, financial scandals, regional differences, and institutional shift, which augmented role of various stakeholders (See Figure 13.1). Addressing corporate malpractices in USA in 1990s, McDonald and Donleavy (1995: 840) states, 'business scandals have resulted in calls for more governmental regulations, however awareness for the need of ethical education has also become apparent'.

Similarly, emphasising practical implication of effective business ethics education, Cornelius et al. (2007: 118) argued that, 'for organisations to embrace ethically and socially responsible thinking, the provision needs to be 'proactive', with fundamental ethics programmes taught by committed and engaged business schools.' These perspectives view ethics education as a critical prerequisite to ensure responsible corporate behaviours. Curriculum development in business ethics is a global concern today due to prevalence of corporate malpractices, and economic downturns worldwide (Fernando

2009). Initially, the idea of introducing these courses in business schools was criticised (Aslop 2003). McDonald and Donleavy (1995) discussed some conventional arguments against these courses including the points that primary purpose of business is profit-maximization, inability of a course to change innate individual values and ethics' subjectivity.

However, these traditional objections are gradually disappearing with changing global corporate landscape (Krehmeyer 2007). Buchanan (2003) argued against some misconceptions related to these courses. Buchanan (2003: 1) comments, 'one argument against teaching business ethics is that, by the time students get to business schools, their values are already well-formed. This argument misses the point: Business Ethics are not personal ethics; rather it's the ethics of a profession, performing a specific role of society. Persons in such roles are judged by how well they perform the associated professional duties, not by personal proclivities'.

Recently, business ethics education has significantly broadened its horizon (Gorenak 2011). Matten and Moon (2004) suggested that today business ethics is synonymous to diverse terms, such as corporate citizenship, business and environment, stakeholder management, sustainability, and CSR. Business ethics courses worldwide have been labeled using these terms (Gorenak 2011).

Christensen et al. (2007) assessed ethics, CSR and sustainability education in prominent MBA programmes that illustrated two key aspects: increasing role of ethics education in strengthening the concept of CSR, and increasing corporation's role in minimising destruction of environmental resources. These findings demonstrate that today's business ethics education revolves around 'CSR' and 'sustainability' (Christensen et al. 2007). According to Bixby et al. (2012: 10), 'CSR, Business Ethics and Sustainability are closely related and can be seen as part of a single continuum.'

Crane and Matten (2010) suggest sustainable corporations are responsive to their diverse stakeholders. According to Petrick et al. (1999: 58-59), 'while many corporations rushed to secure short-term financial gain, their impulsive actions have been linked to social disintegration, low employee morale, predatory financial practices, and emphasis on limitless economic growth over sustainable development.' The significance of building sustainable corporations amplified the 'critical need' of introducing ethics and CSR courses (Krehmeyer 2007).

In this context, skills like ethical leadership and decision making can bestow sustainable competitive advantages on individuals and corporations (Petrick et al. 1999). These are the very skills that effective business ethics and CSR courses represent (Freeman et al. 2009). While emphasising pragmatic transitions in business schools, Krehmeyer (2007: 1) comments,

'Market drivers are pressing business schools to make these changes. These drivers originate from top of organisations, where the need is obvious, through to the recruiters, who are hiring newly minted MBAs'.

Essentially, these courses are playing a constructive role to make students think innovatively (Holland 2004). For instance, Holland's (2004) research of a CSR course taught at De Montfort illustrates how innovative methods can make students familiar with unconventional perspectives of accounting. Holland (2004) suggests that conventional accounting teaching does not encourage students to critically view the reality beyond the boundaries of corporation. For example, the traditional accounting methods only evaluate financial transactions, and it is incapable of evaluating environmental exploitations (Holland 2004). Additionally, most studies emphasise that to attain their ultimate objectives these courses should include innovative methodologies, and proactive initiatives by educational policymakers (Felton and Sims 2005).

Srinivasan et al. (2012) suggested that business schools worldwide are adopting these courses. They suggest there is notable presence of business ethics teaching in Europe, North America and East Asia. However, ethics education is still lagging behind in Oceania, South and Southeast Asia, Latin America, and Sub-Saharan Africa (See Figure 13.2).

Figure 13.2

Business Ethics Teaching Across Regions

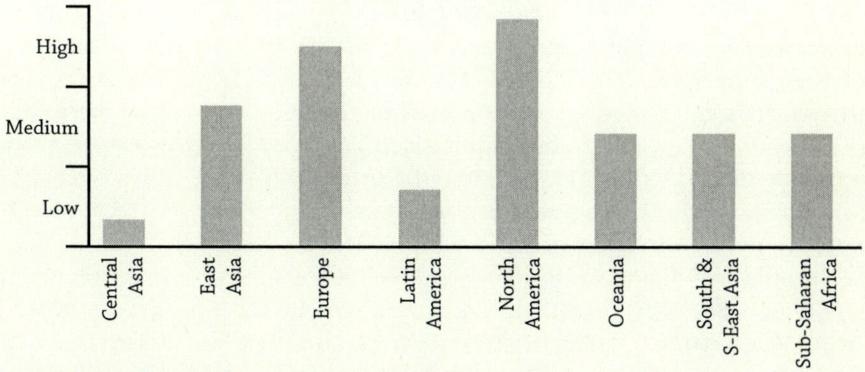

Source: Srinivasan et al. 2012: 5.

Fernando (2009) suggests that due to globalisation, there is increasing demand of business ethics teaching in Indian subcontinent. Corporations in South and Southeast Asia now recognise that technical knowledge on business ethics and CSR is imperative for long-run survival (Fernando 2009). There has been a relatively strong presence of business ethics education in Indian business schools (Srinivasan et al. 2012). In a survey conducted in 2010-11, "out of 57 academics that responded to the survey in India, 14 of them taught ethics in undergraduate programme and 42 of them taught business ethics, CSR, CG or sustainability in MBA programme" (Srinivasan et al. 2012: 5).

Subsequently, Srinivasan (2012) studied the state of teaching, professional training and research in business ethics in South and South-East Asia. Her study comprised a structured survey that focused on state of business ethics education, research and professional trainings in Bangladesh, India, Bhutan, Laos, Malaysia, Pakistan, Nepal, Myanmar, Cambodia, Sri Lanka, Thailand and Vietnam. Srinivasan (2012) suggests some positive trends, such as presence of business ethics is significant in these countries, as in all these countries 'business ethics' is taught either as core or elective module in most prominent universities. In contrast, CSR, sustainability, and CG (corporate governance) are comparably new, and in most cases there are convergences regarding key topics. However, these fields are also evolving. State of ethics education varies across countries. For instance, there are more specialised training centres in India, compared to other countries. However, presence of international consultants is noteworthy in countries like Bangladesh, Malaysia, Thailand, and Sri Lanka. He also suggests lack of specialised institutions is an impediment in implementing business ethics education in Bangladesh, Pakistan, India, and Malaysia.

Cornelius et al. (2007) argued that in order to deliver the expected potentials, business ethics education should be 'proactive'. It's also a matter of discussion how these courses should be designed for effective attainment of their objectives (Sims 2002). Due to unique nature of these courses, the effective methodology of their teaching has been a topic of discussion (Ritter 2006). Several studies emphasised how these courses can be made effective (Sims 2002). The necessity of interdisciplinary approaches and broader stakeholder engagements has been emphasised by several studies to improve the effectiveness of these courses (McDonald 2005).

Gandz and Hayes (1988) suggest business ethics should be taught in business schools as an integrated component in MBA programmes with two-fold attention to 'analytical frameworks' and their 'implementations' to actual business situations. Many studies also suggested that well-designed business ethics teaching can still have insignificant effect unless it adopts an interdisciplinary 'business-school-wide' dialogue about common aims and impediments (Brinkmann and Sims 2001). Srinivasan et al. (2012) put emphasis on practical methodologies to teach business ethics. According to Srinivasan et al. (2012: 19), "The use of short films, documentary and You-Tube clips needs to be deliberately included. Role plays have an enormous potential for active engagement.... Inviting speakers from the industry would allow for more contemporary practices to be discussed in classroom." To sum up, effective teaching of business ethics and CSR requires a coordinated process, involving clear goals, broader engagements, students' participations and proactive dialogues by stakeholders representing the academia, corporations and community (McDonald 2005).

Research Methodology

In this segment, methods used to attain the research objectives will be discussed along with the source of primary data and methods of data analysis. Considering the topic's subjective nature, a qualitative approach has been chosen. The empirical tools applied were 'content-analysis' (based on course-outlines) of eight business ethics and CSR courses taught in four selected business schools in Bangladesh, and face-to-face 'interviews' based on semi-structured questionnaires. The interviewees are 11 professional academics and course instructors at four reputed Bangladeshi institutions. These institutions are University of Dhaka (Institute of Business Administration), North South University (NSU School of Business and Economics), BRAC University (BRAC School of Business), and Independent University of Bangladesh (IUB School of Business). All these are renowned Bangladeshi institutions, having business ethics and/or CSR courses as core or elective modules at post-graduate and undergraduate levels.

This study has used qualitative method for gathering data. Generally, qualitative data is gathered by using qualitative interviews, focus groups and ethnographic observations. There are some rationales behind choosing a qualitative method. The topic is evidently subjective as perceptions regarding the issue can significantly vary, which requires elaborate discussion.

The Sample Frame

The study focused on four business schools in Bangladesh. The major criteria used for the selection of sample frame was whether or not the concerned business school has a business ethics (or/and CSR) course as core or elective module 'at both postgraduate and undergraduate levels'. Moreover, the four chosen universities have renowned business schools in the country, and they have very qualified instructors taking these courses who have substantial teaching experiences in the relevant field.

Research Methods

Many studies explored contents related to these courses. For instance, Cornelius et al. (2007) investigated CSR, corporate identity and ethics teaching of selected business schools using content-analysis of their websites. The content-analysis of this study is based on 'course outlines' of eight business ethics and CSR courses taught at undergraduate and postgraduate levels of four renowned business schools in Bangladesh (see Appendix A-13.1 and A-13.2).

The 'course-outlines' of these courses were collected from respective departments with consents of instructors. The course outlines are important tools for content-analysis, because they contain course descriptions, objectives, methodologies, and expected outcomes. These outlines are rigorously reviewed. Especially, the course objectives and expected outcomes have been highlighted. The major objectives of these courses were scrutinised to comprehend the benefits offered by these courses. Moreover, 'expected outcomes' provided indications regarding what outputs designers of these courses intend to achieve.

The literature review illustrated some key skills that these courses represent (Krehmeyer 2007). It has been investigated whether such competences (e.g. ethical leadership and effective decision making) are being addressed by these courses. The key words have been highlighted and it was analysed how these concepts are being presented. The findings have been depicted in a qualitative and analytic format.

Moreover, a semi-structured interview method has been used for this study. Semi-structured interviews are capable of exploring multifarious data to provide a comparably broader perspective. Although they require extensive conceptual interpretations, they generally provide elaborate perspectives. Additionally, semi-structured interviews elicit flexible discussions on subjective issues. The data collected through semi-structured interviews were audio-recorded and transcribed. The transcripts were reviewed meticulously, and notes were taken of recurring themes. Qualitative and thematic methods were used for data analysis, underscoring relevant words and concepts related to major research questions. The data was accordingly grouped, and organised to illustrate the research findings.

Participants Overview

The literature review suggests that several studies were based on data gathered by interviewing important educational policy makers (Schoenfeldt et al. 1991). Essentially, this qualitative study focused on opinions collected by interviewing 11 course instructors. All these instructors have at least 3 years of experience of teaching business ethics and/or CSR course. Academics from different backgrounds teach these courses in Bangladeshi business schools (Appendix A-13.3). Most participants hold a Ph.D.

Considering their diverse backgrounds, it can be expected that they will offer multidimensional viewpoints, which reflects the multidisciplinary nature of these courses. Moreover, there is a varied number of relevant course instructors in these universities. For instance, at NSU there are six course-instructors who take these courses at undergraduate and postgraduate levels. In contrast, at BRAC, one course-instructor teaches these courses (Appendix A-13.2). However, despite the variety, the common ground among the participants is that all of them have been teaching a business ethics and/or CSR course for a substantial period, and these are the academics who teach these courses at renowned Bangladeshi universities.

Research Questionnaire

It has been discussed earlier that Sims and Felton (2002) proposed four fundamental questions, which should be the foundation of an effective business ethics course. Those four questions and key research questions illustrated in section 1 were considered while developing a questionnaire for the interviews. The research questionnaire for the semi-structured interviews, aimed to elicit convincing answers to research questions. The questionnaire is mainly divided into three segments. The questions in the first segment aim to obtain experts' opinions regarding importance of teaching these courses in Bangladesh. The questions in this segment focus on significance and objectives of these courses. This segment aims to create a basis for subsequent discussions (see Appendix A-13.3). The questions in the next two segments are more technical and specific. These questions ask about the academic's opinions on skills that these courses 'aim to equip' the students with.

Findings from the Content Analysis

The literature review suggested that business ethics courses have been labelled in different ways worldwide (Gorenak 2011). Srinivasan (2012) suggests in South and Southeast Asia, business ethics courses have different titles, such as business ethics, CSR, CG and sustainability. Similarly, in Bangladeshi universities, these courses have been named using different relevant terms. The eight courses used for the study are as follows: Business Ethics, Legal and Ethical Issues in Business, Business Ethics and Leadership (1), CSR, Business Law and Ethics, Business and Environment, Business Environment, and Business Ethics and Leadership (2) (Appendix A-13.1). The course outlines of these courses depict comprehensive course overview, objectives, course-contents, and expected outcomes. The findings of content-analysis have been discussed in next few segments.

Significance, Methodologies and Topics of Business Ethics and CSR Courses in Bangladesh

Most course outlines illustrate their focus on enhancement of individual skills, such as students' ability of critical evaluation of ethical issues and ability to solve ethical dilemmas. Most courses use foreign texts. According to instructors, the main reason behind using foreign texts is absence of relevant texts written by Bangladeshi authors. The course outlines suggest, local articles and case-studies are amply used to compensate absence of local texts. The teaching methodologies, as depicted in course-outlines, are diverse. Apart from lectures, most courses include practical methodologies such as case-studies, group discussions, primary research, lecturing by industry experts, and seminars on relevant issues. As suggested by Srinivasan et al. (2012), these practical methodologies are extremely effective.

According to the 'course contents' of the outlines, a range of topics are covered, including theories of business ethics and CSR, business environment, stakeholders management, CG, and ethical issues in different functional areas of business. For example, the course titled 'Business Ethics', which is offered for BBA students at NSU, encompasses ethical issues related to each functional area of business administration. It encompasses topics like 'Ethics and HRM, Ethics and Marketing, Ethics in Finance, and Ethical Implications of Technology'. This manifests the multidisciplinary nature of these courses.

Business Ethics and CSR Courses in Bangladesh: Focus on Distinctive Skills

A key objective of the study is investigating what distinctive skills business ethics and CSR course intend to equip students with. The course outlines illustrate various skills that these courses offer. These are mainly stated in 'course objectives' and 'expected outcomes' segments. Some of these skills include a better understanding of the macro-environment of business and its various stakeholders, an eloquent understanding of ethical issues in business, ability to formulate codes-of-ethics and CSR programmes independently, greater critical reasoning, and effective decision-making.

According to the reviewed course outlines, a common objective of these courses is enhancing critical awareness and adaptability of students regarding the broader environment of business. Moreover, most courses address the need of appreciating the role of stakeholders. 'The Stakeholder Theory' (Crane and Matten 2010) is a common topic taught in most of these courses.

Moreover, these courses focus on other specific skills such as 'critical reasoning', 'moral judgement' and enhancement of 'ethical decision making'. For instance, some of the stated objectives of the course titled 'Business Ethics' which is offered for BBA students at North South University are:

> To enhance our moral sensibility and expand our capacity for moral inquiry, dialogue and decision making in ways that will be useful in our professional and civic lives...To jointly examine thoughtful ideas and perspectives in the field of business ethics and extend these perspectives to administrative practice and decision making.

Additionally, some of these courses focus on enhancement of more technical abilities related to CSR and business ethics. The course titled 'CSR' which is offered for undergraduate students at Independent University represents topics like 'implementation and integration of CSR into strategy and culture' and these topics are discussed in conjunctions with relevant CSR case studies in different global contexts.

The course outlines demonstrate that these courses are diverse in terms of topics, and most of them have significant global dimensions, focusing on ethical cases related to foreign contexts. This manifests that these courses facilitate analytical discussions on local, as well as, global issues.

Findings from Qualitative Interviews

The previous segment illustrated the findings of content-analysis. Additionally, 11 course instructors of these courses were interviewed using a semi-structured questionnaire. The questions and related discussions revolved around importance of teaching these courses in Bangladesh, the specific skills they aim to equip students with, and the applicability of these skills at professional level. In this segment, findings of the interviews will be depicted.

Importance of Teaching Business Ethics and CSR in Bangladesh

According to the participants, there are several important factors that signify incorporation of these courses into Bangladeshi business schools. These factors include prevalence of corruption, weak corporate governance, inadequate law enforcements, and international pressures. Most participants argued that Bangladeshi business schools should adopt these courses because it is a third world country and corruption is rampant there. There is a strong foothold of corruption in both private and public sectors, which is an impediment for sustainable development. The participants suggest that to counteract corruption, future business leaders should be equipped with effective knowledge on business ethics and CSR, which can enable them to establish sustainable corporations. Dr Akbar Ali (72 years), professor of BRAC University, comments:

> In Bangladesh, it is even more important because we are one of the most corrupt societies... in Bangladesh, there is a belief that corporations are immune to law. If ethical education can be introduced at inception, it can create responsible business people.

Most participants addressed that another important reason why these courses are important in Bangladesh is insufficient corporate law and law enforcement. They emphasised the importance of playing a pivotal role in an environment, which is characterised by weak corporate governance and ineffective legal frameworks. The participants also argued that the legal discourse in the country should be supplemented by individual moral judgments. Shahab Uddin (45 years) of North South University comments,

> The existent legal discourse in the country is quite orthodox, which is characterized by a positivistic notion of law...We try to make students understand the limits of law, which is even more important in a country like Bangladesh. How moral judgments can compensate gap of legal enforcement.

This statement supports Srinivasan's (2012) argument that in many countries of South and Southeast Asia, there is an absence of needed institutions. Another broader issue emphasised by participants is that nowadays there are significant 'international pressures' on corporations to operate ethically. This macroeconomic scenario, characterised by international pressures and global competitions, has made local corporations think more circumspectly about their social responsibilities. The participants suggest that the mounting volume of international trade triggered a demand for updated knowledge of CSR and business ethics.

According to most participants, these courses are important to all business students irrespective of region, due to shifts in global business environment (Gorenak 2011). However, they suggest that business ethics and CSR education has both contextual and global dimensions. They suggest like any regional context the socio-cultural and corporate landscapes of Bangladesh have some unique characteristics. Therefore, curriculum of these courses should be tailored to address those local issues. This perception echoes the findings by Crane and Matten (2004) who suggested that 'globalisation', as well as, 'regional differences' are two key aspects that determine business ethics curriculum. The participants also emphasised several skills that these courses intend to endow students with. These skills have been discussed in next segment.

Business Ethics and CSR Courses: Exploration of Distinctive Skills

A key objective of the study is investigating distinctive skills that these courses aim to equip students with. The participants suggest that these courses aim to endow students with important technical skills, which endorses the theoretical premise of the study (Freeman et al. 2009). Moreover, participants express that these skills are significant in a setting characterised by corruption, and weak corporate law. In such context, abilities like ethical decision making, leadership, and critical evaluation of corporate strategies can add important value into students.

According to participants, some key skills that their courses intend to equip students with are improved decision-making, greater awareness and analysis of broader environment and stakeholders, problem solving ability regarding ethical issues, and ethical leadership. Most participants suggested the courses they teach are multidisciplinary and practical. While responding to the question: How the course CSR differs from other business and management courses?, Tarafdar Rafiqul (42 years) of IUB comments, "The basic difference is there are fewer theories in CSR...there is less theory, more discussions and more practical orientation." Similarly, Muhammad Ali (48 years) of NSU suggests:

> Business ethics is a practical course. Generally these students work for banks, MNCs and other corporations. They require technical capability to make effective decisions. That's something we aim to deliver in a course like this... how to consider numerous scenarios while making decisions.

Most participants emphasised 'enhanced decision-making capability' as the foremost ability that they aim to offer students who go through these courses. The participants suggest these courses aim to improve problem solving skills of students on business ethics and CSR. Most participants argued that these courses provide students with relevant preliminary exposures that can help them take the knowledge to the next level.

While answering what specific skills these courses intend to equip students, Akbar Ali (72 years) comments, "Things like how to conduct an Ethics Audit and Assessment of Ethical Standards can improve specific skills of students. It provides them with a starting in the world of business ethics." Similarly, Muhammad Ali (48 years) of NSU, emphasised skills related to interactions with stakeholders. He commented:

> The course improves their fundamental problem solving skills in the area of how to negotiate in a politically correct way, how to be fair with partners in value-chain and how to manage workers, suppliers and interest groups more effectively.

Most participants emphasised practical benefits that they want to deliver through their courses. Shahab Uddin (45 years) of NSU commented,

> Ultimately, we aim to produce skilled managers. Their job is to apprehend the limits of law and apply moral judgments where there is a vacuum of law. That's the 'skill' this course aims to build in students.

Furthermore, the participants pointed towards broader socio-economic and legal environment of Bangladesh and the importance of 'ethical leadership' that must characterise future business leaders, who can act as change agents. The participants suggested a broader objective of these courses is making students capable of synthesising their skills from different functional areas of business, which is a superior skill that modern business leaders must possess.

Conclusion and Limitations

To conclude, this study represented an endeavour to estimate the scope of skill building of business ethics and CSR courses in business schools. Although the empirical study focused on a small number of institutions in Bangladesh, it extensively reviewed attributes of these courses at global, as well as, local setting. The empirical study represents that prominent Bangladeshi business schools have structured business ethics and CSR courses that are being taught by teachers from different backgrounds. It also manifests that these courses are characterised by multifaceted methodologies. Additionally, the study emphasises that these courses are enormously important for an underdeveloped country like Bangladesh for many reasons, such as growing participation in international trade, prevalence of corruption, and insufficient law enforcement. These factors necessitated formal ethics education for future business leaders who can act as change agents. Essentially, considering this scenario, course instructors of these courses are aiming to equip students with diverse skills, such as enhanced decision making, ability to apply moral judgments in absence of law, ethical leadership, ability to critically analyse broader business environment, and improved knowledge of technical issues, such as Codes-of-Ethics and Ethics Audit. This finding underscores the technical dimension of these courses in making students more competitive that supports the theoretical premise of the study.

The prominent business schools of Bangladesh are adopting these courses, which imply an ascending market demand, and a positive prospect for its corporate sector that requires pioneering business leaders with knowledge on these topics. This study has depicted different aspects of the issue under discussion through review of pertinent literature, experts' opinions and analysis of data. However, this is a small scale study based on four business schools in Bangladesh, which is a developing country in South Asia. Due to limited time frame and limitation of resources, it was not feasible to broaden its scope. Therefore, findings of the study may not represent the trends existent at global level or even in other neighbouring countries in the region (Srinivasan 2012).

Moreover, there are many actors involved in the process of business ethics and CSR education such as teachers, students, and other educational policy makers. This study only focused on perceptions of one key actor of the process: the course instructors. More studies focusing on other important stakeholders can reveal significant patterns on the issue. Perhaps, bottom-up studies focusing on students and corporations can be conducted in future, and findings of those studies can be cross-matched with findings of this study. On a positive note, this study has emphasised some important patterns of business ethics and CSR education in Bangladesh and in general. It can be expected that broader scale studies in future will reveal other significant patterns.

References

Aslop, R. (2003). "Right and Wrong: Can Business Schools Teach Students to be Virtuous?", *Wall Street Journal*, 17 September, R9.

Buchanan, B. (2003). "Teaching Business Ethics: One School's Notes", *Ethikos*, 17(2), September/October.

Brinkmann, J. and R.R. Sims (2001). "Stakeholder Sensitive Business Ethics Teaching", *Teaching Business Ethics* 5(2): 171-93.

Bixby, N., M. Buchanan, M. Cowan, T. Gattiker, S. Lowe, S. Park, K. Sewell and R. Terpend (2012). *White Paper on Teaching Ethics, CSR and Sustainability at Boise State College of Business and Economics.*

Christensen, L.J., Peirce, E., Hartman, L.P., Hoffman, W.M. and Carrier, J., (2007). "Ethics, CSR, and Sustainability Education in the "Financial Times" Top 50 Global Business Schools", *Journal of Business Ethics* 73(4), 347-68.

Cornelius, N., J. Wallace and R. Tassabehji, (2007). "An Analysis of CSR, Corporate Identity and Ethics Teaching in Business Schools", *Journal of Business Ethics* 76(1): 117-35.

Carroll, A. (1979). "A Three Dimensional Model of CSR", *Academy of Management* 4: 497-505.

Crane, A. and D. Matten (2010). *Business Ethics: Managing Corporate Citizenship and Sustainability in the Age of Globalization*. 3rd ed. Oxford: Oxford University Press.

Crane, A., Matten, D. and L.J. Spence (2008). *Corporate Social Responsibility, Readings and Cases in a Global Context*. 1st ed. Oxon: Routledge.

Crane, A. and D. Matten (2004). "Questioning the Domain of Business Ethics Curriculum", *Journal of Business Ethics* 54(4): 357-69.

De George, R. (1987). "The Status of Business Ethics: Past and Future", *Journal of Business Ethics* 6(3): 201-11

Felton, E.L.,Jr. and R.R. Sims (2005). "Teaching Business Ethics: Targeted Outputs", *Journal of Business Ethics* 60: 377-91.

Fernando, A.C. (2009). *Business Ethics an Indian Perspective.* 5th ed. New Delhi: Dorling Kindersley Pvt. Ltd.

Freeman, R.E., L. Stewart and B. Moriarty (2009). "Teaching Ethics in the Age of Madoff", *The Magazine of Higher Learning* 41(6): 37-42.

Gorenak, S. (2011). *Responsible Education and Innovative CSR. Management, Knowledge and Learning, International Conference.* pp.513-521.

Holland, L. (2004). "Experiences from a Student Programme Designed to Euxenite Role of the Accountant in CSR", *International Journal of Sustainability in Higher Education* 5(4): 404-16

Haque, E., N. Farha and M.B. Jalil (2007). "Status of Corporate Governance in Bangladesh", *EWU Working Paper* No. 2.

Krehmeyer, D. (2007). "Teaching Business Ethics a Critical Need", *Bloomberg Business Week*, 25 October.

Khan, A.R. (2009). *Business Ethics.* 2nd ed. Dhaka: Brothers Publication.

Matten, D. and J. Moon, (2004). "CSR Education in Europe", *Journal of Business Ethics* 54: 323-37.

McDonald, G.M. (2005). "A Case Example: Integrating Ethics into the Academic Business Curriculum", *Journal of Business Ethics* 54(4): 371-84.

McDonald, G. and G. Donleavy (1995). "Objections to Teachings of Business Ethics", *Journal of Business Ethics* 14(10): 839-53.

Petrick, J.A., R.F. Scherer, J.D. Brodzinski, J.F. Quinn and M.F Ainina (1999). Global Leadership Skills and Reputational Capital, *Academy of Management Executive* 13(1): 58-70.

Ritter, B.A. (2006). "Can Business Ethics be Trained? A Study of Ethical Decision Making Process in Business Students", *Journal of Business Ethics* 68: 153-64.

Schoenfeldt, L., D. McDonald and S. Youngblood (1991). "The Teaching of Business Ethics: A Survey of AACSB Member Schools", *Journal of Business Ethics* 10(3): 237-41.

Shill, N.C. (2008). "Accounting for Good Corporate Governance", *JOAAG* 3(1): 22-31.

Srinivasan, P., V. Srinivasan and R.V. Anand (2012). "Status of Ethics, Corporate Governance, CSR and Environment Education in Business Schools in India: An Exploratory Study", *IIMB Working Paper* No. 362.

Srinivasan, V. (2012). "Business Ethics in South and Southeast Asia", *Journal of Business Ethics* 104(1): 73-81.

Sims, R.R., and J. Brinkmann (2003). "Business Ethics Curriculum Design: Suggestions and Illustrations", *Teaching Business Ethics* 7(1): 69-86.

Sims, R.R. (2002). "Business Ethics Teaching for Effective Learning", *Teaching Business Ethics* 6(4): 393-410.

Appendices

Appendix A-13.1

List of the Courses Used for the Content Analysis

	Name of the Course	*Course Code*	*University*	*Program*
1.	Business Ethics	BUS 401	North South University (NSU School of Business)	BBA
2.	Business Law and Ethics	BUS 518	North South University (NSU School of Business)	MBA
3.	Legal and Ethical Issues in Business	BUS 515	Independent University Bangladesh (IUB School of Business)	MBA
4.	CSR	MGT 401	Independent University Bangladesh (IUB School of Business)	BBA
5.	Business and Environment	BUS 503	BRAC University (BRAC School of Business)	MBA
6.	Business Environment	BUS 203	BRAC University (BRAC School of Business)	BBA
7.	Business Ethics and Leadership	W620	Dhaka University – Institute of Business Administration	MBA
8.	Business Ethics and Leadership	W502	Dhaka University – (IBA)	BBA

Appendix A-13.2

Participants' List: Name and Particulars of Business Ethics and CSR Instructors

	Name	*University*	*Course*	*Qualifications and Higher Study Information*
1.	Dr. A.K. Mohammad Ali	North South University	Business Law and Ethics	Ph.D. in Company Law University of Manchester, UK. LL.M in International Business Law University of Manchester, UK
2.	Dr. Akbar Ali Khan	BRAC University	Environment and Business and Business Environment	PhD. In Economics Queen's University, Canada
3.	Dr. Shibly Noman Khan	Independent University Bangladesh	Legal and Ethical Issues in Business	Ph.D. in Management University of Queensland, Australia
4.	Mr. Tarafdar Rafiqul Islam	Independent University Bangladesh	Corporate Social Responsibility	MBA, Saint Cloud State University, USA
5.	Dr. Shahab Uddin	North South University	Business Law and Ethics	PhD in International Law SOAS, University of London
6.	Mr. Faisal Wali	North South University	Business Ethics	MBA, Cardiff University, UK (IFC certified BE Trainer)
7.	Dr. Mahbubur Rahman	North South University	Business Ethics	Phd. in Political Science Clark Atlanta, USA
8.	Sheikh Morshed Jahan	University of Dhaka – Institute of Business Administration (IBA)	Business Ethics and Leadership (1)	AM, Duke University, USA
9.	Ms. Dilara Afroz Khan	North South University	Business Ethics	MBA, New York State University
10.	Barrister Ishtiaq Ahmed	North South University	Business Ethics	BAR AT LAW City University, UK LLM, University of London
11.	Ms. Sutapa Bhattacharjee	University of Dhaka – Institute of Business Administration (IBA)	Business Ethics and Leadership (2)	MBA, Willamette University, USA

Appendix A-13.3

Qualitative Interview Questionnaire

General Introduction

Name of the course instructor:
Business Ethics/CSR courses he/she takes:
Name of the institution he/she teaches at:
Age:
Gender:
Ph.D.:
Higher education information:
Do you go to conferences/seminars in Bangladesh or abroad:
Date of the Interview:

1. Evaluating the importance of Business Ethics/CSR courses in Bangladesh and assessing their objectives and key focus areas:

- What is the significance of teaching Business Ethics and CSR courses in Bangladeshi business schools?
- When did you start teaching Business Ethics/CSR? How long your department been teaching Business Ethics/CSR?
- Why do you teach Business Ethics/CSR? How is it different from teaching other business and management courses like organisational behaviour, finance, marketing or management?
- What are the key topics covered by the course that you teach?
- What are the objectives of your course?
- Do you use a textbook? How do you select your reading materials for the course?
- Is there anything you would like to change about the way it is taught?

2. Evaluating the aim of business ethics courses in building sustainable skills in students:

- Does your course on Business Ethics/CSR aim to equip students with specific skills and abilities as the targeted output of the course? (What are those skills or targeted outputs?)
- How are you addressing this issue through your teaching and chosen methodologies?
- What are the expected outcomes of your course?
- In your opinion, why these expected outcomes are important for Bangladeshi students?

3. Evaluating how Business Ethics/CSR courses can help students improve their career prospects from the viewpoint of designers and instructors of these courses:

- How is your course preparing students for their career?
- In your opinion, can your course help students in improving their career prospects? (How, if yes?)
- Once at work, how do you expect students using the course material in their daily activities?
- Do you think knowledge about Business Ethics/CSR gives your students an advantage over other graduates who have not been taught the component?

- How is the general response from the students regarding the course? Do you find them to be interested or enthusiastic about it?
- Have you received any feedback from your previous students regarding the course?
- Do you think you will have to change the course contents and the way it is being taught in the future depending on changes in student's perceptions about Business Ethics/CSR?

General Overview Questions

Finally, is there anything else you would like to add to the discussion that hasn't come up during the interview?

Best Practices in Corporate Social Responsibility

14

TULSI JAYAKUMAR

Mahindra & Mahindra

Rising to be a Socially Responsible Corporate

Background of Corporate Social Responsibility in India

Officially, the focus on CSR (corporate social responsibility) at the policy level began in India with the issuance of the Corporate Social Responsibility Voluntary Guidelines in 2009 by the Ministry of Corporate Affairs. This culminated in the enactment of Section 135 of the Companies Act, 2013, making CSR spending as well as CSR disclosure mandatory for large Indian companies fulfilling certain norms, viz., having a turnover of more than ₹1,000 crore, minimum net worth of ₹500 crore or having a net profit of ₹5 crore or more in a FY (financial year). Such companies are required to spend 2 per cent of their average PAT (profit after tax) in the three preceding financial years towards certain activities designated as CSR activities. Currently, the legal requirement is restricted to an enunciation of how the profits should be spent once they are made, rather than how profits are made themselves. Yet, a 2016 report by the Government of India (GoI) reported that of 7,300 companies in 2014-15, CSR spends by 4500 firms (about 60%), including some Tata group entities and Vodafone India Private Ltd. was declared zero during the period. The reasons given for zero spending included financial restructuring, loss, non-finalisation of CSR areas, delay in board approval for projects, technical and procedural difficulties etc.

This paper looks at the CSR followed by an Indian automobile giant and multinational, 'Mahindra & Mahindra' (M&M), with a view to understand the opportunities and challenges faced by Indian corporates falling under the ambit of the Companies Act. The company selected was the industry leader in 'CSR Best Practice' in 2015. As such, the learnings from the case could provide direction to other companies desirous of emulating best practices.

Corporate Social Responsibility@ M&M

M&M is the flagship company of the Mahindra Group—a US $17.8 billion global corporation set up in 1945, operating in 20 key industries, with an operational presence over 100 countries and employing more than 200,000 people. In 2016, the group was the world's largest tractor brand by volume, India's largest utility vehicle manufacturer, India's no. 1 vacation ownership company, top 5 IT service providers in India, India's largest multi-brand, pre-owned car company and the largest NBFC (non-bank financial corporation) in rural and semi-urban India.

M&M had been a socially responsible corporate since its inception, going beyond the legal and statutory requirements to make responsible investments in the community. The K.C. Mahindra Education Trust was set up in 1954, followed by the Mahindra Foundation in 1969. In 2005, during its 60-year celebrations, the company redefined CSR and pledged to commit 1 per cent of its PAT for its CSR initiatives specifically to benefit the socially and economically disadvantaged communities. Education was selected as the main thrust of CSR, since the company believed it was the main route to solve India's social challenges. However, the company also invested in the areas of public health and environment.

With the implementation of the new Companies Act, 2013, the provisions of the Section 135, Schedule VII, became applicable to the company. The company as such was required to clearly enunciate its CSR policy, along with providing the details of the programmes and activities undertaken by the company in pursuance of this policy.

In 2015, *Economic Times*, together with Futurescape and IIM Udaipur conducted a study of the 'Best Companies for CSR'. Of the 216 companies studied, only 18 per cent met the mandatory 2 per cent CSR norm. The study listed M&M as the top ranked company performing CSR (Majumdar et al. 2015)

CSR Policy of M&M

The CSR vision of the company was defined in line with its core purpose as:

> To focus our efforts within the constituencies of girls, youth and farmers by innovatively supporting them through programs designed in the domains of education, health and environment, while harnessing the power of technology. By investing our CSR efforts in these critical constituencies who contribute to nation building and the economy, we will enable our stakeholders and communities to RISE. The 'core purpose' of the company itself had been redefined

as "to challenge conventional thinking and innovatively use all our resources to drive positive change in the lives of our stakeholders and communities across the world, to enable them to RISE".

The company believed that responsible business practices included being responsible for business processes, products, engaging in responsible relations with its employees, customers and the community and thereby going beyond the statutory and legal compliances. It meant creating societal and environmental value for its key stakeholders.

In accordance with the new Companies Act, 2013, the company pledged to contribute at least two per cent of the average net profits made during the three immediately preceding financial years on CSR initiatives, with effect from 1 April 2014. The company further laid out that up to five per cent of this CSR expenditure in one financial year may be spent on building CSR capabilities. Further, any unspent amount out of the 2 per cent average net profits made during the three preceding financial years may be carried forward to the next financial year.

Corporate Social Responsibility Programmes and Activities

In 2015-16, the CSR programmes and activities of the Mahindra Group spanned 26 different projects activities/projects. These included:

Nanhi Kali: Founded in 1996, Nanhi Kali was a sponsorship programme which provided comprehensive academic (workbooks, study classes) and material (uniforms, bags, notebooks, socks and shoes) educational support to underprivileged girls in India from poor urban, remote rural and conflict afflicted tribal communities through an after school support programme. Since 2005, the project was jointly managed by the Corporate Foundations, namely the K.C. Mahindra Education Trust and the Naandi Foundation.

In FY 2016, the project supported the education of 1,20,466 girls. Of these, 14,918 girls were supported by M&M, while the Mahindra Group as a whole supported 53,049 girls. The balance girls were supported by other corporates and individuals.

The project operated across 10 states including Maharashtra, Chhattisgarh, Andhra Pradesh, Tamil Nadu, Delhi, Rajasthan, Karnataka, Haryana, Madhya Pradesh and Telangana.

The key outcomes of the project included an increase in both enrolment of girls in schools and curtailing dropouts to less than 10 per cent.

Mahindra Scholarships for United World College Students: The scholarships and grants programme of M&M was aimed at enabling students to overcome their financial challenges and pursue their educational dreams. Some of the scholarships had been provided to students to pursue opportunities for post graduate studies in reputed educational institutions overseas, while others had provided students from low income group families to earn vocational diplomas after completing their courses at government polytechnic institutes. The Mahindra Scholarships had enabled enable deserving students to study at Mahindra United World College of India in Pune. The company implemented this programme through the implementing agency, Mahindra United World College of India.

Research Projects of the Indian Council on Global Relations: This programme was aimed at Public policy research and knowledge generation on pressing national issues. The company implemented this programme through the implementing agency, Indian Council on Global Relations.

Mahindra World School Education Trust: The Mahindra World School educational trust was set up to promote education at various levels. It set up the Mahindra World School in Chennai in 2008, a CBSE school with classes from kindergarten to Class XII. The school had 600 children and 50 staff members. In 2016, the company proposed to construct an additional building to accommodate one more section for grade KG-12 which would benefit the community, as part of its CSR activities under this project. The company implemented this programme through the implementing agency, Mahindra World School Education Trust, Chennai.

Promotion of Education—Building a conducive learning environment in urban slums and rural india by encouraging grade specific learning and creating 'responsible citizens': The company, as part of its CSR programme sought to provide for e-learning, infrastructure, books and stationary, uniforms, shoes, promotion of civic education, development of an RLC Centre, road safety awareness rallies, driver training and installation of road safety sign boards. This initiative was seen as benefitting 11,25,739 people.

The company implemented these schemes in both local areas of its operations, as also in other states. Thus, these schemes were implemented in the local areas of operation, including Mumbai, Pune, Igatpuri, Nashik, Nagpur (Maharashtra), Zaheerabad (Telangana), Chennai (Tamil Nadu), Bengaluru (Karnataka), Rudrapur, Haridwar (Uttarakhand), Chandigarh and Pithampur (Madhya Pradesh). These were also implemented in other states such as Rajasthan, Uttar Pradesh and Jharkhand.

Mahindra Saarthi Abhiyaan: Another CSR programme was in the form of a scholarship programme for truck drivers' girl children, who had scored above average marks in 10th grade thereby encouraging them to take up higher education. 1,300 girls were given scholarships under this programme in the local area of Mumbai (Maharashtra). The company implemented this programme directly.

BAJA–Project Based Learning of Auto Engineering Concepts: As part of its CSR initiative of promoting education, the company undertook Baja—a project wherein undergraduate engineering students were provided with a platform in the form of a project that allowed hands on experience in all aspects of automobile engineering and interaction with the corporate world. The project aimed at and benefitted 12,500 students in the local area of Indore (Madhya Pradesh). This project was undertaken through the implementing agency–Society of Automotive Engineers India.

Rise for Safe Roads—Creating zero fatality corridor, Mumbai–Pune Expressway (MPE) over a period of 5 years: This was a first of its kind project creating a zero fatality corridor on the MPE in partnership with various government agencies and training long haul truck drivers for safe driving. As part of this initiative, 1,200 drivers were trained in 2015-16 and a MoU (Memorandum of Understanding) was signed with the Maharashtra State Road Development Corporation (MSRDC). This was done in Mumbai and Pune regions of Maharashtra, and through the implementing agency–Save Life Foundation.

J.C. Mahindra Memorial School: This involved supporting a school providing quality education to the 798 students from low income group families in Khopoli (Maharashtra). It was done through the implementing agency—J.C. Mahindra Memorial School.

ENACTUS—Promotion of Social Entrepreneurship Among Professional Students: Through this initiative, the company reached out to students and promoted social entrepreneurship resulting in the building of successful social business models. Further, the students were able to interact with business leaders and develop entrepreneurial skills. The programme, undertaken on a pan India basis, with the implementing agency–Students in Free Enterprise, benefitted 1,153 students.

A World In Motion (AWIM)—project based learning of mechanical concepts: As part of this initiative to promote education, Class V students were provided with a platform that allowed hands on experience in all aspects of mechanical concepts for building vehicles for road and water. Implemented through the implementing agency, Society of Automotive Engineers India, in local areas of operation—Jaipur (Rajasthan), Mumbai, Nashik (Maharashtra), Rudrapur, Haridwar (Uttarakhand), Chennai (Tamil Nadu) and Chandigarh, the project benefitted 54,449 students and teachers.

Mumbai Public Schools—Promotion of Education: Supporting 28 English medium MCGM schools from KG to 7th Grade, in Mumbai (Maharashtra), the initiative was implemented through the Naandi Foundation and benefitting 15,586 students.

Seva Mandir Trust: Under this initiative, the company aimed at providing quality education to 825 underprivileged children in the age group of 6-14 years, through 23 Shiksha Kendras. It was implemented in the districts of Udaipur and Rajasmand in Rajasthan, through the implementing agency, Seva Mandir.

Mahindra University: The initiative aimed at providing infrastructural support to Mahindra Educational Institutions (MEI) specifically towards construction of a hostel and lab facilities for civil and mechanical engineering colleges at Hyderabad.

Hunnar–Skill Development for Youth Increasing their Scope for Employability: This project aimed at promoting employment enhancement vocational skills and livelihood enhancement projects, provided skill training in auto sales and service in various parts of India including Jhajjar (Haryana), Bulandshahr, Sitapur (Uttar Pradesh), Ajmer, Bharatpur, Jaipur (Rajasthan), Mumbai, Pune, Nashik, Nagpur (Maharashtra), Coimbatore (Tamil Nadu), Bhubaneshwar (Orissa) and Betul, Harda (Madhya Pradesh). Implemented through the implementing agencies–Lend a Hand India, Kherwadi Social Welfare Association, Thakur Education Trust, Dr. Amte Foundation and Centurion University, the initiative led to 26,248 students being trained.

Mahindra Pride School (MPSs): The MPSs were established in 2007, with a view to provide livelihood training to for youth from socially and economically disadvantaged backgrounds. The schools provide training in hospitality craft, IT and sales. In FY 16, the Mahindra Group supported 5 MPSs in Pune, Chennai, Patna, Chandigarh and Srinagar through which 3,135 students were trained. Over 15,000 students had been trained since inception and 100 per cent had been placed till FY 16. M&M had been responsible in supporting the schools in Srinagar and Chandigarh which respectively skilled 523 and 602 students in FY 2016. The implementing agencies for this scheme were the K.C. Mahindra Education Trust Fund and Naandi Foundation.

Mahindra Namaste/Pride School Scholarship: These scholarships aimed at enabling socially and economically disadvantaged youth to undergo livelihood training at Mahindra Namaste Private Limited in Bengaluru (Karnataka). It was implemented through the Naandi Foundation.

Swachh Bharat Swachh Vidyalaya Programme: This initiative had two legs: (i) supporting CII, Delhi to construct eight public toilet blocks in Delhi as part of the Swachh Bharat programme. It was done through the implementing agency Mahindra Foundation (ii) cleanliness Drives, construction and maintenance of toilets were taken up to create 'open defecation free areas' in Mumbai, Pune, Igatpuri, Nashik, Nagpur

(Maharashtra), Zaheerabad (Telangana), Chennai (Tamil Nadu), Bengaluru (Karnataka), Rudrapur, Haridwar (Uttarakhand), Chandigarh, Lucknow (Uttar Pradesh), Noida, Delhi, Patna (Bihar), Bhubaneshwar (Orissa).This initiative was implemented directly by the company.

Under this CSR initiative, 1,170 toilets were constructed and 54,213 people benefitted in schools and the villages.

Multi-disciplinary Medical and Healthcare Services for Disadvantaged Sections of Society: The programme covered medical camps, mobile dispensaries, holistic HIV/AIDS programmes, health and wellness for traffic personnel, provision of healthy meals, cancer screening camps, health awareness camps, ear camps, TB care and medical check-ups and eye testing for truck drivers, driving test programme and 24 hour ambulance for road accident victims. Promoted in the local areas of operation in Maharashtra, Telangana, Tamil Nadu, Karnataka, Rudrapur, Uttarakhand, Chandigarh, Uttar Pradesh, Noida-Delhi, Bihar and Orissa, the initiative benefitted 1,76,721 people. It was implemented through implementing agencies—Sevamob, Life Education and Developmental Support, Cancer Patients Aid Association, Kripa Foundation, BSA Training Academy, Nashik Accident Medical Emergency Foundation, etc.

Lifeline Express: The company had regularly partnered with Impact India Foundation to sponsor the Lifeline Express–a hospital on wheels, catering to medical needs of rural people in remote areas who did not have access to quality medical facilities. This included diagnostic, medical and surgical treatment for preventive and curative interventions, including cataract, cleft lip and palate and deafness correction. It also provided treatment for dental and epilepsy treatment. Breast and cervical cancer screening was also offered. The programme implemented through Impact India Foundation benefitted 15,642 people in Rajasthan and Uttar Pradesh.

Healthcare Projects: With a view to promote preventive healthcare, the company initiated two healthcare projects: *Palcare*—Supporting the setup of a palliative care programme for people with chronic illnesses such as cancer, Alzheimer's, kidney failure, lung conditions and stroke.

Karo Trust: providing financial and psychological support to patients suffering from critical and life threatening illnesses. This project was implemented through implementing agency–Mahindra Foundation in partnership with the Jimmy S. Bilimoria Foundation and *Karo* Trust in Mumbai (Maharashtra).

Disaster Relief: The company had provided consistent and timely support to relief and rehabilitation initiatives in those parts of India affected by natural calamities by either directly contributing to the Prime Minister's or Chief Minister's Relief Fund or by directly engaging in rebuilding villages.

In 2015-16, this initiative took the form of relief and rehabilitation provided towards the Damu Nagar fire tragedy in Mumbai by providing immediate fire emergency services including water lines to fire brigade. This also included distribution of drinking water and meals for 3 days along with distribution of basic household amenities to families and books and stationary for school children affected by the fire. This relief benefitted 1,065 households which was implemented directly by the employees under the ESOPs (employee social options programme). Another such initiative was the Tamil Nadu flood relief, involving distribution of food, blankets, rations and utensils to 7,340 people by employees directly.

Jeevandaan—Blood Donation including Life Support for Thalassemia Patient: An ESOPs driven initiative that is held regularly across locations/plants, it includes a robust Thalassemia Programme to provide an uninterrupted blood supply for Thalassemia patients. This programme was implemented in all its local areas of operation and resulted in 14,889 units of blood collected in 2015-16.

Navdrushti—Eye Care and Vision Corrections: This initiative comprises of awareness drives, eye testing, distribution of spectacles and cataract surgeries for the deprived sections of society. Implemented through implementing agencies–Vision Spring, Ganga Mata Eye Hospital, Netra Jyoti Foundation and Tulsi Eye Hospital, Swajan Social Development and Health Education, the initiative benefitted 21,530 people in 2015-16.

Healthcare for the Differently-abled: This initiative aimed at providing mobility aids, nutritional support, conducting health camps and supporting livelihood development of persons with disability. Implemented in the local areas of operation in Maharashtra, Karnataka, Uttar Pradesh, Uttarakhand, through implementing agencies–The Association of People with Disabilities, Ganga Mata Eye Hospital and Comfort Dental Clinic, Spastics Center (Ashayen) and Suhrud Mandal, it benefitted 490 people.

Project Hariyali: Since 2007, the company was committed to increase the green cover by a million trees on an ongoing basis. The following projects/activities were part of this scheme:

- *Araku Project*: This involved tree plantation to increase green cover and improve the livelihood of farmers. In FY 16, the project planted 1.23 million trees in totality. This CSR grant enabled the planting of 8,50,000 trees in the tribal Araku valley belt in Andhra Pradesh.
- *Increasing Green Cover & Maintenance of Green Zones*: 2,03,674 trees were planted under this scheme in the local areas of operation in Maharashtra, Telangana, Tamil Nadu, Karnataka, Uttarakhand and Chandigarh.

Project Hariyali was implemented through implementing agencies—Naandi Foundation, ESOPs and Nashik Muncipal Corporation.

EHS+: M&M partnered with implementing agency-OSC to establish an EHS+ centre for training small and medium enterprises in the industrial sector, with an aim of promoting environmental sustainability in Pune (Maharashtra).

Mpowered–Rural Electrification through Solar Power: The initiative led to remote villages of Belwa and Basahi being electrified with home lighting and e-hubs for livelihood generation avenues. With the company implementing this directly, it benefitted 66 households and 330 people.

Jaldoot-Providing Safe Drinking Water to Schools and Villages where Water is Scarce and Contaminated: This initiative aimed at construction of water tank, borewells, provision of hand pumps, installation of RO plants and provision of water coolers in the local areas of operation in Mokhada, Palghar (Maharashtra), Rudrapur (Uttarakhand), Jaipur (Rajasthan) and Bengaluru (Karnataka). Implemented through the implementing agencies Vasai Janhit and Suryodaya Foundation, Swajan Social Development and Health Education Samiti and ESOPs, the scheme benefitted 11,061 people.

Donation to the Corpus of the K.C. Mahindra Education Trust: The company implemented this initiative directly with the objective of supporting schools and providing scholarships. This was implemented in Mumbai.

Krishi Mitr–Rural Development aimed at Improving Income Generation for Farming Communities: The programme, with the objective of rural development, included soil testing, advisory services, drip irrigation, community farming, seed culture farming, agri extension services, infrastructure development and capacity building resulting in improvement in agricultural productivity. Implemented in Mankepada, Raigad (Maharashtra), Sagar, Tikamgarh (Madhya Pradesh) and Ajmer, Alwar (Rajasthan), through implementing agencies–Swades Foundation, BAIF Development Research Foundation, Srijan, Rajasthan Rural Institute, Karm Foundation, Lok Nayak Jay Prakash Narayan Leprosy Eradication Trust, Sadguru Foundation, Dr Panjabrao Deshmukh Krishi Vidyapeeth, the initiative benefitted 49,635 farmers.

Integrated Watershed Management Programme (IWMP): The company entered into a PPP (public private partnership) with Government of Madhya Pradesh for watershed development at Damoh and Bhopal for increasing the ground water table by 30 per cent, resulting in increased agricultural productivity and improved living standards. Implemented directly by the M&M IWMP team, the scheme led to 1,812 and 112 million litres of incremental rainwater harvesting capacity at Damoh and Bhopal respectively covering 83 villages and 12,900 households.

Shiv Jal Kranti—Water Management in Drought Areas of Aurangabad, Marathwada Region: This project aimed at building new water storage structures and repairing of old structures leading to increased water availability during the dry season. Fifty six (56) structures were repaired or built in 34 villages, benefiting 38,357 people in 2015-16, through the implementing agency–Dialsa Foundation.

Seed the Rise: This initiative aimed at raising awareness and funds to support poor and marginalised farmers in drought hit regions of the country. This was implemented in Vidarbha and Raigad districts of Maharashtra through implementing agencies–Naandi Foundation, K.C. Mahindra Education Trust, Digital Green and Swades Foundation.

Wardha Farmer Family Project (WFFP): It aimed at enriching farmers lives through various agri productivity initiatives. Implemented through Naandi Foundation in Vidarbha, the project benefitted 305 farmers.

MRV Biogas Plant: This project involved production of Bio Gas/fertiliser for the local community. A tripartite agreement with Naandi Foundation and Mahindra World City Developers Limited was signed to set up a biogas plant which would convert food and other waste into energy which would be used in the local community. A testing lab has been set up and trials are on and 300 people benefitted in 2015-16.

Water Management—Rural Development Projects Strengthening Water Resources: This initiative aimed at fortification of check dams and water structures increasing water availability for irrigation for the local farming community and desilting of water structures creating greater catchment area during monsoon. Implemented directly in Igatpuri (Maharashtra) and Zaheerabad (Telangana), the project benefitted 50,328 people.

Sports Scholarship: This initiative aimed at promotion of sports through coaching and provision of sports kits for tribal youth. Implemented by the company directly in Nasik (Maharashtra) and Jaipur (Rajasthan), 2,000 sportsmen/women received scholarships and 50 received kits in 2015-16.

Adhata Trust: The company, through the implementing agency–Adhata Trust, provided medical assistance, social support and recreational activities for senior citizens through six community centres in Mumbai.

Janani Uthan—Skill Development for Women: This project sought to setting up Mahila Silai Centres and computer education for women to increase income generating activities for women in local areas of operation, Rudrapur (Uttarakhand) and Jaipur (Rajasthan). It was implemented through implementing agencies—Society to Create Awareness towards Life and Environment, Swajan Social Development and Health Education, and benefitted 2,800 women.

Infrastructure Support during the Kumbh Mela: The company provided infrastructure support for pilgrims and safety gear for police personnel in Nasik, through its employees directly under the ESOPs. This benefitted 50,000 people.

Supporting the Socially and Economically Backward: This programme aimed at supporting orphans, elders and low income groups through various initiatives throughout the year. Implemented locally in Noida (Delhi), Bhubaneshwar (Orissa), Mumbai (Maharashtra), Haridwar (Uttarakhand), Chandigarh, Pithampur (Madhya Pradesh) and Jaipur (Rajasthan) through implementing agencies–National Centre for Promotion of Employment for Disabled People, Adhata Trust, Ramakrishna Sevasrama and ESOPs, the scheme benefitted 12,773 people.

Other Projects: The company also supported deserving projects of reputed NGOs in the areas of education, health, environment and flood relief, such as those by NAGAR, Ammada Trust, St Jude's, Yuvak Biradari, World Vision, and Mahindra Foundation in Mumbai (Maharashtra).

Discussion

Given the mandatory nature of CSR in India, it would be important to analyse and distinguish Mahindra's CSR from the largely non-strategic CSR which is carried out by most Indian corporates. This would help point out the gaps if any, and also highlight industry best practices.

The company's average net profit for the preceding three years in 2016 was ₹4247.5 crore. The prescribed CSR expenditure (2% of the average net profits) for the company was ₹84.95 crore, which was equal to the amount spent by the company towards CSR activities in FY 2015-16. Thus, the company exhausted its required CSR spend.

Schedule VII of the Companies Act, 2013 contains the list of activities which may be included by companies as qualifying for CSR (Government of India 2014). The list amended in February 2014 included:

- Eradicating hunger, poverty and malnutrition, promoting preventive healthcare and sanitation and making available safe drinking water.
- Promoting education, including special education and employment enhancing vocational skills specially among children, women, elderly, and differently-abled and livelihood enhancement projects.
- Promoting gender equality, empowering women, setting up homes and hostels for women and orphans; setting up old age homes, day care centres and such other facilities for senior citizens and measures for reducing inequalities faced by socially and economically backward groups.

- Ensuring environmental sustainability, ecological balance, protection of flora and fauna, animal welfare, agro-forestry, conservation of natural resources and maintaining quality of soil, air and water.
- Protection of national heritage, art and culture including restoration of buildings and sites of historical importance and works of art; setting up public libraries; promotion and development of traditional arts and handicrafts;
- Measures for the benefit of armed forces veterans, wars widows and their dependants.
- Training to promote rural sports, nationally recognised sports, paralympic sports and olympic sports.
- Contribution to the Prime Minister's National Relief Fund or any other fund set up by the Central Government for socio-economic development and relief and welfare of the Scheduled Castes, the Scheduled Tribes, other backward classes, minorities and women;
- Contributions or funds provided to technology incubators located within academic institutions which are approved by the Central Government.
- Rural development projects.

Table 14.1 lists out the various CSR schemes/projects carried out by the company in the year 2015-16, the sector under which the CSR project is covered as per Schedule VII, the budgeted outlay and the actual amount spent on the programme (in ₹ crore). The company undertook 43 programmes in various areas/activities, spending more than its budgeted outlay of ₹84.95 crore.

Table 14.1

M&M CSR Projects: Details alongwith Amounts Spent

S. No.	*CSR Project/Activity Identified*	*Sector in which the Project is Covered (As in Schedule VII)*	*Amount Outlay (Budget) for Each Programme*	*Actual Amount Spent on the Programme*
1.	Nanhi Kali	Promoting education	5.69	5.69
2.	Mahindra Scholarships for United World College Students	Promoting education	6.19	6.19
3.	Research Projects of the Indian Council on Global Relations	Promoting education	2	2

4	Mahindra World School Educational Trusts	Promoting education	2	2
5	Promotion of Education	Promoting education	1.87	1.87
6	Mahindra Saarthi Abhiyan	Promoting education	1.54	1.54
7	BAJA	Promoting education	1.08	1.08
8	Rise for Safe Roads	Promoting education	0.92	0.92
9	J.C. Mahindra World School	Promoting education	0.66	0.66
10	Enactus	Promoting education	0.45	0.45
11	A World in Motion	Promoting education	0.45	0.45
12	Mumbai Public Schools	Promoting education	0.28	0.28
13	Seva Mandir Trust	Promoting education	0.27	0.27
14	Donation to the Corpus of the KC Mahindra Foundation	Promoting education	1.62	1.62
15	Mahindra University	Promoting education		
16	Hunnar	Promoting employment enhancement vocational skills and livelihood enhancement projects	4.68	4.68
17	Mahindra Pride School	Promoting employment enhancement vocational skills and livelihood enhancement projects	2.5	2.5
18	Mahindra Namaste/Pride School Scholarship	Promoting employment enhancement vocational skills and livelihood enhancement projects	1.44	1.44
19	Swachh Bharat Swachh Vidyalaya Programme	Promoting preventive healthcare and sanitation	5.09	5.09
20	Multi Disciplinary Medical and Healthcare Services for Disadvantaged Sections of Society	Promoting preventive healthcare and sanitation	3.26	3.26
21	Lifeline Express	Promoting preventive healthcare and sanitation	1.36	1.36
22	Healthcare Projects	Promoting preventive healthcare and sanitation	1.25	1.25
23	Disaster Relief	Promoting preventive healthcare and sanitation	0.94	0.94

contd...

.contd...

24	Jeevandan	Promoting preventive healthcare and sanitation	0.61	0.61
25	Navdrushti	Promoting preventive healthcare and sanitation	0.55	0.55
26	Healthcare for the Differently-abled	Promoting preventive healthcare and sanitation	0.26	0.26
27	Project Hariyali	Ensuring environmental sustainability	4.47	4.47
28	EHS+	Ensuring environmental sustainability	1.63	1.63
29	M-powered	Ensuring environmental sustainability	0.67	0.67
30	Jaldoot	Providing safe drinking water	1.55	1.55
31	Krishi Mitr	Rural development	5.47	5.47
32	Integrated Watershed Management Programme	Rural development	2.87	2.87
33	Shiv Jal Kranti	Rural development	1.5	1.5
34	Seed the Rise	Rural development	1.05	1.05
35	Wardha Family Farmer project	Rural development	1.00	1.00
36	MRV Biogas Plant	Rural development	0.9	0.9
37	Water Management	Rural development	0.38	0.38
38	Sports Scholarship	Promotion of rural sports	0.25	0.25
39	Adhata Trust	Promoting the setting up of old age homes, day care centers and such facilities for senior citizens	0.7	0.7
40	Janani Uthan	Promoting gender equality, empowering women	0.25	0.25
41	Infrastructure Support during the Kumbh Mela	Protection of culture	0.12	0.12
42	Supporting the Socially and Economically Backward	Measures to reduce inequalities faced by socially and economically backward groups	0.06	0.06
43	Other Projects	Promoting education/ promoting preventive healthcare and sanitation	0.14	1.09

Table 14.2

CSR Projects of Mahindra & Mahindra Classified as Per Schedule VII, Companies Act, 2013

Nature of CSR Activity Under Schedule VII	*Number of Projects of Mahindra & Mahindra Under these Heads*	*Amount Committed to these Projects (in ₹ Crore)*
Eradicating hunger, poverty and malnutrition, promoting preventive healthcare and sanitation and making available safe drinking water.	9	14.87
Promoting education, including special education and employment enhancing vocational skills specially among children, women, elderly, and differently-abled and livelihood enhancement projects.	18	48.64
Promoting gender equality, empowering women, setting up homes and hostels for women and orphans; setting up old age homes, day care centres and such other facilities for senior citizens and measures for reducing inequalities faced by socially and economically backward groups.	2	0.95
Ensuring environmental sustainability, ecological balance, protection of flora and fauna, animal welfare, agro-forestry, conservation of natural resources and maintaining quality of soil, air and water.	3	6.77
Protection of national heritage, art and culture including restoration of buildings and sites of historical importance and works of art; setting up public libraries; promotion and development of traditional arts and handicrafts.	1	0.12
Measures for the benefit of armed forces veterans, wars widows and their dependants.		
Training to promote rural sports, nationally recognised sports, paralympic sports and olympic sports.	1	0.25
Contribution to the Prime Minister's National Relief Fund or any other fund set up by the Central Government for socio-economic development and relief and welfare of the scheduled castes, the scheduled tribes, other backward classes, minorities and women.	1	0.06
Contributions or funds provided to technology incubators located within academic institutions which are approved by the Central Government.		
Rural development projects	7	13.17
Other projects	1	1.09
Total Projects	43	85.92

Table 14.2 analyses the various M&M projects on the basis of the Schedule VII activities, as also the proportion of overall spends on such activities. The highest spend was on promoting education, including special education and employment enhancing vocational skills specially among children, women, elderly, and differently-abled and livelihood enhancement projects. More than 50 per cent of the CSR spend was devoted to this area/activity. Eradicating hunger, poverty and malnutrition, promoting preventive healthcare and sanitation and making available safe drinking water with 17 per cent of the CSR spend and rural projects with about 15 per cent of the CSR spends were the second and third largest components in overall CSR spend.

Seventeen (17) of the 43 projects were undertaken in the local areas of operation of the company, while the remaining projects were located in the rest of India. The company spent 16.35 crore (about 19%) in local areas of operation.

Just about 1 per cent of such CSR spend was expended by the company through direct implementation. Ninty nine (99) per cent of CSR funds were spent through implementing agencies or through the corporate foundation.

How can we view the large spends on education and rural health and projects, especially in local areas? The company, being an Indian multinational in the automobile sector with its production of automobiles and tractors, would do well to create shared value. CSR, while not directly connected with the areas of business interest needs to be aligned to synergistic business interests for it to constitute strategic CSR.

We find that M&M's CSR can be construed as 'strategic CSR'. While the company spent a certain proportion of its funds on multiple CSR projects and schemes, the bulk of CSR was on ramping up the health and education within India, since it is healthy and educated adults who could add to the working population, possess purchasing power, and thereby spend on the products manufactured by M&M. This also was the logic for concentrating a large proportion of the funds on the rural projects.

The Act provided that the Company should give preference to the local area and areas around it where it operates, for spending the amount earmarked for CSR. However, strategic considerations prevented the company from concentrating its spend in areas of local operations and around its manufacturing hubs. The company's products sold all over India, and as such the earmarking of CSR spends for local areas alone would not have made strategic sense.

An Ernst & Young study in 2013 pointed out that about 60 per cent of the top 50 Indian companies in the S&P BSE 100 Index 'managed' CSR from within the organisation, either through dedicated CSR departments or handling the responsibility through the human resources function or the corporate communications department. About 40 per cent had established their own non-profit entity to manage and execute such CSR initiatives. As regards implementation, partnership of NGOs (non-governmental organisations) was the most preferred route, with few companies implementing CSR initiatives directly.

The board level CSR committee at M&M was responsible for monitoring CSR policy from time to time, as also managing CSR modalities. However, 99 per cent of the implementation was done through implementing agencies. This brings to the need for expert managerial professionals in the CSR space with the requisite competencies who could implement CSR effectively, thereby ensuring the efficiency of CSR spends.

The company won the following accolades for the best practices in the ESG dimension in 2015:

- Receiving 'Sustainable Plus Platinum Label' for FY 15 from CII-CESD;
- Receiving 'Excellence in Sustainable Supply Chain Award 2015' in the CII-ITC sustainability awards;
- Ranking first in CSR in 'The Best Companies for CSR' study conducted by *The Economic Times* (Futurescape and IIM Udaipur);
- Receiving 'Golden Peacock Award for Risk Management' from the institute of directors;
- Retaining the status of getting listed on the Dow Jones Sustainability Index – 2015 under the 'Emerging Market Index' for the consecutive third year with improvement in percentile scores;
- Retaining its position in the top 10 in the India 200 Carbon Disclosure Leadership Index 2015;
- The Mahindra Group Sustainability Report was short listed amongst the finalists of Asia Sustainability Reporting Awards by CSR Works.

Conclusion

Mahindra is a large Indian corporate, both from the agency and resource-based views. Following the agency approach, it had standardised tools for performance evaluation and monitoring, and multiple stakeholders, while following the resource-based view, the company had a formal organisational structure and a professional management team running it, as well as clearly defined business objectives and markets that provided opportunities for reaping economies of scale.

The size of the firm has an impact on its CSR manifestation. CSR in large firms is usually driven by business case rhetoric, viz., risk reduction, brand enhancement, anticipation of regulation and socially responsible investment. Further, it is vulnerable to external pressure. However, its background as a family managed business meant that its CSR priorities were internally driven based on the owners' values in setting priorities (Porter and Kramer 2011). Thus, we witness M&M's CSR being in the field of promoting education right since its inception. In this sense, it displayed a small firm orientation. Over time, the CSR priorities came to be determined by owners/top management in conjunction with professional managers, based on synergistic business interests.

As a large company, M&M demonstrates an extensive web of stakeholder relations leading to a wide range of CSR foci for the firm. M&M may need to focus on few, widely distributed CSR projects, which may have a larger impact than multiple small projects. It may be possible to club the efforts towards promoting education into one-two nation-wide projects, rather than having commitments towards 18 different projects.

The company has managerial expertise to undertake strategic planning of CSR. Further, it exhibits a range of approaches from proactive (for instance Nanhi Kali) to reactive (for instance, Rise for Safe Roads). The company may need to pay greater attention to implementation issues. While the company has its own foundations, a large number of projects are being implemented through multiple partner agencies. The company will need to put in place mechanisms for effective monitoring and evaluation of these multiple agencies.

As regards direct implementation, the company has in place a scheme for ESOPs. Mahindra employees have been encouraged to volunteer for various CSR projects in the areas of health, education and the environment through the ESOP. While employee buy into corporate CSR is critical for its success, and employees can be used to communicate such CSR more credibly, it is imperative to link key performance indicators of employees in various verticals to their performance on twin objectives: business objectives and the sustainability objectives. The company's sustainability objectives could thus be integrated with its larger business objectives.

While the company is currently measuring the impact of its CSR on corporate social performance through impact assessment measures, it is important to relate such CSP to CFP (corporate financial performance). This will help the company to rationalise the multiple programmes, and concentrate on those programmes, which have the maximum impact both on society and for the company. The company may further carry out an analysis of the perceived and required CSR at the local community level, and this may inform its further CSR spends.

The Companies Act 2013, with its mandated CSR spends, will lead to an increase in the amount of CSR spending in India. Companies would do well to pay attention to the areas and activities that come under the purview of their CSR spend, so that firms can benefit in a synergistic manner. As the case of M&M demonstrates, strategic CSR has the potential to create shared value for multiple stakeholders, including the company itself.

References

Government of India. (2014). *The Gazette of India*. Ministry of Corporate Affairs. 28 February. Retrieved from *http://www.mca.gov.in/Ministry/pdf/CompaniesActNotification3_2014.pdf.*

Indian Express (2016). "Government Makes Public CSR Spending of 7334 Companies", *Indian Express*, 17 November. *http://indianexpress.com/article/india/india-news-india/govt-makes-public-csr-spending-of-7334-companies-4381030/*

Mahindra & Mahindra (2016). *Corporate Social Responsibility Policy*. Retrieved from *http://www.mahindra.com/resources/pdf/csr/CSR-Policy-2016.pdf.*

Majumdar, U., N. Rana and N. Sanan (2015). "Mahindra & Mahindra Tops CSR List in India as Companies Scale up Operations", *The Economic Times*, 26 October. Retrieved from *http://economictimes.indiatimes.com/news/company/corporate-trends/mahindra-mahindra-tops-csr-list-in-india-even-as-companies-scale-up-operations/articleshow/49330470.cms.*

Porter, M.E. and M.R. Kramer (2011). "Creating Shared Value", *Harvard Business Review* 89(1-2): 62–77.

Others

Annual Report 2015-16. Retrieved from *http://www.mahindra.com/resources/pdf/about-us/Annual-Report-2015-16.pdf*

Corporate Social Responsibility in India. Potential to Contribute towards Inclusive Social Development, 2013. Retrieved from *http://www.ey.com/Publication/vwLUAssets/EY-Government-and-Public-Sector-Corporate-Social-Responsibility-in-India/$File/EY-Corporate-Social-Responsibility-in-India.pdf.*

15

JIBITESH RATH and P. SHYAM

Corporate Social Responsibility @ National Mineral Development Corporation Ltd

Business and Social Vision of National Mineral Development Corporation (NMDC)

NMDC is a CPSE (central public sector enterprises) under the Ministry of Steel, Government of India, primarily engaged in the business of exploring minerals and developing mines to produce raw material for the industry. Today, NMDC is the largest Iron ore producer in the Country with four operating mines in Bailadila (Chhattisgarh) and two in Bellary-Hospet range (Karnataka), Diamond Mining Project, Panna in Madhya Pradesh among other operations. NMDC is also entering into manufacturing of steel by setting up a greenfield integrated steel plant at Nagarnar.

Being a responsible corporate citizen, it has been a pioneer in addressing its responsibility towards society. Its CSR (corporate social responsibility) programme is as old as the company itself. NMDC believes that the well being of society at large is a prerequisite for the progress of business and prosperity of the organisation.

While pursuing its business vision of expansion in ongoing activities in India and abroad, as also by diversifying into new areas of mineral exploration, NMDC seeks to add value to its CSR effort by aiming for eradication of illiteracy, minimising child and maternal mortality, poverty alleviation and affordable healthcare in the surrounding villages of its project areas.

Policy on CSR, Including Board Approved Policy

As already enunciated earlier, the philosophy underlying the CSR programme in NMDC is belief that the well-being of society at large is a pre-requisite for the progress of business and prosperity of the organisation. Keeping this in mind, policy makers in NMDC have framed a broad based, well thought out and transparent policy document with respect to its CSR programme.

Objectives

With the aforementioned philosophy and the principle of inclusive growth forming their core thought, the board of directors have laid out the following policy objectives of CSR in NMDC keeping the following focus areas in sight:

- Literacy/education/cultural development.
- Safe drinking water/healthcare and sanitation.
- Skill development for sustainable income generation and livelihood
- Agriculture and infrastructure development
- Promotion of sports
- Relief during the natural calamities etc.

Budget

The following are the guidelines for allocation and expenditure of CSR budget of NMDC:

- The budgetary provision in a FY (financial year) towards CSR initiatives shall be at least two per cent of the net profit of the company.
- If the allocated budget remains unutilised, it is carried forward to the succeeding year.

Consultative Mechanism

NMDC has spawned a unique and widely acclaimed consultative mechanism covering all the stakeholders right from village/community level to district level and extending right up to state government level coordination.

This consultative mechanism has been the subject of praise by no less an authority than the Department of Public Enterprises, Government of India, which has recommended NMDC's consultative mechanism for replication by other CPSE's.

Implementation

Coupled with this consultative mechanism, NMDC has a three pronged approach to directly implement CSR programme and these are:

- In partnership with State governments by entering into a MoU (memorandum of understanding) with the concerned State governments,
- Through reputed and experienced NGOs (non-governmental organisations)/SPs (service providers) or fellow public sector enterprises, on nomination basis, and

This has given the CSR programme at NMDC, immense flexibility and easy operability.

Monitoring

CSR proposals, as well as the corresponding budget proposals are examined by the CSR and Sustainability Committee of Directors, headed by an independent director and recommendations of the Committee are finally put up for approval of the board. Implementation is monitored through a system of joint inspections with the relevant service providers/NGOs/state government officials, and the monitoring of CSR programmes is done by CSR and Sustainability Committee during its review meetings.

Innovative Practices in CSR

NMDC's CSR has been acclaimed as an example, by the Department of Public Enterprises, Government of India, for other CPSEs to emulate. The comprehensive consultative mechanism adopted by NMDC's CSR programme has, especially been the object of praise. The inclusiveness of the CSR programme is enhanced by this multi-level consultation process. The involvement of stakeholders starts at the grass roots community level, followed by District level interaction and culminating in coordination with State governments has ensured conceptual clarity, effective implementation and proper monitoring of the CSR programmes in NMDC. This innovative consultative structure has given NMDC's CSR, a distinct edge, as also the variety of initiatives.

CSR Awareness among Employees

Given the long tradition of CSR in NMDC, it is common belief that each and every employee is aware of the Corporation's CSR effort. This awareness is further strengthened by the use of all channels of communication like house magazines, special issues of the in-House magazines, project joint Councils, Apex Joint Councils, SC/ST (scheduled castes/scheduled tribes) welfare association meetings, as also other welfare association meetings and of course periodical updates on the Corporation's website, to name a few.

Details of Contribution towards CSR in the Last 3 Years (including Efforts Towards Social Inclusion, Health Education, Skill Development etc.)

NMDC has been at the forefront of CSR and has been one of the biggest CSR spenders among CPSEs, as is borne out by the statistics for CSR expenditure in the last three financial years given in Table 15.1.

Table 15.1

CSR Spending by NDMC, 2012-13 to 2015-16

Sl. No.	Financial Year	CSR Expenditure in ₹ (Crore)
1	2012-13	101.10
2	2013-14	131.42
3	2014-15	188.65
4	2015-16	210.09

CSR Activities in the Recent Past

Following are some of the flagship CSR initiatives of the company:

Shiksha Sahayog Yojana

Shiksha Sahayog Yojana is a one of its kind initiative in the country, which NMDC has been implementing since 2008-09, for the SC/ST students who are natives of the Bastar division (which is presently divided into seven Districts) in Chhattisgarh state and residents of eight peripheral villages around Donimalai Project in Bellary District, Karnataka state and whose family income is less than ₹6,000 per month. This initiative was introduced in the backdrop of a high dropout rate among students hailing from the local tribal communities, despite the efforts of the Government's Sarva Shiksha Abhiyaan. This was primarily due to the inadequate educational facilities for students near their immediate neighbourhood, which discouraged students from continuing their education beyond primary level and parents also had no incentive to send a helping hand, who was supplementing their efforts in agriculture or other vocations.

The number of students benefiting from the scheme were around 7,500 in 2008-09, and it increased to 18,000 in the year 2014-15.

NMDC had adopted the process of direct crediting of scholarships into the bank/post office accounts of the beneficiary students. It would not be out of place to mention that this was a pioneering practice introduced by NMDC's CSR programme, which was later on adopted by the Central and State government authorities/agencies.

The scheme has been enriched with innovative activities like debate competitions, sports events, study tours, science exhibitions etc. to give opportunity for overall personality development of the students.

A study conducted by NMDC shows that the scheme has encouraged students to continue their studies. The scheme has also helped in improving attendance in schools and ensured better results.

Balika Shiksha Yojana

Balika Shiksha Yojana is a novel CSR initiative having a triple purpose of assisting girls from socio-economically disadvantage sections of society to pursue professional education, contribute to empowerment of women and also help in addressing the situation of acute shortage of medical and paramedical staff in Bastar Division. This program was initiated by NMDC in the year 2011-12. Initially, 25 girl students from socio-economically disadvantaged background were sponsored by NMDC for B.Sc (Nursing) and GNM (general nursing & midwifery) courses at Apollo Institute of Nursing at Hyderabad, the education arm of Apollo Hospitals. The success of the programme led to the enhancement of the number of students sponsored from 25 to 40. As on December 2016, 32 students were being sponsored for the three year GNM course and 8 students were being sponsored for the 4 year duration B.Sc Nursing programme. Till date, 225 students have been sponsored by NMDC for pursuing nursing courses.

This scheme has been framed directly in response to the needs of the communities surrounding NMDC projects. The need was assessed based on interaction with the local district administrations who had voiced their concerns about lack of adequate trained nursing professionals in the local hospitals/PHCs (public health centres), where only 33 per cent of the requisite nursing staff was available to render medical services to the local communities. Added to this was the concern about the inability of local tribal girls to pursue the professional courses in nursing, etc. due to socio-economic constraints.

Mid Day Meal Programme

Mid day meal is a programme of the Government of India which aims at addressing the dual problem of malnutrition as well as the issue of absenteeism and drop out among school children.

NMDC has been supporting the mid day meal programme in surrounding areas of the Donimalai project in Karnataka in partnership with Akshaya Patra Foundation since 2008-09 by providing monetary support to the mid day meal scheme to provide nutritious and wholesome meal during the school hours which includes items like chapatti, eggs etc., in the menu and has also contributed 2 dedicated vehicles for meal distribution.

In all, 8,000 school children in 38 schools of Sandur taluk in Bellary district are getting benefitted from the scheme.

Residential School at Nagarnar, Bastar, Chhattisgarh

Remote village locations, tough geographic terrain and various socio-economic reasons often prove to be a hindrance for acquiring education. As a result, many children from remote and backward villages of Bastar division do not get a chance to study.

In order to address this issue and provide local tribal children in Bastar region with a conducive learning environment, NMDC established a residential school at Nagarnar in the year 2010-11.

Teams of NMDC employees, both male and female personally visited remote hamlets in the left wing extremism affected villages of Bastar region and counselled the parents of children of school going age, convincing them to send their children to school. Consequently, most of the students who were admitted in the school were 1st generation school goers from their families, hailing from the deep jungle hamlets.

At present, the school strength is 513 students up to class IX with one higher class being added every year. Plans have been finalised to expand the school up to 10+2 in future. The initiative has created a positive impact in the area and admission to the school has become a much sought after goal amongst the local community.

Polytechnic College at Dantewada, South Bastar

Continuing with its efforts to provide technical education to the local youth, NMDC has established a Polytechnic College at Dantewada in year 2010-11 within the premises of education hub.

Plans are afoot to initiate new trades in the institute, which currently has an intake of 126 students per year in mechanical and electrical streams. As on December 2016, 418 students were pursuing their Diploma course in the Polytechnic (after taking into account lateral entry of 10 students in each branch in the second year of the diploma course).

The college has been granted exemption from central counselling to encourage professional technical education among students from Dantewada district/Bastar division. It is the only 'polytechnic college' in Chhattisgarh which is totally operated by a PSU (public sector undertaking) without any financial contribution from the State government of Chhattisgarh.

Education Hub

Factors like geographic terrain coupled with prevailing law and order situation have seriously hampered the chances of local children to get quality professional and technical education over the years. In the wake of this reality, Government of Chhattisgarh came up with a solution for establishing an 'education hub' at Geedam, Dantewada district which could act as an educational hub with institutions ranging from primary school to professional institutions like polytechnic, teacher training institute, livelihood college etc., in a single campus. The objective was to provide conducive environment to the local children for overall intellectual and physical development by providing them with quality educational facilities.

NMDC has actively partnered with the State government in this unique initiative and is supporting it in several ways. Some of the initiatives supported by NMDC in education hub are:

- *Astha Gurukul*: It is a residential school primarily for children affected by naxalite related violence apart from SC/ST/OBC and other underprivileged students from the local communities. NMDC has funded creation of physical infrastructure and facilities viz. Academic block, residential complex, staff quarters in Astha Gurukul. NMDC also supports regular operations of the school.
- *Hostel for Boys and Girls*: Construction of 1000 seater hostel for boys and girls respectively has been funded by NMDC in the Education Hub.
- *Polytechnic College at Dantewada*: The college has been established and is being operated by NMDC within the premises of Education Hub.
- *Saksham*: It is a residential school which has been established for children with special needs. The idea is to educate and train them at all levels and facilitate their schooling with appropriate aids and materials. NMDC has been supporting Saksham by bearing the regular operational expenditure of the school and has also financially contributed towards creation of the physical infrastructure. NMDC also takes pride in affirming that saksham school was one of the institutions visited by the Hon'ble Prime Minister during his visit to Dantewada in May 2015.

Integrated Village Development (IVD)

The initiatives under the IVD component have been successful in touching every aspect of the rural life and have started to show positive results in the direction of transforming these villages as model villages.

Various component of the IVD programme are:

- Agriculture and livelihood support services.
- Vocational training programme, and
- Nutritional support for children in 46 Anganwadi centres.

Starting with just 2 villages in 2009, the programme has expanded to 18 villages so far. The number of people getting covered under the intervention has also increased from 1,600 persons to 20,000 persons.

Innovative Programmes Launched and its Expected Positive Impact on General Public

Apart from continuing some of the existing novel initiatives, NMDC has initiated a few innovative CSR programmes, which are as follows:

- An elaborate sporting programme in the villages around NMDC's Bailadila Projects. The said programme is expected to provide an opportunity for the tribal youth to channelise their energies towards constructive activities like sports, exhibit their sporting talent and keep alive some of the sporting traditions of the local area.
- A cleanliness campaign in 16 villages around NMDC projects in Bailadila region under mission Swachh Bharat, with the objective of bringing about behavioural changes with respect to cleanliness through sanitation and hygiene promotion campaigns, capacity development of local government stakeholders and civil society and introducing a system of rewards and recognitions for incentivising cleanliness, as a way of life.

The Way Ahead for NMDC's CSR

NMDC's CSR is operating in a dynamic and fast changing world. Laws/Guidelines are regularly being amended, people's expectations are also increasing and the developmental needs of the nation are shifting over the years.

NMDC is now being asked to take up sunrise initiatives in the areas of Swachh Bharat, Skill India etc., besides, keeping up its good work in traditional focus areas. This is a challenge, for which, NMDC's CSR is gearing up.

Apart from the above, the need for transparency, inclusiveness and accountability in operating NMDC's CSR are also being addressed by strengthening the communication mechanisms with all stakeholders, automation of reporting systems and voluntary evaluation of effectiveness of CSR initiatives, to name a few.

Intangible/Unquantifiable Effects of CSR

Not all benefits of CSR activities are tangible or quantifiable. The intangible/non-quantifiable benefits of CSR are much higher and NMDC takes pride of these

Though NMDC has never sought to directly link its CSR programme to any of its business objectives, the only successful land acquisition for a green field project in the last decade of Indian corporate history, can invariably be attributed to the CSR efforts of NMDC in the backward Bastar region of Chhattisgarh, over the years.

Besides being a major contributor of revenue to the State and Central governments by way of taxes and levies, NMDC has over the years silently contributed to the steady socio-economic development of the Bastar region, as well as the areas around its other operational projects.

16

HARENDRA R. PATEL

Employee Engagement in Corporate Social Responsibility Activities

A Case of Birla Copper-Hindalco Industries Ltd.

Whatever your passion, whatever your gift, join US in giving back.

—CSR team, Birla Copper

Every day, all around the world, there are people in need. Helping meet those needs are hundreds and thousands of volunteers. Here are just a few.

—Birla Copper

Corporate Social Responsibility (CSR) in India

The Companies Act, 2013 had introduced the idea of CSR to the forefront, integrating it into the core operations of a company. It also suggested that CSR needs to go beyond the concept of philanthropy and providing goods and services. It is an undeniable fact that the private sector plays a major role in the way our economy, environment and society is shaped.

CSR is a concept whereby companies integrate social and environmental concerns in their business operations and their interaction with their stakeholders on a voluntary basis. CSR is all about a company knowing, managing and improving its impact on the economy, the environment and the society and work on the 3Ps model (planet, people and profit).

About the Organisation

Hindalco Industries Ltd., Unit: Birla Copper was established in April 1997 at Dahej village, Tehsil Vagra, District Bharuch of Gujarat. It is one of the largest single location custom copper smelters in the world with production capacity of more than 500 kt per annum.

Main Products

The business produces wide range of products and services catering to five industry segments: non-ferrous metals, precious metals, fertilisers, chemicals and power.

Product range includes copper cathode, CCR (continuous cast rod), precious metals (gold, silver, PGM), other minor metals (bismuth bi-sulphate, copper telluride, selenium), phosphatic fertilisers, sulfuric acid, aluminium fluoride, besides a host of other by-products e.g., phospho gypsum, copper slag, fly ash. The product caters to diverse end-use segments encompassing power and infrastructure, construction, railways, gems and jewellery and agriculture. Cathodes produced at Birla Copper are registered at London Metal Exchange as "Grade A" rendering global acceptance.

In fertiliser business, the company produces and markets Birla Balwan DAP (di-ammonium Phosphate [N-18% P2O5-46%]) and value added products which contain major nutrients nitrogen, phosphorous and minerals. DAP is basically used as basal dose which gives nutrition for roots, creating immunity for crop resulting into better growth and quality yields.

CSR Initiatives of the Company

To achieve the social objectives, the company's rural development activities span five key areas—education, healthcare, sustainable livelihood, infrastructure and espousing social causes—and the single-minded goal here is to grapple with the 'quality of life' challenges that underserved communities face, and working towards making a meaningful difference to their lives.

The Aditya Birla Centre for Community Initiatives and Rural Development provides the vision for the company's CSR initiatives under the leadership of its Chairperson, Mrs Rajashree Birla. The CSR committee of directors at the board level comprises:

- Mrs Rajashree Birla, Chairperson.
- Mr Askaran Agarwala, Director.
- Mr Jagdish Khattar, Independent Director.
- Permanent Invitee: Dr (Mrs) Pragnya Ram, Group Executive President, Corporate.

The company has undertaken grass root development in Vagra tehsil, District Bharuch, covering 69 villages, reaching out to 1.05 lakh population through "Integrated Programme for Rural and Community Development".

Under the CSR initiatives of the company, the project work was started from two pilot villages i.e., Dahej and Lakhigam in the year 1997.

Before implementing, the projects went through various stages of design, development and planning. Different research methodology, tools and methods were used for the collection of data in order to arrive at a particular conclusion related to the project. For the collection of data different NGOs, reputed institute, agencies like TCS, XISS, Faculty of Social Work, MS University etc., were engaged to generated the analytical reports of the various projects.

The company has received various awards and appreciation for its CSR initiatives in the financial year 2015-16 such as the award presented by FICCI, India CSR Award, and BT-CSR Excellence Award.

Social Vision of the Company

To actively contribute to the social and economic development of the underserved communities, lifting the burden of poverty and helping bring in inclusive growth. In so doing, build a better, sustainable way of life for the weaker sections of society and raise the country's HDI (human development index).

—Rajashree Birla, Chairperson, Aditya Birla Centre for Community Initiatives and Rural Development.

Our CSR programmes are aligned with our group social vision and business CSR policy. Our aim is to reach out to last man in the society and bringing positive changes in the life of the deprived people.

— Sanjay Sarkar, President and Chief Operating Officer, Aditya Birla Group.

We are committed to the surrounding community for improving human dignity, promoting services to deprived and improving socio-economic condition.

— Harendra R. Patel, Joint President-Human Resource , Birla Copper.

Social Objectives of the Unit

- Ensure quality healthcare services and education facilities to local community.
- Increase community participation specially for women & youth through skill development livelihood programmes.
- Improve basic village infrastructure.
- Contribute towards social empowerment by engaging all sections in the task of village development.
- Create and sustain a culture of cooperation for inclusive growth and development.
- Encourage and form village level institutions to monitor and drive the developmental projects.

CSR Focus Areas

Education Upliftment

Name of the Project	*Rational of the Project*	*Status of the Project*	*Proposed Target*
Education material distribution to rural students in 69 villages of entire Vagra tehsil (1st to 8th Std students of 85 government schools)	Poor economic Condition	Improvement in: Literacy rate: 37 to 73.62%; Women literacy rate: 32 to 76.02%; School enrolment: 86 to 100%; School attendance: 65 to 95%. School dropout reduced from 22 to 2%	Literacy rate: 80%; Women literacy rate 80%; School enrolment: 100%; School attendance: 100%; School dropout: 0%.
Regular school health check-up camp for rural students on 8 parameters like weight, height , chest, ent, stomach infection, mental retardation, skin/hair problem	Healthy students , healthy generation		
Provide transportation to rural students (daily school commute, board exam, exposure visit, sports programme, science and maths exhibition)	To reduce school dropout and continuing education		
Bicycle distribution to needy girls	Reduce girls school dropout	250 bicycle provided to rural girl students	Bicycle support to 400 girls
Science teacher provided	Quality of education		
Career guidance & counselling/goal setting programme	Develop career oriented approach and goal achievement	3,000 students	10,000 students
Rural sports (sponsored at tehsil and cluster level)	Physical and mental development		

Healthcare

Name of the Project	*Rational of the Project*	*Status of the Project*	*Proposed Target*
Health awareness programme (health talk for adolescent girls and women, sanitation, de-addiction drive, HIV/AIDS, family planning)	Improving health indicators by generating awareness		
Immunisation (routine, MMR, pulse polio)	Reducing IMR	IMR 48 per 1000 MMM 148 per 1,00,000	
Healthy baby show	Motivate for complete immunisation	Routine immunisation increased from 73 to 100 per cent Tracking on mothers increased 78 to 100 per cent	Immunisation 100 per cent
Health camps (general, multi specialty, blood donation)	Addressing preventive and curative health issues	Institutional delivery increased from 73 to 100 per cent	Institutional delivery 100%
Mega eye cataract surgery camp	To cure cataract patients and help old age people to live independently	365 cataract operations done	3,000 cataract operations
Individual toilet construction	To develop habits to use toilets and prevent from diseases and make village open defecation free	Constructed 500 individual toilets in the surrounding five villages Sanitation facility increased from 62 to 82 per cent	Individual toilet construction: 1000 Sanitation: 100 per cent
Health improvement (gym centre established for rural people and yoga classes initiated)	Keep the community healthy and fit		

- *A Safe and Healthy Work Environment*: We invest in our employees' health and well-being, offer flexible work practices, and provide a safe workplace.
- *An Inclusive and Diverse Culture:* We recruit a diverse workforce and foster an inclusive culture where everyone feels welcomed, valued, respected, and heard.
- *Providing Training and Development Opportunities*: We offer training, mentoring, and development programs and encourage our employees to build a career with Aditya Birla Group.
- *Rewarding Our People*: We provide a competitive rewards package and we recognise our employees' achievements and contributions.

Employee Engagement Gap

At Birla Copper before year 2013, 30-40 per cent employee involvement or participation was seen in CSR activities. The accountability, ownership, leadership skill, satisfaction level and team work was missing.

A challenge in front of the HR department of an organisation was how to engage the employees in the ethical behaviour and CSR activities of the company.

Methodology Used

- Effective communication highlighting CSR aims.
- Use of existing communication channels like posters, pamphlet distribution, social media, intranet sites, mail reminders.
- Encouraging Employees through recognition or appreciation certificates and mails.

Motivation and Benefits: The Employee Perspective

- They feel pride and generate positive feeling.
- They got a platform from where they can contribute for noble cause.
- Ownership and accountability generated among employees.
- Strengthen relation with stakeholder and reduced grievances.
- Help to develop self discipline among employees.
- Strengthen inter personal relation among employees.
- Generate healthy environment.

Our Stories

Birla Copper Employee Support for Blood Donation Camp

A blood donation camp is organised once in a year in association with Red Cross Blood Bank and Rotary Club-Bharuch, where more than 100 employees and family member successfully donate blood. As every donation saves up to 3 lives, the drive is able to make an impact on more than 300 lives. The camp is concluded with the donors being served with light refreshments, donor badges and a certificate of appreciation.

Our employees volunteer themselves in making this camp successful by getting involved in making arrangements like seating on registration desk, providing hospitality etc., as per the requirement.

Dahej is the most vibrant industrial hub where all big industries are doing CSR work. For last 3 years Rotary club & Red Cross Blood Bank is appreciating us for large participation in comparison of other industries.

Share the Warmth Campaign

Suchendra Sarkar, President of Surbhi Mahila Mandal along with the employees frequently visit the Orphanage of mentally challenged girls in Bharuch and spent quality time with them by inspiring them to learn, and to celebrate life. This project involves distribution of bed, warm clothes or good & services to women who are residing thereby providing them with better standard of living. The objective is to extend a helping hand to mentally challenged girls and women to make them feel like they are at home.

Birla Copper Employee Support Swatch Bharat Champaign

Committed to the cause of environmental sustainability, the unit organised a 'Cleanliness Drive' in Bharuch town, under its CSR ambit. The cleanliness drive comes as a humble endeavour to contribute towards the Government of India's initiative, 'Swachh Bharat Abhiyan'. Realising the significance of such campaigns, total 14,000 volunteers came out in support to prevent the growing strain on planet Earth's natural systems and spent 4 hours each and cleaned 14 km area.

It was a meaningful effort to contribute towards building a cleaner India. Employees and their family members voluntary joined together and stepped forward vigorously and collaborated for the noble cause and the drive was a great success. Their determination also proved to be a great source of motivation for the on-lookers. The company was also awarded with the Certification of Appreciation by District Administration, Bhaurch Nagarpalika. The event is also registered in the Limca Book of Record.

Go Green Drive

Continuing with its endeavour to preserve environment, the cunit launched a Tree Plantation Drive 'Go Green' at its nearby village, school campus and township. Around 40 employees participated in the tree plantation drive and planted 120 saplings.

The aim was to promote environmental conservation and sustainability. The sole purpose for the plantation activity was to create a ripple effect and to drive home the message that this is going to be a sustained effort, not a one-time activity.

Be Independent, Make Difference

To promote gender equality and empowerment of women CJST has taken up various initiatives to make the women more self-reliant. Various skill development programmes like stitching, beautician course, macron handicraft etc., have helped these women to a great extent to earn their income.

Our local employee helps in marketing and setting up exhibition of the product manufactured by SHG group and rural women. Their visits and purchasing of items encourage and motivate the SHG group to do their best.

Espousing Social Causes

We work with communities and try to address social issues through our innovative interventions like DAAN Utsav, Disaster relief donation, celebrating different sports and culture programmes in which our employee participate wholeheartedly making the events successful.

In sports, every year, cricket tournament is played between plant employee and village youth for fun and building healthy relationship. Our local employees also support and contribute in Mass Marriage programme organised under the CSR.

Birla Copper Employee Visit to Govt. School of nearby Village:

Mr Harendra Patel (Joint President-HR) along with employees visited nearby Village Dahej, Gujarat, and spent quality time with the children by inspiring them to learn and to celebrate life. He stressed upon the importance of education & health as vital factors for one's holistic development and success in the future. Children full of enthusiasm and confidence shared their passion and their success stories. Various activities were organised to build team spirit amongst the children. A painting competition was organised for various age groups and winners were duly awarded. The company also renovated the 150 year old school under the CSR programme.

Employee Speak: Why I Volunteer?

We are blessed with what we have received and now it's a time to give back. We get a platform from where we can reach to local community in our busy schedule in the form of time, money or talent. We feel

motivated that we are the part of participation and contribution for noble cause.
—Dinesh Rathi, WCM, Birla Copper.

It motivates and inspires us to share the good fortune with others. It feels really good in giving back to the local community in terms of time, money or talent. Passion to reach out to underserved community gives satisfaction at the end of the day.
—Rajan Mishra, Copper-3 (Mech.), Birla Copper.

It helps us to keep in touch what's going on in community. Giving comes in many forms and in many ways; it's up to you how you choose to contribute. In their view, it's the right thing to do, involving everyone for a change.
—Subodh Vaghela, Finance, Birla Copper.

It is preparing our coming generation to contribute for noble cause. The effective communication of CSR team helps us to have an idea of various programs/activities in which we can volunteer ourselves, spend time and spread smile.

—Rajesh Bhattasana, Copper-3 (Automation), Birla Copper.

Volunteering brings life to us; it connect us directly to the issues which are in society and we feel connected to be a part of this effort which Birla Copper CSR team takes.
—Suchandra Sarkar, President of Surbhi Mahila Mandal, Birla Copper Township.

Everybody can be great because anybody can serve. We don't need a college degree to serve. We don't have to make our subject and our verb agree to serve.... We only need a heart full of grace. A soul generated by love.
—Sobhana Patel, Surbhi Mahila Mandal, Birla Copper Township.

We are not doing great things; we are doing small things with great love and affection.
—Usha Singh, Surbhi Mahila Mandal, Birla Copper Township.

Every place is a goldmine. We just have to search for that place where we feel connected to make a change in society where we live.
—Jaya Mishra, Surbhi Mahila Mandal, Birla Copper Township.

For some people, volunteering is about giving but for us it's a way of living. It is providing us the platform where we can contribute and feel connected to community.
—Manisha Patel, Birla Copper Township.

Conclusion

Connecting the unconnected is what we do. We work with others to build thriving communities, improve people's lives, and support the long-term success of our business. Successful programmes on social responsibility rely heavily on enlightened people management practices. In this context, our HR department is the coordinator of CSR activities for establishing effective relationships with stakeholders and orienting the employees and the organisation towards a socially responsible character.

In Birla Copper, more than 180 CSR programmes are organised every year in which employee voluntarily participate and give contribution for social change. It encourages our employees to take part in social initiatives close to their hearts to make a positive social impact. The focus of the company is on the long term development of cordial and peaceful relation between employees and employers. HR works closely with the sustainability function to continue to find creative ways to weave a culture of sustainability into the organisational fabric.